'This ground-breaking book explores the neglected, everyday practicalities of management, focusing on the role of key artefacts in ordering organisational life. In doing this it exemplifies what the authors characterise as "third-person phenomenology". Locating their study in the tradition of ethnomethodological work, the authors offer stimulating reflections on the character of this radical enterprise, treating it as a "first sociology".'

Martyn Hammersley, The Open University

'Authored by two of the leading researchers in the field of ethnomethodology, this book makes a unique contribution not only to ethnomethodology but to management and organizational studies in general. Its innovative study practice provides highly original and provoking insights into the often closed world of senior management in organisations.'

Graham Button, formerly Pro-Vice Chancellor for Arts, Computing, Engineering and Sciences, Sheffield Hallam University, and Laboratory Director, Xerox Research Centre Europe, Grenoble

'Anderson and Sharrock investigate the "shop floor problem" – usually a problem *for* managers who want to know what other workers actually do in day-to-day practice. Drawing upon their own experiences as managers and with managers, they observe that the "shop floor" for managers is largely constituted by records that enable action at a distance. In addition to giving a rare entry into the mundane work of management, the book introduces keen insight into ethnomethodology and social theory through their "third-person phenomenological" perspective.'

Michael E. Lynch, Cornell University, USA

# Action at a Distance

This book examines the nature of work and management, centring on documents as a class of management objects which have been relatively understudied in ethnomethodological research. Treating documents and similar artefacts as ordering devices, the authors describe consociation – the social organisation of patterns of coordinated action in situations where the usual resources of face to face communication are absent. With a focus on senior managers, this volume provides a description of the interior configuration of the world of senior management as the encountered, everyday experience of managing, drawing on first person experience rather than ethnographic fieldwork to shed new light on the importance of third person reflection upon practical understandings. An innovative study of the social character of such management objects as spreadsheets, strategic plans, computational models and charts, *Action at Distance* will appeal to scholars of sociology with interests in ethnomethodology, the sociology of work and method in the social sciences.

**Bob Anderson** is the former Pro Vice Chancellor for Research at Sheffield Hallam University. As CEO of University Campus Suffolk, UK, he led the founding of what is now the University of Suffolk. He is currently an Associate in the Horizon Research Institute at Nottingham University.

**Wes Sharrock** is Professor in the Department of Sociology at Manchester University, UK.

# Philosophy and Method in the Social Sciences

Engaging with the recent resurgence of interest in methodological and philosophical issues in the human and social sciences, this series provides an outlet for work that demonstrates both the intellectual import of philosophical and methodological debates within the social sciences and their direct relevance to questions of politics, ethics or policy. Philosophy and Method in the Social Sciences welcomes work from sociologists, geographers, philosophers, anthropologists, criminologists and political scientists with broad interest across academic disciplines, that scrutinises contemporary perspectives within the human and social sciences and explores their import for today's social questions.

**Series Editor**
Phil Hutchinson, Manchester Metropolitan University, UK

**Titles in this series**

**Clarity and Confusion in Social Theory**
Taking Concepts Seriously
*By Leonidas Tsilipakos*

**Evolution, Human Behaviour and Morality**
The Legacy of Westermarck
*Edited by Olli Lagerspetz, with Jan Antfolk, Ylva Gustafsson and Camilla Kronqvist*

**The Constitution of Social Practices**
*By Kevin McMillan*

**Action at a Distance**
Studies in the Practicalities of Executive Management
*By R.J. Anderson and W.W. Sharrock*

For more information about this series, please visit:

https://www.routledge.com/Philosophy-and-Method-in-the-Social-Sciences/book-series/ASHSER1373

# Action at a Distance
Studies in the Practicalities of
Executive Management

R.J. Anderson and W.W. Sharrock

LONDON AND NEW YORK

First published 2018
by Routledge
2 Park Square, Milton Park, Abingdon, Oxon OX14 4RN

and by Routledge
711 Third Avenue, New York, NY 10017

*Routledge is an imprint of the Taylor & Francis Group, an informa business*

© 2018 R.J. Anderson and W.W. Sharrock

The right of R.J. Anderson and W.W. Sharrock to be identified as authors of this work has been asserted by them in accordance with sections 77 and 78 of the Copyright, Designs and Patents Act 1988.

All rights reserved. No part of this book may be reprinted or reproduced or utilised in any form or by any electronic, mechanical, or other means, now known or hereafter invented, including photocopying and recording, or in any information storage or retrieval system, without permission in writing from the publishers.

*Trademark notice*: Product or corporate names may be trademarks or registered trademarks, and are used only for identification and explanation without intent to infringe.

*British Library Cataloguing-in-Publication Data*
A catalogue record for this book is available from the British Library

*Library of Congress Cataloging-in-Publication Data*
Names: Anderson, R. J. (Robert John), 1946- author. |
    Sharrock, W. W. (Wes W.) author.
Title: Action at a distance : studies in the practicalities of executive
    management / R.J. Anderson and W. W. Sharrock.
Description: 1 Edition. | New York : Routledge, 2018. |
    Series: Philosophy and method in the social sciences |
    Includes bibliographical references and index.
Identifiers: LCCN 2017059126 | ISBN 9781138504141 (hbk) |
    ISBN 9781138504165 (pbk) | ISBN 9781315145846 (ebk)
Subjects: LCSH: Management. | Executive ability. | Leadership.
Classification: LCC HD31.2.A543 2018 | DDC 658.4—dc23
LC record available at https://lccn.loc.gov/2017059126

ISBN: 978-1-138-50414-1 (hbk)
ISBN: 978-1-138-50416-5 (pbk)
ISBN: 978-1-315-14584-6 (ebk)

Typeset in Times New Roman
by Swales & Willis Ltd, Exeter, Devon, UK

# Contents

*List of figures*      ix
*List of tables*      x
*List of appendices*      xi
*Preface*      xii

**PART I**
**Foundations**      1

1 The world of the senior manager      3

2 Management as a common sense construct      19

**PART II**
**Studies in the practicalities of executive management**      27

3 Representations and realities      29

4 Representations without metaphysics      44

5 Intersubjectivity and the arts of financial management      53

6 The contingencies of due process      74
   Appendix      86

7 Sensitivity analysis as practical modal realism      87
   Appendix      99

8 Benchmarking as reality conjuncture      100
   Appendix      111

| | |
|---|---|
| 9  Does it wash its face? | 118 |
| Appendix | 135 |
| 10  Plans and their situated actions | 138 |

**PART III**
**Conclusion**     157

| | |
|---|---|
| 11  Ethnomethodology: a First Sociology? | 159 |
| *Index* | 176 |

# Figures

| | | |
|---|---|---:|
| 3.1 | The design process | 32 |
| 5.1 | Complete set of worksheets | 60 |
| App.6.1 | CU Governance of Operational Processes and Management of Curriculum Planning and Academic Standards | 86 |
| App.9.1 | Cost model sheet 1 | 135 |
| App.9.2 | Cost model sheet 2 | 136 |
| App.9.3 | Cost model sheet 3 | 136 |
| App.9.4 | Cost model sheet 4 | 137 |

# Tables

| | | |
|---|---|---|
| 5.1 | CU Board HESA agenda item | 59 |
| 5.2 | HFSA financial evaluation | 60 |
| 5.3 | CU loan covenants | 61 |
| 5.4 | Projected out-turns 2007–12 | 62 |
| 5.5 | Cash flow statement | 63 |
| 5.6 | Income and expenditure structure | 64 |
| 5.7 | Calculation of net cash flow | 66 |
| 5.8 | Calculation of cash flow | 69 |
| App.7.1 | CU Strategic Plan: Financial sensitivity analysis | 99 |
| App.8.1 | Population data (FTE) | 113 |
| App.8.2 | Financial data | 113 |
| App.8.3 | Sustainability | 114 |
| App.8.4 | Input measures I | 115 |
| App.8.5 | Input measures II | 115 |
| App.8.6 | Output measures | 116 |
| App.8.7 | Next steps | 117 |
| 10.1 | CU planning schedule | 143 |
| 10.2 | RCA governance | 147 |
| 10.3 | RCA sustainability | 149 |
| 10.4 | RCA network growth | 150 |
| 10.5 | RCA external drivers of growth | 151 |
| 10.6 | RCA internal drivers of growth | 152 |

# Appendices

6.1 CU Governance of Operational Processes and Management
of Curriculum Planning and Academic Standards     86
7.1 CU Strategic Plan: Financial sensitivity analysis     99
8.1 An initial benchmarking exercise for CU     111
9.1 Screenshots of course costing model     135

# Preface

This book addresses a number of somewhat under-emphasised themes in the ethnomethodological literature. The first is *consociation*, the social organisation of patterns of coordinated action which extend in space and time. Although formal and informal organisations, groups and institutions have often been the sites of ethnomethodological investigations, only occasionally has their character as socially constructed collectivities been studied. Instead, investigations have tend to narrow in on the interactional features of joint action. Picking up themes from some of the earliest work within Ethnomethodology and from our own previous studies, we ask how hierarchically, temporally and spatially extended sequences of action are achieved as the accomplished lived-work of organisational life. How are accountable joint action sequences produced by members of organisations in those circumstances where the usual resources of face-to-face communication cannot be invoked?

Second, we focus on senior managers and executives, a group which has been almost entirely overlooked. In particular, we look at *executive management as a finite province of meaning*; that domain of organisational action construed in terms of the expectations, motivations, attitudes and shared understandings of the group usually described as providing overall direction and leadership to the organisation. In doing so, we offer an initial description of some aspects of the interior configuration of the world of executive management as the encountered, day-in, day-out experience of managing – what their experience of managing comes to as a course of life's work.

Third, we centre our discussion on executive documents and related objects, a class of phenomena which has had a relatively low profile in ethnomethodological reports. By treating these and similar artefacts as *ordering devices*, we bring out their central contribution to the accomplishment of organisational consociation. In particular, we draw attention to how their socially organised features are made available to members of the local setting and so facilitate the production and reproduction of standardly structured, uniquely performed patterns of action; that is, how predictable types of action are brought off through the specificities (the 'haeccities') of any particular occasion. Following Dorothy Smith's original lead, we aim to re-emphasise and extend the availability of documents and the like as first-class resources for ethnomethodological analyses.

Fourth, our turn to the world of senior management returns to Ethnomethodology's distinctive cast as a *'First Sociology'* and the use of first person experience as a resource for analysis.[1] Since its inception, and for entirely understandable reasons, Ethnomethodology has steadily increased its dependency on the standard sociological research strategy of intensive or extensive ethnographic fieldwork. This dependency has had many disciplinary and other benefits, but equally, we suggest, has encouraged an homogenisation of the types of materials gathered and the analytical approaches used. By eschewing fieldwork and replacing the evidence it provides with the analytically reconstituted practical understandings of the executive manager, we hope to re-claim a place for third person reflection on first person experience.

Fifth, and this is perhaps more a reflection on the nature not just of Ethnomethodology but all contemporary social science, we have undertaken these investigations because the phenomena are *interesting in themselves*. We have been drawn to them not because they provide instantiations of other issues of interest to government agencies and funders nor because they are an accessible means by which to demonstrate 'impact', 'value', 'multi-modal methods', or some other virtue. Husserl's injunction 'Back to the things themselves!' was a lodestone for Garfinkel when re-thinking what he later termed 'classical' or 'constructionist' Sociology. In this book, we take the injunction in a slightly different way, namely as an instruction to address whatever phenomena the social world makes available to us as objects for analysis in their own right rather than as signifiers for something else. It is our curiosity regarding the social character of such management impedimenta as spreadsheets, strategic plans, computational models, charts and so on which encourages us to be indifferent to any macro-sociological significance to be attributed to them. Their intrinsic interest alone is justification enough for wanting to study them.

## The organisational setting

At the time to which the studies relate, County University (CU) was a Higher Education initiative designed to help raise standards of educational attainment in a region of England where they had traditionally been below the national average. It was led by a partnership comprising the Higher Education Funding Council (HEFCE), two regional universities, Regional University North (RUN) and Regional University South (RUS), the Regional Development Agency (RDA), the County Council (County), the city (City) and the Further Education College in the city (College). Start-up funding was provided by HEFCE, RDA and County. The core educational provision, HEFCE funded student places, was transferred by College. In addition, provision was provided in four other local Further Education Colleges. The model of the institution was a 'hub and spokes' with the hub in the city and the spokes being the Further Education College partners.

The formal structure of CU was a Company limited by Guarantee with a Board of Directors representing the partners. The Members of the Company were the two regional universities. Until it could reach a student population of 4,000 and bid for independence, CU was 'Godfathered' by RUN and RUS. As well as chairing the Board in rotation, the universities offered advice and support with regard to educational and operational matters.

The project began its operational life in 2005 and appointed its CEO at the start of 2006. Soon after, a small management team was put in place. The target date for its first intake was September 2007. As well as setting up the academic and operational infrastructures, two critical tasks had to be accomplished in the first phase of CU's existence. Academic staff had to be recruited to teach the courses. It was expected that the vast majority at the hub would be transferred under TUPE arrangements from the College. Staff in the partner colleges would remain with their current employer. At the same time, a programme had to be initiated to provide purpose-built facilities for the hub. This programme depended on a complex set of 'deals' involving funding from RDA and land owned by College and City. The first teaching and administrative building was opened in 2008 with student accommodation and further teaching facilities following slightly later. In 2016, CU became an independent university.

The materials on which the studies in this book are based are taken from the first five years of CU's operation. Where necessary, specific contextual detail is provided as part of the presentation of individual studies.

## Acknowledgements

We owe an enormous debt of gratitude to the current Vice Chancellor of CU for permission to use the materials which form the basis of this book. We would also like to thank all the staff at CU for their help and support.

We would like to thank Graham Button for helpful comments on a number of chapters.

Wes Sharrock would like to thank Manchester University for granting him leave of absence during 2016 when the bulk of the book was written.

Bob Anderson would like to thank Derek McCauley, Tom Rodden and Horizon Digital Research for support throughout the preparation of the book.

We would like to thank Louis Bucciarelli and MIT Press for permission to reproduce the diagram on page 32 from L. Bucciarelli, *Designing Engineers*, MIT Press, 1984.

## Note

1 And hence to the concerns discussed in Howard Schwartz's unjustly disregarded gem "Data: Who Needs It?" (Schwartz 2002).

## Reference

Schwartz, H. 2002. "Data: Who Needs It?" *Ethnographic Studies*, no. 7 7–32.

# Part I
# Foundations

# 1 The world of the senior manager

This book is about one of the things that make large-scale organisations possible, namely the ability of senior managers to influence the actions of others when both are separated in time or physical and organisational space. Note the phrasing. Action at a distance is *one* of the things required for large-scale organisations – not the only thing and perhaps not even the most important thing. It is necessary but not sufficient. Nor is it only senior managers who have this ability. Everyone else in organisations does too – at least in principle. Bringing about action at a distance is something which anyone can do provided they have the means for it, and a great many do.

So why study senior managers? In part, it is because while organisations and their administrations have been widely studied by ethnomethodologists and sociologists, the routine, daily work of the most senior managers has been somewhat neglected. However, to use a phrase that will crop up time and time again, their work is 'shop floor work' too. Second, and this is related, the professional literatures (both academic and other) have tended to obscure the lived reality of all levels of management – but especially those at executive levels. On the one hand, they depict these managers as the dominant force in organisations and are replete with advice, instruction and recipes for how to become a 'rainmaker' and use various charms to work managerial magic. On the other, they are held to be hapless vehicles of fiscal, economic and social forces which, by dictating the choices they have and the decisions they make, lead them to impose a uniformity of structure on organisational arrangements. Although we have met some senior managers who do seem able to perform miracles and we have seen many twist and turn in the face of demands placed on them by market, financial, or shareholder forces, in our experience, the most senior managers no more control the organisations they 'lead' than any other group does, and seeing things through the prism of a struggle for power and control misrepresents what organisational life feels like. This is because, most of the time, daily life for senior managers is no less and no more ordinary than for anyone else. It is that ordinariness we want to examine here.

Action at a distance can sound a bit like one of those feats of magic we just mentioned, so we had better explain what we mean by it. Briefly, it is the ability of social actors to cause others who are not immediately co-present with them to act in certain ways. Executives and senior managers in large organisations try to do this all the time, and good ones are pretty effective at it. What they and all the others engaged in action at a distance are doing is creating the organisation as a consociate social structure.[1] As we discuss below, studies of managers generally emphasise the construction of what Alfred Schutz (1967b) called the 'we-relationship' of established face to face interaction. This relationship is important but our interest is more turned towards that other dimension of the 'we-relationship', the coordination of joint courses of action over organisational distance. Consociate features are those mediated by ties exercised over space and time, where such ties are not (or not always) supported by immediate face to face interaction.

Of course, we are not the first to study consociation in organisations. Nor are we the first to study the role of senior managers in constructing it. Armies of social and management scientists have marched into large organisations determined to discover management's part in them and how it works. Our investigative approach is different though. Or, at least, we think it is. We call it a 'third person phenomenology' because it attempts to provide an analytic or observational account of first person experience. Previous examples of third person phenomenology can be found in Anderson et al. (1988), Anderson and Sharrock (2014), Sharrock and Anderson (2011). The studies in this book continue this line of work.

Third person phenomenology is one mode of ethnomethodological investigation. As we set out in Chapter 12, we think of Ethnomethodology as a *First Sociology*, a conception which underpins third person phenomenology. The idea of Ethnomethodology as a First Sociology means a third person phenomenology of executive management must differ from standard sociological and Management Science descriptions. Equally, it is different from the approaches associated with Conversation Analysis and 'ethnomethodologically-informed ethnography'. Again notice the phasing. It is different, not better *tout court*. Judgements about which sociological approach is better than which turn on the interests motivating them and the objectives they set themselves. All we are saying is we think a third person phenomenology is better suited for the kinds of studies we want to undertake. It would not, indeed could not, satisfy every set of sociological interests.

Our aim in this introductory chapter is to lay out why we have adopted the approach we have and describe some of its presuppositions. We will do this first by using two very standard tropes on what is a familiar theme in the literature; the adoption of external and internal viewpoints on senior management as fragmented activity. We will then introduce third person phenomenology as a mode of Ethnomethodology and what we think it offers. Of course, the real value of the investigative approach will only be cashed out in the studies it facilitates, but by offering some guidance now, we hope we will make it easier for readers unfamiliar with our investigative strategy to see the rationale motivating it and the logic of the descriptive steps we take.

## The external logic of fragmentation

However we arrange the mosaic of conventional wisdom on management, ever since Henry Mintzberg's classic paper (1975), we have known of the disparity between that wisdom and what research reveals managers actually do. Whilst what Mintzberg called 'folklore' has managers deciding, supervising and reviewing the activities under their purview, research shows they play a variety of roles which broadly fall into what he calls the interpersonal, the informational and the decisional. Somewhat later, at the beginning of an equally classic discussion, John Kotter (1999) itemised this variety by listing the events in one individual manager's day.[2] Though this description was presented as news for Management Science, anyone who has spent any time with managers knows their days are filled by an endless procession of events, encounters, talk, meetings, document reading and travel; in short, a slew of activities in which, as well as doing what 'folklore' says, they 'chat about hobbies, hold spur-of-the-moment meetings, and seek out people far from their chain of command' (Kotter 1999: 148).

An encyclopaedic summary was provided by Colin Hales (1986) who reviewed a great deal of the management research literature and came to very similar conclusions as Kotter. Here is his precis of the evidence he collated:

(T)he known features of managerial work may be summarised as follows:

1. It combines a specialist/professional element and a general, 'managerial' element.
2. The substantive elements involve, essentially, liaison, man-management and responsibility for a work process, beneath which are subsumed more detailed work elements.
3. The character of work elements varies by duration, time span, recurrence, unexpectedness and source.
4. Much time is spent in day-to-day trouble shooting and ad hoc problems of organisation and regulation.
5. Much managerial activity consists of asking or persuading others to do things, involving the manager in face-to-face verbal communication of limited duration.
6. Patterns of communication vary in terms of what the communication is about and with whom the communication is made.
7. Little time is spent on one particular activity and, in particular, on the conscious, systematic formulation of plans. Planning and decision making tend to take place in the course of other activity.
8. Managers spend a lot of time accounting for and explaining what they do, in informal relationships and in 'politicking'.
9. Managerial activities are riven by contradictions, cross-pressures and conflicts. Much managerial work involves coping with and reconciling social and technical conflict.
10. There is considerable choice in terms of what is done and how: part of managerial work is setting the boundaries of and negotiating that work itself.

(Hales 1986: 104)

6   *Foundations*

To understand what holds all this frenetic work together, Kotter says you have to understand the challenges managers face. Most of the time, managers are engaged in:

- figuring out what to do despite uncertainty and an enormous amount of potentially irrelevant information;
- getting things done through a large and diverse group of people despite having little direct control over most of them.

(Kotter 1999: 148)

These two challenges are resolved through processes he calls 'agenda setting' and 'network building'. The endless procession we mentioned just now is all in the service of getting the manager's networks to execute his or her agendas. The image this style of analysis presents is one where even though managers might appear to be pushed from pillar to post and live highly uncoordinated lives, in reality what they do is a highly rational response to the organisational context in which they are operating. This rational response is the means through which they exercise the control they are presumed to have. One not so fanciful way of summarising this account of managerial experience might be to suggest it is a constant striving to cope with the consequences of an organisational version of the Second Law of Thermodynamics.[3] Over time, everything tends towards entropy. The threat of progressive disorganisation is the normal state managers are battling. Under this conception, such disorganisation appears as a succession of problems generated by the dissipation of energy and resources as well as the degeneration of processes and the substitution of goals, all of which require 'fixing'. Agenda setting and network building in the face of a perennial threat of entropy are presented as the only rational strategy.

## The internal logic of fragmentation

The descriptions given by Kotter and Hales are observer depictions. They are third person overviews of what management and decision making looks like. However, as Charles Perrow (1965) among others has suggested, we should not assume that such summaries necessarily catch how those engaged in management see their activities and the conditions they are operating within:

> (S)ocial scientists will do well not to neglect a basic, pedestrian characteristic of the organizations they study – the nature of the work performed or, more generally, the techniques available and in current use for achieving organizational goals.
>
> (Perrow 1965: 996)

Ignoring the pedestrian particularities of any example, both the specifics of what is being managed and the context in which it is being managed, risks losing the *in vivo* sense of daily management life (what it looks like on the inside for those on the 'shop floor' of management) as well as the features the general categories of activity just mentioned take when they are actualised.

As we have said, spend any time with any kind of manager and you will very likely compile a list of daily happenings which is not markedly different to the lists offered by Kotter and Hales. However, the way managers describe them is likely to be very different. In that difference is a clue to why we think a new way of describing management life is needed. Here is a set of observations gleaned from executives we have known:

> While different activities have different rhythms, all seem 'bursty'. Periods of attention are followed by periods of disattention when the focus shifts to another topic, another problem to be dealt with. Routine maintenance of ongoing tasks is largely an unrealisable ideal. Activity becomes frenzied when an important deadline draws near. Task organisation is driven by deadlines.
>
> There is no sense of a stable set of daily priorities. Activities are constantly having to be shuffled as different tasks or action lines are pushed to the top of the To Do List. One forcing function is a deadline. Another, just as common, is the pressure of someone else's demands. Other people's deadlines – and not just a superior's – can set your work schedule. At other times, unforeseen urgent problems pop up and demand attention.
>
> The only way to get things done is to keep focused and see everything and everyone associated with any particular decision, solution, or objective being worked on as a possible resource for you to achieve the outcome you want. But, of course, everyone else does this too! Recognising this shared attitude not only helps find compromises and ways through problems, it also alerts you to the dangers of being 'mugged' into agreeing to something the implications of which you haven't fully understood. When consulting about a decision, care needs to be taken about where a conversation might lead and what you will or will not want to agree to. An agreement now may later force a decision you would rather not make. These judgement calls are about people and events but more importantly they are also about possible implications and especially their interpretation by others.
>
> You can only get things done by getting others to do what you want. That means you have to engage and enrol them by getting them to fit in with what you want to do and, particularly, doing so (more or less) willingly. Whilst you might want to construct 'win-win' outcomes, plotting in advance how to do this is mostly a waste of time. It is only rarely that you know the range and ordering of other people's problems, and so you can't align your needs with theirs in advance. Win-win outcomes are found, if they are found, as you see what other people's problems are when trying to solve your own.

No solution, outcome or management decision is ever optimal. The best you can hope for is 'good enough' or 'what we can live with'. Pushing a 'good enough' solution so it becomes optimal for you will take at least as much time and effort again as one which you can live with. This is because solutions, decisions and outcomes are always arrived at by trade-offs. The more you push for your best outcome, the more you push others away from theirs. The further they get from their optimal outcome, the more resistance you will encounter.

## Re-thinking management work

The language of the descriptions just given is heavily loaded with terms describing what management looks like, what it feels like and how you have to orient to it. These are, you might say, the subjective complement of Kotter's and Hales' objective descriptions. They capture the experience of management life while Kotter and Hales try to represent the observable behaviour exhibited in precisely the same tumult. Inside and outside, subjective and objective, analytic and expressive are all useful enough distinctions. But they force an opposition we might not necessarily want or need and raise the question whether it is possible to construct an analytic account of the manager's subjective perceptions. In other words, is it possible to construct third person descriptions of first person experience?

### *Ethnomethodology and third person phenomenology*

We have said third person phenomenology is a mode of Ethnomethodology. In what follows, we summarise the central aspects of Ethnomethodology in order to draw out what a third person phenomenology might be. We will not give a detailed introduction nor summarise its intellectual biography. Instead, we will assume some familiarity with the broad background.[4] In particular, we will take as given a number of claims about Harold Garfinkel's conception of Ethnomethodology and his abiding sociological interests, as well as the ways these were worked though in the development of Ethnomethodology. We will state these baldly. Buttressing arguments for them can be found in most well-informed introductions.

1   Sociology's ambition is to describe how social order is sustained. Its accounts can be framed in many different ways. What creates these differences are differences in the premises used for the framing. This dependency means we cannot use the results of analyses to evaluate the relative persuasiveness of frames.
2   The descriptions given should be methodologically rigorous. That is, the theoretical structures developed and the investigations undertaken to demonstrate their empirical application should be clear, logical, systematic and consistent. The aim, ultimately, is to have sociological descriptions which bear comparison with those of the natural sciences. Key to this rigour is transparency of assumptions. No assumptions should be utilised in a theoretical construction or in the design of an investigation which have not been explicitly marked.

3   Garfinkel's own interests were in proceduralising sociological theories or models to see how effective they were in making social structures empirically visible. His method was to treat theories and models as sets of instructions for making social structures observable and analysable. In large measure, these modes of proceduralising were based on canons of rigour he derived from Felix Kaufmann (1958) and Alfred Schutz (1962). The first of these canons describes what we might call 'the sociological gaze' and was summarised in his notion 'the praxeological rule':

> The seen but unnoticed backgrounds of everyday activities are made visible and described from a perspective in which persons live out the lives they do, have the children they do, think the thoughts, enter the relationships they do, all in order to permit the sociologist to solve his theoretical problems.
> (Garfinkel 1967: 37)

The person-in-the-sociologist's-society is what Schutz called an 'homunculus', a theoretically constructed puppet, operating in a theoretically defined environment. The homunculus and environment are constructed by systematically applying the second canon, 'conceptual play', in ways provided for by the discipline's standard practices:

> By conceptual play is meant that the investigator undertakes the solution to a problem by altering imaginatively the features of the problematic situation and then following through the consequences of this alteration without suspending respect for the basic rules of his discipline.
> (Garfinkel 1956: 188)

In empirical investigations, the specification of the actor and the environment are to be clearly stated and consistently applied. Where attempts to use the specifications fail to make social structures sufficiently accessible, the onus is on the sociologist to vary the original premises on which the theory had been built, not to introduce ad hoc adjustments to save the theory. By continually returning to the premises and varying them, over time the rigour of theory should be improved.

1   Following Schutz's (1967a and 1967b) interpretation of Weber in the light of the findings of Phenomenology, the central analytic task for any theory of social action is to describe the role of what Husserl (1970 and 1983) called '*noesis and noema*' in configuring the phenomenal fields in which action takes place. Through this structuring, actors resolve the problematic possibilities of appearances and determine the meaning of objects and actions in a setting. Sociology calls this resolution 'The Definition of the Situation'. For Sociology, social order depends upon the *systematic reproduction* of shared definitions of the situation so that actions are mutually intelligible. Each actor can see the fit between what the other is doing and the ends being sought.

2  By far the most sophisticated theory of social action had been provided by Talcott Parsons (1951; Parsons and Shils 1951). Garfinkel set himself the task of proceduralising Parsons by treating his theory as a set of instructions for producing instances of the systematic reproduction of shared definitions of the situation.

## The 'discovery' of ethno-methods

In Parsons' conceptual structure, the basic element of social life is the 'unit act'. This has five elements.

a  An actor.
b  A situation made up of an environment of conditions.
c  Goals or ends to be achieved.
d  A standard for the assessment of means.
e  A mode of orientation towards the elements in the unit act.

The mode of orientation provides the grounds on which to define the situation and hence the selection of appropriate means to attain desired ends. When means are fitted to ends, provided they are in accord with scientific standards of efficacy, action is rational. Under the conception of the environment in which action takes place as a social system, the most important element is the population of others whom we encounter. These others are assumed to be actors who themselves have modes or orientation and definitions of the situation. Given both parties are rational social actors, each has expectations of what should be done based on their definition of the situation, motivations and so on. This is the double contingency. Garfinkel's question is 'How are these expectations aligned?'

For populations of actors to engage with one another on a continuing basis and so create the patterns of social relationships making up the social system, activities have to be coordinated. Providing a systemic basis for coordination is the nub of the theoretical problem. Two things are critical here. First, the solution must be systematically reproduced and not simply random. Second, that reproducibility must be an outcome of the structural arrangements obtaining within the social system itself. In Parsons' view, relying on actors' ability to coerce each other to coordinate actions would be an unstable solution. It would result in the infamous Hobbesian 'war of all against all'. Orderly social life would become impossible. What was needed was what he called 'motivated compliance'. Actors had to want to coordinate with each other. Motivated compliance with shared requirements would be a stable solution. Parsons provides for motivated compliance by introducing the assumption that actors are socialised into a common culture. This culture is composed of sentiments (norms and values) with regard to what ends are acceptable, expectations about how those ends should be achieved (that is, what means are allowable) and definitions of what roles actors are to play and what situations and actions mean. Equipping actors with a shared culture resolves the double contingency by providing them both with a common definition of the situation and solves the problem of coordination. They are assumed to see things the same way. In *Toward a General Theory of Action* (Parsons and Shils 1951), the structural process of socialisation ensures the patterns or norms, sentiments and definitions which make up a culture are shared. The unit act is possible because of the way the social system works.

We now have all the pieces. Social action is defined in terms of means/end rationality. Social actors are socialised rational actors sharing a common culture. The sharing of a common culture provides the mutual understanding and shared expectations required for actions to be coordinated because it allows each to understand the other's objectives and choices. This understanding covers expectations, defines roles and identifies the norms or rules of behaviour to be followed.

Coordination of action turns on agreed definitions of the situation. The theory says they are agreed, but, Garfinkel wondered, how is this agreement brought about? Given that all they have to go on is how things appear,[5] how from the myriad of different ways any situation might be defined, do they decide that *this* is the definition they are both using? To try to make this visible, Garfinkel picked out just two of the pieces we listed: means/end rationality and mutual understanding. The trouble is they are conceptually entangled. It is the assumption of the means/end rationality of some action which makes it understandable. To try to untangle them, Garfinkel takes a radical step. By exercising the right of the theorist to conceptual play, he proposes to change the original assumptions and drop the presumptions that both rationality and mutual understanding are intrinsic to social action. This is done in two steps. First, the presumption is set aside for actors. They are no longer assumed to have a shared culture by means of which they see the rationality of action. Next, the assumption of mutual understanding is set aside. Without the assumption of the rationality of action, there can be no prior mutual understanding.

If we construct encounters on the basis of these revised presuppositions, on Parsons' theory, actors should find each other's actions 'specifically senseless'. They will have no cultural resources to make sense of what is going on. On the other hand, if, somehow, they do manage to achieve coordination and sustain their interaction, whatever understandings they arrive at must have been constructed there and then in the encounter and not derived from a predefined culture. Garfinkel sought to apply that proposition.

In a series of studies which have become known as the 'breaching experiments', Garfinkel operationalised his revised premises. In a first experiment, as part of a mock-up of a consultation, participants were subjected to what they did not know were random questions and equally random responses to their answers. Given the questions and answers were random, objectively the environment they faced was 'senseless'. Although the resulting encounters were difficult and disturbing, the breaching actions did not cause interaction to fail. Instead, participants put considerable effort in trying to find some grounds where whatever the experimenter did or said could be found to be reasonable and meaningful. What under Parsons' theory should have brought the interaction to a halt, turned out not to.

For Garfinkel, this finding had a very profound implication. Although actors were assumed to have a shared culture which provided them with definitions of the situation and associated rules of behaviour, no analysis had been given of how on different occasions actors jointly know which definitions and rules to apply. How did the sharing of the definition of the situation and hence the identification of the appropriate rules come about? The assumption of a shared culture had obviated this question and so had effectively hidden what appeared to be of critical importance.

In subsequent studies, Garfinkel attempted to make visible just what the means and rules for arriving at a definition of the situation were. People were set the task of giving detailed glosses on their conversational utterances. Each proffered gloss was then the subject of demands for more clarification, resulting in yet further detailed glossing which again was challenged. The experiments resulted in an open process of branching questions and answers. In other examples, people were invited to play simple games in which, by flouting what might be thought of as the basic 'rules of the game', the investigator deliberately tried to disrupt the interaction and cause it to be abandoned. The aim was to see if these assumed basic rules really were prescriptive. Did violating them mean the game would collapse?

Once again, difficult though the encounters were, social interaction did not fail. In both sets of studies, definitions of what was going on and interpretations of what role the experimenter was playing and what was being done, were adjusted, extended, or even suppressed, and in some cases ignored altogether. Actions were allowed to run unchallenged if they made no material difference to what it was assumed everyone was trying to do.

The conclusion Garfinkel drew from all these studies was both simple and radical. We need to step beyond the assumption of a shared culture and scrutinise the phenomenon which had been hidden by that assumption. Instead of accepting that understandings, meanings and rules are, by definition, shared, we have to study how social actors display what they take to be going on, what their understandings of the particular situation is, and how mutual understanding is arrived at. However the phenomenal field which makes up the gestalt of their experience is structured, the character courses of action in that field have must be the outcome of what actors do to bring about this mutual intelligibility or, to use Garfinkel's term, its 'accountability'. The methods they use for achieving this must be conceptually prior to the assumption of a shared culture because finding a culture is shared depends upon them being successful. Using a term which was fashionable at the time, Garfinkel christened these methods 'ethno-methods' and their study 'Ethnomethodology'.

To summarise: the phenomena which Ethnomethodology investigates are the methods by which social actors routinely, normally, and in the midst of social life, co-produce the accountability of the courses action they are jointly engaged in. On the basis of the findings of the breaching experiments, it is postulated accountability is achieved within the flow of these courses of action. Since the production of shared accountability is an outcome, all social theory needs to equip its social actors (its homunculi) with are methods for producing the displayed or observable rationality of activities – that is, their 'accountability'. But to do this, all they have to go on are appearances. The analytic description of how from within the flow of ordinary life, actors jointly resolve the *noesis and noema* of social action to produce mutual intelligibility and the coordination of sustained structures of action is what we mean by third person phenomenology. It aims for an observer's account of what the orderliness of social action looks like from the inside; what we call its 'interior configuration'.

## The ethnomethodological gaze

To realise the possibilities of a third person phenomenology, we have to stipulate a set of analytic principles on which to base investigations. To the 'praxeological rule' and 'conceptual play' mentioned earlier, we will add the following:

1  The task of co-producing the accountability of action is a universal feature of all social activities. It is as central to science, professional work, leisure, theatre, religion, or wherever else as it is to ordinary life. It is a pervasive and irredeemable part of sociality.
2  Seeing and understanding the rational accountability of action is contingent on the circumstances in which it is produced. Accountability is *reflexive* on the settings for which it is produced.
3  Settings are self-organised in that the definitions, meanings and norms being made visible by the actions of participants to the setting are constituted in and for that setting as the course of action unfolds.
4  The knowledge, understandings, interpretations and meanings contained in the accountability of the setting cannot be formally specified; that is, itemised in a way which abstracts them entirely from their circumstances. Rather, they are indexical to the setting. Among the methods participants use are ones for resolving this indexicality.

Harvey Sacks once formulated the investigative outlook which results from adopting the above premises as the following view of social actors:

> [W]hat I have been proposing could be restated as follows: For Members, activities are observable. They see activities. They see persons doing intimacy, they see persons lying, etc. It has been wrongly proposed they do not see, for example, 'my mother', but what they 'really see' is light, dark, shadows, an object in the distance, etc. And that poses for us the task of being behaviourists in this sense: Finding how it is that people can produce sets of actions that provide that others can see such things.
>
> (Sacks 1995: 119)

This is what third person phenomenology explores: how do social actors jointly display and recognise the accountability of their activities and so enable the reproduction of the pervasive orderliness social life exhibits?

The premises set out above shape the sociological approach Ethnomethodology uses to find and analyse its materials. It focuses on how the observability (the accountability) of courses of action is produced, made visible and recognised within courses of action themselves. Demonstrating how this is done can only be through describing how actors constitute and display what they take appearances to be.

Under the general approach just described, investigations are framed first by withdrawing the assumption that 'how things are' is known and shared as the premise for activities. Instead, it is assumed what is known and what is shared are produced as a practical accomplishment in and through courses of action. As a result, we arrive at the following general set of 'study policies' or maxims:

1 Treat activities as reflexively accountable;
2 Treat settings as self-organising and common sense as an occasioned corpus of knowledge;
3 Treat social actors as enquirers into those settings and accounts.

These maxims provide a simple (if not the simplest) set of presuppositions for investigations. In turn, they have their counterparts in how actors are construed. Social actors are defined in terms of their use of methods. That is, social actors are analytic types, 'homunculi' as we called them earlier, constructed in terms of:

1 A maxim of self-explication: Unless otherwise required, actors assume meaning of action is discoverable within the action itself. This maxim implies the operation of two further interpretive rules:

   a  A syntactic rule: Actors assume the courses of action being undertaken are normatively oriented.
   b  A semantic rule: Actors assume the meaning of any segment of a trajectory of action can be derived from the meaning of other element(s).

2 A maxim of egologicality: This maxim refers to the structure of the pre-predicative world for the perceiving subject. In the flow of experience, the world I perceive is *my* world and its meaning (what it is *for* me) is organised by my interests and relevances. In coming to an understanding of social action, unless otherwise required, actors assume a distribution of knowledge, interests, motivations and relevances such that if they do what they expect others to expect, others will do as they expect; and they assume others assume that too. Egologicality is the rationale that produces the famous 'reciprocity of perspectives' which Schutz identified as the condition for stable social interaction (Schutz 1962).

This approach postulates social actors as enquirers into settings and into the accounts given of them. This is simply a recasting of Sacks' conception of members as oriented to observables. What we are enquiring into are the methods and procedures, the mechanisms and devices, by which what is experienced in routine social life as the taken-for-granted factuality and reality is constructed as the stable features of social life they are taken to be.

## The interior configuration of management

Garfinkel labelled the *in-situ* co-production of the meaning of action 'lay sociology' to contrast it with the provision or renderings of the meaning of courses of action which 'professional Sociology' produces as outputs of its disciplinary work. The relationship between lay and professional Sociology is a dependency. Professional Sociology builds its theoretical and explanatory structures on the accountability of action produced by lay sociology. As investigators of social settings, professional sociologists transform common sense accounts provided by participants into sociological conceptualisations. As a consequence, the work of lay sociologising goes largely unnoticed in Sociology. It goes unremarked in common sense too since the competences required to produce such meaning are taken for granted by social actors themselves. Cultural competence is assumed and so attention is directed away from the details of its performance. The following characterisation of this assumption was offered for natural language and conversation, though it is generalisable to all cultural practice:

> We understand the mastery of natural language to consist in this. In the particulars of his speech a speaker, in concert with others, is able to gloss those particulars and is thereby meaning differently than he can say in so many words; he is doing so over unknown contingencies in the actual occasions of interaction; and in so the recognition *that* he is speaking and *how* he is speaking are specifically not matters for competent remarks. That is to say, the particulars of his speaking do not provide occasions for stories about his speaking that are worth telling; nor do they elicit questions that are worth asking, and so on.
> (Garfinkel and Sacks 1970: 344; emphasis in original)

As with talk, so with senior management. In the midst of the flow of management action, the competences practising senior managers acquire are made unremarkable by their routine and effortless deployment. Because they are so routine, because they are so ordinary, they do not need to be talked about. But it is precisely being taken for granted in this way which makes them sociologically interesting. To bring out that interest, we have to make them visible, observable and analysable.

We propose to do this by treating some of the artefacts senior managers use, for example, documents, charts, reports, models and the like, as devices which reveal the detail of management reasoning. In this way, we will make visible some of the common sense methods managers use to display and share their understandings of situations, settings and actions and thereby co-produce consociate organisation;

methods which they take for granted in the welter of their daily management lives. The gestalt created through these understandings is the interior configuration of management as they experience it.

In the next chapter, we use the notion of 'management as a common sense construct' to scope an array of topics for investigation using this approach. In the following chapters, we show how we frame these management objects to bring out the common sense competences on which their use relies. It is our framing which makes third person phenomenology not only different from other social science approaches but from other prominent forms of Ethnomethodology as well. We have said resolving the double contingency is the fundamental problem for any systematic sociological analysis. All sociologies premise their resolution in the presumption of intersubjectivity. We use the maxims set out earlier to define or stipulate an actor's (a senior manager's, in our case) analytic orientation to the intersubjective character of the constellation of (management) objects they attend to. The methods used under that analytic orientation resolve the problem of mutual intelligibility and so configure their first person experience. These methods provide a way of 'sense assembling' the context for their actions; something we might call 'common sense management-as-a-mode-of-reasoning'. Our ambition is to provide a third person description of this first person experience – to repeat the phrase, its interior configuration. The objects we examine (i.e. the documents, charts, spreadsheets and so on) are the objects on and through which this reasoning is deployed. Our challenge is to display that reasoning.

It is important to recognise our gaze is not turned to how the objects are used in other ways, especially how they might figure as interactional resources in formal meetings, briefing sessions, planning sessions and the like. These are important questions when considering senior management work, but not the ones we are concerned with. We are focused on the interpretive work which the consociate nature of organisations imposes on executives; the work of making sense, interpreting, finding the accountability of management objects in order to be able to put them to the uses for which they were designed whenever and wherever they are used. Our scrutiny is confined just to the objects themselves. We are not looking at how documents get talked about or used by senior managers and others who work with them. Rather, we want to reveal (in Chapter 11, we refer to this as 'disclosing') the presuppositions required for their competent comprehension and use. As Garfinkel and Sacks pointed out, in their routine daily use these presuppositions are not talked about because they are not worth talking about, even though they are heavily traded on in senior management work for the formulation of artefact-related matters. They are central elements of what 'any executive knows' (at least in this organisation at this juncture) and so are passed over without comment. Transcripts and ethnographic descriptions offer rich materials for the analysis of managerial life and bring out many interesting features of management work. However, they do not reveal the modes of reasoning we are interested in.

Consociation is the achievement of intersubjectivity over time and distance. Its successful achievement is necessary for stable organisational life. This book looks at some of the ways managers bring off that achievement.

## Notes

1 The term is Aron Gurwitsch's (1979). We say more about consociate social relations in Chapter 2.
2 Mintzberg and Kotter both talk of 'managers', though their focus is largely on the most senior cadres.
3 As Roger Penrose recently put it, what the Second Law seems to be reminding us is 'the familiar and rather depressing fact that, when left to themselves, things simply become more and more manifestly disordered as time progresses!' (2016: 243).
4 The literature is large and growing. The key texts are Garfinkel (1967, 2002 and 2006), We have contributed ourselves (Sharrock and Anderson 1986, Sharrock and Lynch 2003) but other general accounts each with their own viewpoint can be found in Heritage (1984) and Livingston (1987). Recently, Lynch (2015) has given a distinctive view of Garfinkel's work and the current state of Ethnomethodology.
5 Providing a philosophical basis for constitution of objective experience from appearances was Husserl's life's work (Husserl 1970, 1983). For a clear exposition of the implications of Husserl's philosophy for Sociology, see Schutz (1967b, especially Part II, and 1967a). In line with his strategy of 'misreading' philosophy in the service of mounting sociological investigations, Garfinkel asks about the constitution of social facts (definitions of the situation, norms etc.) from appearances.

## References

Anderson, R. and Sharrock, W.W. 2014. "The Inescapability of Trust." In *Trust, Computing and Society*, by R. Harper (ed.), 144–171. Cambridge: Cambridge University Press.
Anderson, R., Hughes, J. and Sharrock, W. 1988. *Working for Profit*. Aldershot: Gower.
Garfinkel, H. 1956. "Some Sociological Concepts and Methods for Psychiatrists." *Psychiatric Papers, vol. 6* 181–195.
——. 1967. *Studies in Ethnomethodology*. Englewood Cliffs, NJ: Prentice Hall.
——. 2002. *Ethnomethodology's Program*. New York: Roman and Littlefield.
——. 2006. *Seeing Sociologically*. Boulder, CO: Paradigm.
—— and Sacks, H. 1970. "On the Formal Structures of Practical Actions." In *Theoretical Sociology*, by J.C. McKinney and E.A. Tiryakian, 337–366. New York: Appleton-Century-Crofts.
Gurwitsch, A. 1979. *Human Encounters in the Social World*. Pittsburgh, PA: Duke University Press.
Hales, C. 1986. "What Do Managers Do?" *Journal of Management Studies, January* 88–115.
Heritage, J. 1984. *Garfinkel and Ethnomethodology*. Oxford: Blackwell.
Husserl, E. 1970. *The Crisis of European Sciences and Transcendental Phenomenology*. Evanston, IL: Northwest University Press.
——. 1983. *Ideas Pertaining to a Pure Phenomenology and to a Phenomenological Philosophy*. The Hague: Martinus Nijoff.
Kaufman, F. 1958. *The Methodology of the Social Sciences*. Atlantic Highlands, NJ: Humanities Press.
Kotter, J. 1999. *John Kotter on What Leaders Really Do*. Cambridge, MA: Harvard Business Review.
Livingston, E. 1987. *Making Sense of Ethnomethodology*. London: Routledge and Kegan Paul.
Lynch, M.E. 2015. "Garfinkel's Legacy: Bastards All the Way Down." *Contemporary Sociology, vol. 44, no. 5* 604–614.

Mintzberg, H. 1975. "The Manager's Job: Folklore and Fact." *Harvard Business Review* 49–61.

Parsons, T. 1951. *The Social System*. London: Routledge and Kegan Paul.

—— and Shils, E. (eds). 1951. *Toward a General Theory of Action*. Cambridge, MA: Harvard University Press.

Penrose, R. 2016. *Fashion, Faith and Fantasy in the New Physics of the Universe*. Princeton, NJ: Princeton University Press.

Perrow, C. 1965. "Hospitals: Technology, Structure and Goals." In *Handbook of Organisations*, by J. March (ed.), 910–971. Chicago, IL: Rand McNally.

Sacks, H. 1995. *Lectures on Conversation vols I & II*. Oxford: Blackwell.

Schutz, A. 1962. "Concept and Theory Formation in the Social Sciences." In *The Problem of Social Reality, Collected Papers Vol. 1*, 48–66. The Hague: Martinus Nijhoff.

——. 1967a. "Phenomenology and the Social Sciences." In *Phenomenology: The Philosophy of Edmund Husserl*, by J. Kockelmans (ed.), 450–472. New York: Doubleday.

——. 1967b. *The Phenomenology of the Social World*. Evanston, IL: Northwestern University Press.

Sharrock, W.W. and Anderson, R.J. 1986. *The Ethnomethodologists*. Chichester: Ellis Horwood.

——. 2011. "Discovering a Practical Impossibility: The Internal Configuration of a Problem in Mathematical Reasoning." *Ethnographic Studies no. 12* 47–58.

—— and Lynch, M. (eds). 2003. *Garfinkel and Ethnomethodology vols I–IV*. Los Angeles, CA: Sage.

# 2 Management as a common sense construct

## Introduction

During the early 1960s, the British government considered setting up a Business School similar to those at Harvard, MIT and elsewhere in the US. In making his contribution to the discussion, J.H. Smith (1960), then one of the UK's leading industrial sociologists, argued strongly for the inclusion in the syllabus of a course on the sociology of organisations. Those being prepared for senior roles in organisations, he asserted, needed to be exposed to an objective, scientific understanding of the social factors influencing the practice of management to complement explanations given by Management Science, Economics and Psychology. The centrepiece of the proposed course was the consideration of 'management roles and their determinants (technical, economic)'. Thirty-odd years later, reflecting the passage of time and changes in Sociology's conception of itself, Keith Grint (1995) repeated the appeal but this time more in terms of the need to understand the nature of power in organisations. Once again, the character of the management role was to be central. Although much in Sociology and the sociology of organisations has changed, it seems the criticality of the function and role of management remains a continuing pre-occupation.

To position our discussion of senior and executive management, this chapter will take the general notion of 'management' as its point of departure and develop an approach based upon the framework outlined in Chapter 1. To do so, it draws inspiration from Egon Bittner's classic paper 'The Concept of Organisation' (Bittner 1965). By pointing out the resources which the sociologist uses to understand organisations are the same as those which members of the organisation use to form their understandings, Bittner, following the line of argument we set out in Chapter 1, suggested if Sociology wishes to offer a technical description (such as those in various accounts of 'bureaucracy') to capture the characteristics of the rational organisation of activities in enterprises and elsewhere, the features it includes in its description will reflect the features which members of the organisation include in their common sense constructions of the same rational organisation. Whilst the sociologist's depictions will be directed to illuminating and resolving sociological considerations and problems, members of the organisation will be concerned with their own. Bittner proposed the linkage between the sociological construct and the construct used by members of the organisation points to a hitherto unexamined sociological topic, namely the concept of rational organisation as a socially organised common sense construct.

In studying common sense constructs, Bittner warned it would be important to ground the investigation in three ways. We must be prepared

> to treat every substantive determination we shall formulate as a case for exploring the background information on which it in turn rests ... *and describe the mechanisms of sustained and sanctioned relevance of the rational constructions to a variety of objects, events and occasions relative to which they are invoked.*
>
> (Bittner 1965: 181; emphasis in original)

We must look beyond the definitions and usages of those within the organisation whose official task it might be to formulate the nature of the organisation. Such persons are, in his view, simply 'toolsmiths', and we would not restrict the description of the use of a tool simply to the modes of deployment envisaged by its creator.

Equally, we must look beyond those aspects of the organisation which most obviously express the idea of rational organisation and, instead, examine whatever happens to be brought under the scheme:

> *The consequence of this step is that the question of what the scheme selects and neglects is approached by asking how certain objects and events meet, or are made to meet, the specifications contained in the schedule.*
>
> (Bittner 1965: 181; emphasis in original)

Such considerations laid the groundwork for the sociological investigation of the methodical uses of 'organisation' as a common sense construct. From his own initial reflections, Bittner suggests organisation might be looked under three broad headings:

1. As a gambit of compliance whereby whatever is needed to be done or whatever has been done can be brought under the relevant rule or rules governing that species of activity through the deployment of 'organisational acumen' – the know-how, know-what of how things get done in any particular organisational context.
2. As a model of stylistic unity by means of which the extended complex structures of activities are bounded and integrated as a proper ordering of interdependencies. This ordering is not the expression of a sense of organisational discipline provided through sanctioned or compelled conformity to whatever may be the prescribed courses of action but of what Bittner calls 'piety', wherein what is done is done because those who do it see it as an appropriate structure of coordinated actions.

3   As corroborative reference wherein the local meaning of whatever one is engaged in can be set in the context of an understanding of the surrounding gestalt. Taken as a collection of individual elements, the meaning of individual tasks or activities may be fragmentary and determined locally. In response to the entropic possibilities of such fragmentation, the notion of rational organisation can be used to solve the synecdoche problem for organisational order by co-relating each part within the whole.

These formulations describe 'organisation' in terms of the normative orders formulated by members of the organisation. Such usages, however, are not to be taken in too Panglossian a way. No organisation exhibits homogeneity of outlook on how things are and who is or should be doing what. Indeed, the normativity of the social order is as much to be seen in the finding of its breach as in its demonstrable observance. The contestability of normativity leads to another consideration. The schemes of interpretation are themselves organisational objects and subject to organisational processes. They are reflexive on the strategies for managing and shaping activities wherein they are used as a resource by *whoever* wishes to make *whatever* sense they can of the state of organisation.

In the studies we present in this book, we take organisational consociation to be the achievement of the intersubjective accountability of actions through the use of senior management as a common sense construct. We treat the determination of what activities mean as the outcome of complementary methods to achieve the recipient design of action. That is, we treat co-participants as being oriented to the mutuality of complementary methods for constructing and finding the accountability of activities. This strategy allows us to adapt the principles set out in Chapter 1, and to adopt the following investigative postulate: *members of an organisational setting see each other's actions as providing displays of what the meaning, sense, logic, rationality, purpose and so on of those actions are to be taken to be.* Describing methods of recipient design as the exhibition and determination of the displayed accountability of organisational activity is how the modalities of management in general as a common sense construct can be made visible and investigated. The variety and contestability of such interpretations is one of the quotidian facts of organisational life.

## 'Management' as a management construct

Conventionally, management as a course of action type is defined by two related elements:

1   A position in a formal division of labour and its associated bundle of activities, rights, obligations, orientations and responsibilities;
2   Correlated with the above, a position in a power structure based in forms of authority and legitimation.

Discussions of the function of management, the culture of management and the practice of management are usually couched as the interplay of rules associated with formal position and the constraints set by the actualities of power. This is often done by counter-posing idealised descriptions of management work, the barriers and enablers facilitated by the operation of formal and informal organisational relationships, and the balance of capacities and control between the powerful and the powerless. It was in terms of just these contrasts that Smith and Grint presented 'the role of management' as the leading term in sociological explanations of the nature of organisations.

In explicating the counter-posed idealised descriptions, sociological accounts of 'management' as the title of a category of actors set details of a course of action type within a mosaic of related conceptualisations. Within such schemes we find:[1]

1   Categories of other types of actor who, together with 'management' make up the personnel in any setting;
2   Inferences about shared motivations constituting reasons for action;
3   Lists of typical interests and relevances organising action;
4   Presumptions about horizontal structures of relevances and interests structuring attention and priorities;
5   Assumptions about a reciprocity of perspectives which allows typical actors to shape the trajectories of their actions as complements or counterpoints to those of others;
6   Repertoires of standardised courses of action allowing any instance to be accommodated within the scheme and which provide for the securing of serial ties between actions.

Unsurprisingly, given the position we have just outlined, these components have their counterparts in the common sense notions of management found within any organisation. However, whereas sociologists might propose that their depictions are reflective and have a degree of 'disinterestedness' and 'generalisability', the adoption of the praxeological rule requires us to treat the members of the organisation as permanently and irredeemably immersed in the specifics of resolving what, in the particular context they are in at any point, they should do next in relation to the courses of action, problems and tasks in hand as they attempt to achieve their desired ends, whatever those might be and however they are to be brought about. The member's depiction is always to be constructed *in media res*.[2]

Our studies describe just some of the modalities of 'accountable senior management' found in organisations. These modalities provide locally perspicuous epitomisations of 'what top management is up to *now*' or 'what executive management is in *this* organisation'. The ones we pick out are:

1   Management as observable and trackable schemes of operational values;
2   Management as displays of continuity of purpose;
3   Management as discoverable due process.

In scoping these three, we are not claiming they are the only modalities to be found nor are we claiming such epitomisations are universally shared. What we are saying is that these modalities can be found and, where found, are socially available accounts of management action. Each stands for a budget of enquiries into how management and other organisational courses of action configure the organisation and so constrain the open texture of interpretability. Strong family resemblances hold between the concepts of organisation and management in professional and lay accounts of organisational life. We should not be surprised, then, to find resonances between the two constructs in cases of both sociological and lay use. Our analysis of actual materials demonstrates these resonances at length.

A final preliminary thought; in looking through the studies we present in later chapters, it would be a mistake to line up the management object being described with just one of the modalities we have listed. Whilst we might emphasise a particular modality in our discussion, the performative possibilities of management objects – that is, what they can be used to do – are open. They can serve whatever purposes an organisational actor may have at any particular point.

## *Exhibited schemes of values*

Management researchers and commentators attest to the prevalence of what might be termed 'rationalisation drift'. Whereas the formal structures, policies, practices enshrined in its charter provide an initial, technical rationale for the complex of activities encompassed within the organisation, over time they become hedged around by other structures, policies and practices which derive their rationale from the institutional environment outside the organisation. *In extremis*, as Meyer and Rowan (1977) suggest, technical rationalisation is reduced to myth and ceremony. An element in such drift is value subscription and ascription, the normative orientations guiding the patterning of courses of action which form the essence of the management and organisational cultures on which researchers report.

Members of organisations, both managers and non-managers, understand the phenomenon of rationalisation drift and use it as a common sense metric for the interpretability of senior management courses of action.[3] The calibration of 'real' and 'claimed' value orientations motivating management strategies is achieved through what senior managers are seen to be doing. Such deductions may stem from comparisons between what is said in public pronouncements and what is seen to be done in day-to-day problem solving, in the prioritising of investments, or in the 'rationalisation' of delivery structures. Similar evidence can be found in the re-configuration of planning objectives, the announcements of new partnerships to be entered into, or recruitment and staffing decisions. Determining the extent of drift in value rationalisation and the projection of its local and global consequences rests on a construal of senior management activities as exhibiting schemes of value which motivate action. On the basis of such judgements, members find patterns in activities which indicate, for example, pressure for change and increased momentum in its realisation. Such determination enables members

24  Foundations

to re-design their own activities to articulate appropriate complementary or countervailing values in the familiar processes of formal and informal conformity and conflict which social science observers detail.

## *Displays of continuity of purpose*

Helmuth von Molke's epigram about the first casualty in battle being the plan may be a management cliché but it remains true for all that. No matter whether in their infancy or well established, all organisations are complex force fields. Internal and external pressures to undertake particular courses of action can often be at odds or downright contradictory, as may be the priorities being pressed by various stakeholders and partners. A plan may be developed which 'satisfices' across all these demands, only for implementation to be stymied by subsequent shifts in the driving forces or by a sudden emergence of an entirely new dominant demand. Changes in the force field rarely give rise to complete 'ground-zero' re-planning, though. Rather, a strategy of adaptive integration is the more likely response with extensive personal, management and political energy as well as time being expended on 'flexing up' the plans currently in place and being implemented. As top managers are wont to say, rebuilding the plan is the very last thing anyone wants to do.

The extent to which activities can be found to display continuity of purpose whilst accommodating foreseen and unforeseen exigencies is a judgement members of the organisation make in virtue of what they take senior managerial responses to mean. Standard responses range from the replaying of strategic option choices through the rolling back of initiatives and programmes to what might be painful adjustment to what have become known as 'Rumsfeld problems'.[4] The extent to which change and continuity are seen to be equilibrated, and what is implied by where the balance is being set, is key to a member's understanding of the stress and turbulence to which the organisation is currently (and might in the future be) subject and, hence, what their own response should be. Managers orient to both the understandings and the likely responses simply because if 'unmanaged', they can add further energy to whatever convulsions are already going on. Major delays in building programmes, for example, can have implications for the scheduling of organisational re-structuring and hence career projections or market opportunities. Equally, the emergence of major, unplanned cost requirements can twist the ordering of decision streams. Things that were planned to be done later may have to be done earlier; some things that were high priority may have to be dropped. From whatever they do to address the issues which arise, members of the organisation can see how far the solutions being put in place maintain a clearly recognisable continuity of purpose. Because of the scale of most Rumsfeld problems and the extent of organisational re-direction they demand, those who are not senior managers in the organisation are often quite well aware of the challenges they pose and have a good sense of their implications. Seeing what senior managers do to deal with them and what, therefore, those solutions imply is critical to forming expectations in regard to organisational stability, the trajectories of action and the likely availability of resources to undertake them. In turn, all are key components of the ordinary member's structure of organisational relevances.

## Discoverable due process

Governance and who is responsible for it has been much discussed of late as headline after headline has trumpeted alleged improprieties in the ways organisations, large and not so large, public and private, are run. For the sociologist, governance provides yet another locale where the tendency for formal policies and actual practices to diverge may be on view. As with other studies of rationalisation drift, the aim is to mark and track both the forces at work on managers which encourage or impel movement away from strict observation of the formal rules and procedures, and the reasons offered for so doing. These reasons are held to point to the causes and consequences of the warping, morphing, or erosion of what counts as 'good management culture' in the organisation.

Members of organisations also orient to a sense of propriety, that is, to a sense of the proper bases on which decisions and actions should be taken, and hence seek to find due process being honoured in what is being done; the right things are being done in the right way. This sense does not come from a detailed knowledge of the Memorandum of Understanding, Articles of Association, or any other formally defined remit under which the organisation might have been created. Instead, as Bittner pointed out, it comes from a generalised sense of what ought to be done before what, what ought to be used as a reason for what, and who should or should not be doing what. This generalised understanding allows members of the organisation to decide what managing is and define what senior managers are doing by the extent to which their actions can be fitted under it. This is senior management as discoverable due process.

All members of organisations are engaged in management to some extent. They are involved in going to meetings; they are involved in scheduling activities; they are involved in determining local and global priorities; they are involved in the resolution of problems. Thus, for them, the determination of discoverable due process is as much about what 'we' are doing and how 'we' are doing it as it is about what 'they', the formally designated most senior managers, might be up to. One of the most important ways such judgements can be made is by seeking to bring the activities currently under way within the scope of whatever organising format is available for the situation in hand. Members of the organisation can see if there is a fit between 'the agenda' and its meeting, 'the record' and the decision outcomes, statements of 'the evidence' and the definition of its implications, 'the next steps' to be taken and the allocation of tasks and responsibilities. From such fits, they can see just how far managerial due process is being adhered to. That finding becomes their evidence for the accounts they offer.

One last point is worth bringing out. In sociological and other discussions of governance, the moral order of due process is often what is at issue. Are the tenets ascribable to the actions taken the ones which ought to be in place? For members of organisations, such moral considerations are only occasionally a matter of concern. Rather, their interests centre on the extent to which the interpretation of due process arrived at chimes with the projectability of the trajectories of actions being undertaken elsewhere under the organisational frame of reference. Are we arriving at similar decisions in much the same way? Will this decision lead to revision of earlier decisions? Will this course of action generate turbulence for that course of action, and so on? The practicalities of management as governance are the practicalities of activity management as a normative order – that is, as a system of activities which can and should be fitted together in particular ways.

## What next?

By treating management as a common sense construct, we can develop suites of topics through which to explore the co-production of the accountability of senior management action. Such accountability is produced within the flow of management activity. This is the configuration of senior management from within. The means we use to make this configuring visible is the structuring of documents and related management objects as devices for ordering activities. In the next two chapters we lay out what we mean by this. In subsequent chapters, we show how, under the three modalities we have just outlined and through the use of an array of documentary and other objects, organisational consociation is produced by means of recipient design of senior management activity as the display of mutual intelligibility.

## Notes

1 Obviously, we are following Schutz (1962) in this specification.
2 For the purposes of exposition, we will allow this (caricatured) contrast to run. On another occasion, we would wish to look at what things impinge upon and shape the way sociological descriptions might be given. The working sociologist is no less *in media res* than the working member of the organisation. It is simply the array of things they are in the midst of is different.
3 We mean 'metric' here in Lindsay Churchill's sense (no date).
4 Donald Rumsfeld, Defence Secretary under George W. Bush, famously distinguished between 'known unknown' and 'unknown unknown' exigencies associated with a formulated plan. It is the latter which pose 'Rumsfeld problems'. These can often require major strategic re-orientation.

## References

Bittner, E. 1965. "The Concept of Organisation." *Social Research*, vol. 32 239–255.
Churchill, L. No date. *Notes on Everyday Quantitative Practices*. New York: Russell Sage Foundation.
Grint, K. 1995. *Management: A Sociological Introduction*. London: Polity Press.
Meyer, J. and Rowan, B. 1977. "Institutionalized Organizations: Formal Structure as Myth and Ceremony." *American Journal of Sociology*, vol. 83, no. 2 340–363.
Schutz, A. 1962. "Common Sense and Scientific Interpretation of Human Action." In *The Problem of Social Reality*, 3–47. Dordrecht: Martinus Nijoff.
Smith, J.H. 1960. "Sociology and Management Studies." *British Journal of Sociology*, vol. 11, no. 2 103–111.

# Part II
# Studies in the practicalities of executive management

# 3 Representations and realities

## Re-positioning documents

In the previous two chapters, we set out an approach to the study of management which comprised an analytic stance and a general formulation of the domain, namely modalities of the common sense construct of management. At several points in that introduction, we were at pains to emphasise how different as an articulation of the ethnomethodological gaze, third person phenomenology is to conventional Sociology. In this chapter, we give a relatively straightforward illustration of that difference in orientation and interest by looking at how the idea of 'documentary representation' has been applied in Sociology. We will do so by considering Louis Bucciarelli's (1994) reflections on engineering pedagogy and textbooks and John Law's (2011) deconstruction of a social survey. The purpose is not to offer a deep critique of either analysis but rather to put our finger on just how these fairly conventional (at least these days) analyses construe the representations they describe as opposed to own interests.

Having marked the contrast in this way, we use the next chapter to home in on the phenomena we take as the theme of our analysis: senior management's reasoning about and with documents, schedules, charts, schemas and other depictions of organisational activities. The majority of management work is carried out in, around and through these kinds of 'management objects'. In our studies, we anchor depictions of the ramified complexities of managerial realities in the details of a range of examples. To paraphrase a term very familiar from elsewhere in Sociology, our focus is on documentary and other methods of order construction. The objects we will use are from the more formal class of 'inscriptions' strewing desks and floors, heaped on shelves and arranged in drawers, pinned to walls and stuck on screens – in fact, found everywhere in organisations. They make up one category of 'the missing masses' of mundane artefacts (Latour 1992) constituting the materials of managerial life.

Except, of course, they haven't really been missing. As Matthew Hull's (2012) extensive review reveals, even if we narrow the scope to bureaucratic or formal documents, the social sciences have had an abiding (if not actually very focused) interest in them as signals, symbols and cyphers of a vast array of features of organisational life. Documents have been studied for how they reflect organisational form, the distribution of power, organisational culture, and so on. Only recently, Lindsay Prior (2008) exhorted the social science disciplines to shift their interest. Using a phrase for which we have a somewhat nostalgic affection, he urged us to take documents as a topic for analysis rather than a resource.[1] The kind of shift Prior had in mind was away from seeing documents as objects for 'secondary research' where, as passive records, they are counted and summarised, and towards addressing what Actor Network Theory (ANT) calls their 'performativity'. The questions to be asked were about the role particular documents play in the networks of 'actants' engaged in organisational or other courses of action. Such a repositioning would force attention to the ways in which documents express or 'enact' particular perspectively organised readings or representations rather than simply being information carriers. By deconstructing documents, analysts would be able to demonstrate their role in creating and sustaining generalised metaphysical outlooks, perspectives, or world views attributable to various cultural practices and how these outlooks reinforce the dominant structures of power and authority within the cultures in which they are found.

In a previous discussion (Anderson and Sharrock 2012), we argued at some length that ANT often begins with an interestingly formulated investigative proposition and somehow, step by step, becomes embroiled in needless controversialising. What seems to engender this slide is a predisposition to view social phenomena solely as exemplifying some sociological (and, in the case of representations, often philosophical too) puzzle or contention. As a result, what the phenomenon might be to those immersed in the social context in which it is found becomes displaced by the significance it has for the sociologist. Whilst we applaud Prior's call for a re-thinking of the sociological possibilities of documents, we do not think he has exorcised this predisposition. Instead, we believe blandly heeding his suggestion is likely to lead, indeed already has led, to much the same strategy of displacement – a displacement of the uses that documents have for participants in the settings to one where the documents are assessed in terms of the sociologist's interest in the correspondence between representations presented in documents and the realities those documents purportedly represent or surreptitiously insinuate. The point of this chapter is to show this substitution does not involve a legitimate alternation of one point of reference for another, but involves, rather, the elaboration of the sociologists' interests *at the expense* of those of the participants. In the next, we will set out an alternative way of starting from this re-positioning, one which uses the approach described in the first two chapters.

## What engineers don't learn about engineering

In *Designing Engineers*, Louis Bucciarelli (1994) tells the story of Beth, a young and presumably recent engineering graduate. Beth is attempting to solve an ongoing problem with a desalination plant installed in a Middle Eastern country. Beth herself is at her desk at a US site of the engineering company. She is working under conditions which are not really favourable for getting on with the desalination plant job because she has more than one project on the go at the same time. She is constantly interrupted and is called upon to move from one to another by the demands of her colleagues and clients. She cannot make up the time she loses to these distractions during the day by working longer hours because of her domestic commitments. The computing resources and data available were not created by her to deal with the task, but have been supplied 'by the field'. This is 'real life' engineering carried out on a serious project (i.e. not a practice or rehearsal one) and is just how any experienced engineer might recognise their working life to be. The trouble is Beth's working life is nothing like the accounts of engineering which Beth will have encountered during her formal training. For Bucciarelli, this means there must be something wrong with engineering schooling. So, Bucciarelli asks, how on earth could Beth learn to operate as a competent practising engineer under conditions like this? It can't be that Beth is unique. Her education has been much the same as other engineers and they too have learned to cope with the fragmentation and messiness of their working lives. The one thing Bucciarelli is sure is wrong about engineering schooling is that it doesn't teach engineers their work will be messy in the way that Beth's work has been shown to be. Beth is having to work in messy circumstances, but on her engineering courses she didn't learn this is how it would be. In fact, for Bucciarelli, she learned the exact opposite. Engineering texts and curricula provide a picture of engineering at odds with Beth's experience. Bucciarelli's view is that in engineering, trainees aren't taught a realistic idea of their eventual work. Instead, they are taught how to operate in an 'object world' which is very different to the practical reality they are notionally being trained for.

Bucciarelli argues that the way the engineering design process is taught involves presenting engineering work as if it takes place in an 'object world', an abstract environment which includes only the abstract objects with which engineers are concerned and pays no attention to the working relations amongst the engineers doing the work. The object world is a place where everything is neat, tidy and precise, and can be depicted in the terms provided by mathematics and formal diagrams. Bucciarelli asserts this can be shown in the materials, such as textbook imagery, used in the training of engineers. Textbook diagrams like the one shown below, set out a standard schematic (standard to the ways of engineering education, that is) of the end-to-end steps of the design and implementation process.

In Bucciarelli's eyes, this diagram shows what sort of environment 'the object world' of engineering is, one which shows design and implementation as a *neat and tidy*, smoothly continuous and peacefully *deliberative process* (seemingly very different from the harassed, perturbed and impromptu state of Beth's situation). In Bucciarelli's eyes, the textbook diagram is misleading since it projects an image of what engineering work that is not true to its realities. Thus,

> We might conclude that design practice is an extremely orderly, rational process in which creative thought can be contained in a single box that yields a conceptual design or designs, which after detailed evaluation and analysis within some more boxes can be given real substance, tested, put into production, and then marketed for the profit and the benefit of all humankind.
>
> (Bucciarelli 1994: 111)

## 32  The practicalities of executive management

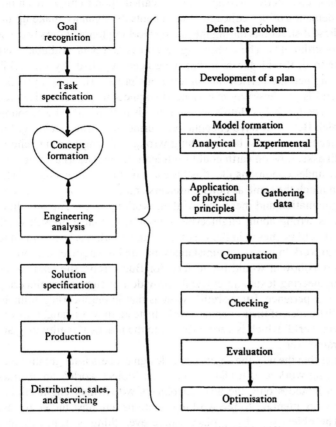

*Figure 3.1* The design process (Bucciarelli 1994: 112)

Moreover, the diagram gives the impression that the whole process of design and development is almost an automatic process:

> a halting flow, a chaining of cause and effect; it might even be viewed as a conveyor belt, a machine through which the design is moved and acted upon, transformed and embellished at each stop. The only suggestion of possible messiness comes in the looping of some of the lines around the blocks. This indicates *feedback* and makes *designing* an iterative process.
>
> (Bucciarelli 1994: 111; emphasis in original)

He continues:

> A prerequisite to talk about feedback or interaction is the temporal ordering of the segmented states of design. This entails definition of a clear beginning and end – the top and bottom if the figure in this case. The object as design

process is then closed and bounded. Time, though not explicitly shown, is implied; it starts at the top and extends downward. We might even assume that each block ought to be allotted an equivalent amount of time. The orderly segmenting of process, with the design proceeding down (falling) through this linear sequence of stages, suggests a form of determinism.

(Bucciarelli 1994: 111)

The misleading picture of engineering is supposedly manifest in the details of the diagram. What is allegedly wrong with it is that it depicts the *social reality* of projects in line with the structure of the engineer's object world and not in terms of Bucciarelli's sociological viewpoint. The significance of the diagram is set by its ontological implications.

Bucciarelli picks out three ways in which we are potentially misled.

*Time*: The diagram is not explicit about time though time is implied by the serial organisation of the process boxes. The worry seems to be that the diagram's normative structures, for example, standardised measures of time, are not specified. The diagram gives no way to set our expectations about the length of steps in the process. If readers are not told how long the respective steps are, won't they nonetheless default to supplying timings to the diagram for themselves and thus tend to assume that elapsed time (however measured) for each stage or box must be the same? Such an assumption would 'fill in' the normative gap. The trouble is that making that assumption would be at odds with what all engineers know about the process the diagram depicts. For example, it would imply that project scale and complexity have no effects on the pacing of the process and hence not only can the design of a drone and the Dreamliner be depicted in the same general form, but each step in any development process must take the same amount of time. We think it is Bucciarelli, not the diagram that is doing the misleading here – there being no reason to think that the temporal features of the diagram relate to fixed periods of time. Assuming that each stage in the process takes the same time would be as foolish as taking the scale conventions of a spatial map to apply to the walls of houses shown in the map just as they do to the distances between topological features and the lengths of paths. As Roy Turner once pointed out, it would be naïve to imagine that an icon on a map implied the walls of suburban houses were 22 feet thick. It is not a cartographical convention that all features on a map are drawn to the same scale. Many do not apply to the legends that picture the conventions of the map. Readers of maps and engineering diagrams – perhaps even engineering trainees – know this, and it would be at least as (we think more) reasonable to assume that the absence of time-scales indicates that the diagram carries no implications about the time a given step in an engineering design process takes.

*Structure*: Bucciarelli complains 'the only suggestion of possible messiness' seems to come with the 'looping of some lines around the blocks'

(1994: 111). Somewhat grudgingly, this is accepted as identifying two crucial and emphasised features of the design process; iteration and feedback. Both can be seen in the diagram, but simple illustration of a possibility is not enough for Bucciarelli. He sees the comparative thinness of the lines making the loops as downplaying their importance. Moreover, the inconsistency between the presence of iteration and the implication that each block might be given the same amount of time is disregarded by Bucciarelli. Since iteration is a repetitive process, the loops show only the presence of iterations and nothing of the number of iterations there might be, nor of the clock-time any single iteration might take.

*Determinism*: The diagram expresses a regimented order to design tasks. Bucciarelli prefers to read this as portraying those working through the process as being compelled to follow the steps as laid out. But, if we see the diagram as a general schematic designed to have as wide an application as possible then it could equally be said to identify an extensive, if not comprehensive, range of *engineering* activities that may be involved in any engineering project and differentiated into separate phases in some of them. The sequencing might then illustrate dependency not control. Being able to start on a given kind of task might be dependent upon having already begun or even completed a prior task. The succession of tasks and their dependency may reside in the kinds of tasks they are. For example, the ability to carry out some tasks may depend upon having something to work with. Testing prototypes is dependent upon the availability of prototypes to be tested. The work of running paper through a photocopier to determine the rate of failure for that type of machine and the quality of the images being produced cannot begin until prototype machines have been produced. Rather than intimating any kind of determinism, the diagram could be seen as an aid to decision making. It offers a categorisation of the kinds of activities which need to be planned for in carrying through a design project. It acts as an aid against overlooking the need to provide for what will, at some point, become a necessary activity, and may suggest answers as to where in the sequence that might be placed. At what point, for example, will it be necessary to start producing prototypes if testing operations are to start on time? Answering that question presupposes answering another question, namely what other design tasks will need to be completed before prototype construction can start?

For us, what Bucciarelli see as inadequate and hence misleading features of the process diagram could just as easily be described as the sort of characteristics a general introductory text commonly show, and should be understood as offering a (comparatively) simple and abstract characterisation of the main constituents of the standard design process. Since it wasn't offered as a sociological description of the concrete social organisation of complex projects, why should we expect it to give an adequate description in those terms? This is what we mean by the substitution effect. Actually, though, it goes much deeper. In a later discussion, Bucciarelli and Kroes (2014) argue not only do descriptions of engineering processes give a false view of what Engineering is like, but, as we have already noted, also that the whole curriculum which trainee engineers follow constantly reinforces a particular view of Engineering and engineering practice. This view depicts Engineering as a body of

> discipline specific ways of modeling [*sic*] a product's behaviour, with special methods developed for problem solving and established notions about what constitutes a robust solution, with their own body of codes for use in what constitutes a robust solution, with their own body of codes for use in design, with their own forms of prototypical hardware and supplier's catalogues – all the resources an engineer has to call upon in practice – to constitute what we label an object world.
> (Bucciarelli and Kroes 2014: 188)

Such a view does not offer students

> a realistic picture of engineering practice – in particular with regard to the role of social features and social values. These values enter engineering practice because engineering work nowadays requires ongoing teamwork – a mode in which engineers with different disciplinary backgrounds, responsibilities and interests (from different object worlds) – must work together. This gives engineering work a social dimension because negotiations between engineers then becomes an unavoidable aspect of their work.
> (Bucciarelli and Kroes 2014: 190)

On Bucciarelli and Kroes' rendering, then, what the engineering object world expresses is the false view that Engineering is an instrumental, rational, not to say ratiocinative, convergent enterprise; when looked at 'sociologically', any engineering effort is essentially a locally contexted negotiation featuring compromise across an array of multi-valued, multi-cultural and multi-faceted perspectives. The importance that Bucciarelli attaches to the diagram is as an articulation of an erroneous metaphysics.

Given what we have just said, we should not be surprised at the way actual learning materials themselves are viewed. For example, Bucciarelli and Kroes cite this from a textbook:

> The main objective of a basic mechanics course should be to develop in the engineering student the ability to analyse a given problem in a simple and logical manner and to apply to its solutions a few fundamental and well-understood principles.
> (Beer et al. 2006: xiii, quoted in Bucciarelli and Kroes 2014: 191)

## 36  The practicalities of executive management

The interpretation Bucciarelli and Kroes give of this statement is that:

> The mechanics problem is given – not to be formulated by the student; it demands a simple and logical analysis – not a conjectural, inferential thinking up and about; and it is to be solved using a few fundamental and well-understood principles – not trying several, alternative, perhaps conflicting approaches and perspectives. The working life of an engineering student, hence graduate, from this perspective is neat, well posed, deductive, and principled.
> 
> (Bucciarelli and Kroes 2014: 191–192)

Once again, substitution is at work. That the word 'basic' might be key is overlooked, with basic considerations often being uncomplicated versions of advanced ones, along with the possibility that being basic is an important part of its design as a text for beginners. Rather than taking the text on its own terms, Bucciarelli and Kroes are more interested in extrapolating from it toward what they see as a general mind set, one which defined by 'object world thinking' or an 'engineering mentality'.

Unlike novels, textbooks are not generally designed to be read from beginning to end. Rather they are to be used piecemeal, perhaps in conjunction with taught courses. As a consequence, they embody the underlying idea of an orderly learning progression. Dependencies can be assumed in the sequencing of learning; there are things which one learns first (which is what 'basic' perhaps intends) and other things which one learns later. A Mechanics textbook is unlikely to claim it shows students how to solve tough, unsolved, multi-dimensional engineering problems right from the start. Instead, its expressed purpose is to enable students to see connections between Mechanics and Engineering (and assess their own grasp on these simplified matters by tackling interesting though simple problems). 'Time', 'timing' and 'timeliness' are not elements in the organisation of teaching and learning that Bucciarelli and Kroes seem to think relevant to construing teaching materials.

We don't say that texts don't portray Engineering as a neat and orderly process. But, for us, this is part of their ostensible purpose as an aide to training. Our question would be not about the sociological implications of the ontologies we can see in them, but how they have been designed to enable *students* (which is its intended audience) to learn to operate some previously unfamiliar tools of the trade, among which, presumably, are some principles and some of the mathematics of Mechanics. On this view, much of what is presented in the texts is about what can be done in and with Mechanics. What is being learned under the title of 'problem solving' is how to use Mechanics to work out solutions to calculable problems. This is not about how to generate and solve complex engineering problems, but more how to use Mechanics to solve the kind of problems which can routinely be solved by calculation. What is being learned is to do for yourself what those competent in Mechanics can already do.

The worry sociologists like Bucciarelli and Kroes have is not that the Engineering profession is in general crisis because no one knows how to organise large projects or deliver them on time and to budget as a result of their having been trained to think of Engineering in a way which is at odds with the way Engineering really is. Rather, it is that although engineers obviously can and do manage these things (i.e. a proportion of engineering projects get completed), their education has given them a false and thus inappropriate 'model' of Engineering, one that has somehow had to be unlearned and replaced by a viewpoint in which Engineering is a socially organised practice (which, in Beth's case, seems to mean that tasks are worked on in fragmented ways). For us, there seem three pretty obvious responses to this concern:

1   Perhaps what Bucciarelli and Kroes have in mind is what most professions call the accumulation of experience and so does not take place during university training but is acquired afterwards in and through engaging in real world engineering.
2   Alternatively, perhaps it does take place during training, for an educational process can be instructive about many matters that are not specifically taught. There is much which is taken in *along with* what is specifically taught. So, perhaps there are opportunities within and alongside the training process to gain these understandings.
3   Or again, perhaps acquiring the skills, competences and understandings required happens at innumerable junctures in the training process rather than by undertaking specific learning tasks at specific points. In that sense, engineers might learn these things everywhere and nowhere.

There is also a fourth possibility. Perhaps Bucciarelli and Kroes are simply looking in the wrong place. The 'turn to the social' in much professional education has often involved inserting Sociology into courses in Medicine, Engineering, Accountancy, Architecture and so on. These interjections have by no means been universally welcomed or successful. Certainly, there is no evidence that knowing about the sociology of accountancy makes anyone any more competent in the practice of accountancy or, in the case of Engineering, being taught about social institutions, social groups, cultures, identities, norms and values (and thereby about the negotiated character of engineering projects) makes anyone any more capable as a member of an engineering project team.[2] Bucciarelli and Kroes presume that if something is not being taught in so many words, it cannot be being learned. But engineers must have learned some things they weren't taught in so many words, for, as Bucciarelli and Kroes argue, those words are kept out of training materials so as to perpetuate the illusion that engineering work is done under 'object world' conditions. Perhaps it is that, whatever Bucciarelli and Kroes think should be taught, is actually being learnt in and through all the other parts of the student's non-engineering ordinary life, as well, of course, through engaging in group exercises, personal projects, assignments, reading the newspaper and the like. This leads us to the suggestion that perhaps the object world of Engineering is not as hermetically sealed as we are being led to believe. The claim that it is begs the question of how over several years in the classroom, at the lab bench, using textbooks, solving problems and undertaking projects engineering students actually do learn how 'to engineer'. Rather than asking about the metaphysics of engineering education, this question focuses on the actualities of learning to be an engineer.

## The metaphysics of surveys

John Law is not as puzzled as Bucciarelli and Kroes, but he is similarly impressed by the idea that representations (mis)represent an essentially untidy social reality as if it were a neat and tidy one. He knows how people acquire their 'object worlds' and other conceptual frameworks. These are conveyed in and reinforced by ordinary, routine activities – what Law calls 'practices'. This acquisition and reinforcement is mostly done by stealth. In the nations of the developed 'North', the dominant conceptual framework is a 'one world metaphysics' associated with the natural and mathematical sciences. The ways we find out about the social, physical and natural worlds around us through our participation in everyday affairs all reinforce this one world metaphysics. On Law's estimation, we are being inveigled – by diffuse effects – into thinking that this one world metaphysics is mandatory.

Take a publication as pedestrian as the *Eurobarometer*, a bi-annual report devoted to surveys of opinion among citizens of EU member states (Law 2011). Each report deals with a distinct theme or topic. Law asks us to look at one report on attitudes to farm animal welfare in different parts of Europe. In it we find statements such as '58% of EU citizens want to be better informed about farming conditions.' The map given with this statement shows how the 58% is distributed among the member states. Through this data, Law says, 'We are being told explicitly about how people think, and about country differences' (2011: 8).

That much seems fairly obvious. But now comes the critical shift: 'There is also a bunch of hidden assumptions embedded in these results and in the survey more generally, and it is these that are interesting in the present context' (Law 2011: 8).

We've used the word 'inveigled' advisedly, for Law worries that these 'hidden' assumptions are being passed off on the readers of the *Eurobarometer*. The idea seems to be that if the reliance on these assumptions in the interviewing were pointed out, people might then question, even reject, the 'one world' assumption along with (presumably) the whole business of social surveying.

For Law, it is not what the survey reports about concern for farm animal well-being that is of any significance to his analysis. What matters is only that the assumptions surreptitiously reproduce through communication the standard 'one world' conception of reality. This is the same substitution of sociological import for concern about the ostensible uses of the document that we saw with Bucciarelli and Engineering education.

So, just what are these 'hidden' assumptions about the how the interviewing was done which Law derives from the published report of the interviewing results?

It's being assumed, one, that the person speaks an *appropriate national language*; its being assumed, two, that she knows what an *interview* is (and please don't make the mistake of thinking that this is self-evident. The 'interviewee' is a twentieth century invention); its being assumed, three, that she's *arithmetically competent* (she can, for instance, answer "seven" on a scale from one to ten, with some idea what this might imply); its being assumed, though, that she possesses some more or less *stable attitudes* which influence her behaviour; and its being assumed, five, that those attitudes intersect with information which further influences her behaviour.

(Law 2011: 8–9; emphases in original)

Law admits that his own claim these "assumptions" are 'hidden' seems pretty fatuous since they are blindingly obvious, However, their importance to him lies in the fact these matters are assumed rather than being individually enumerated in the text that assumes them.[3] This means that they are, rather, 'at work under the radar'. What they are at work on is reinforcing assumptions readers are to make about the character of the survey respondents talked about in the findings:

This is *how the person is being enacted in the survey*. Let me put that more strongly. It is how the survey person is being *done*. It is what the survey person is made to be. And other kinds of people aren't getting into the survey at all.

(Law 2011: 9; emphases in original)

The bundle of properties identified defines what 'a respondent' is for the survey. We could grant this much and still be nonplussed about the point being made. Where does the one world metaphysics come in?

The answer is: they [the one world metaphysics] are being done by stealth in the survey. They are taking the form of what we might think of as blank realism. In surveys nation states are containers filled with people. So the UK becomes a space with 48 million people in it. Not *terra nullius* but *terra plenus*. The space isn't empty. It is filled with people. But it's the same metaphysics. And here's what's interesting. No one noticed or commented on the fact that the collectivity is being created in this way. Which, surely, is precisely the art of the whole mechanism.

(Law 2011: 9; emphases in original)

Here we have it. Just as (so Law seems to believe) the ontology of the natural sciences is a material world full of individual fundamental particles, the *EuroBarometer* creates an analogous world of social individuals. These individuals are the basic component of the social world. As a result, what to all intents and purposes looks to be a bureaucratic compendium of summarised views and opinions about animal welfare is *actually* a mechanism for reproducing the one world metaphysics of Western Science as expressed in the territorial possessiveness that is at the core of our political consciousness. Once grafted on in this way, it defines the reality of the political environment in which we live (which is that of populations distributed amongst national territories) as the *only proper way* of organising things.

What is most notable in Law's reflections is the attenuated character of the 'reality' at issue here. The very conception of metaphysics by stealth makes it sound as if what people might take to be novel, obscure, difficult, or unattractive ideas are somehow being smuggled into their conceptual frameworks. This overlooks the rather obvious fact that for Law to extract those assumptions, they have to be recognisable *from the* Eurobarometer *presentation* in the first place and, indeed, recognisable as 'the same — and therefore unremarkable —assumptions again' (for example, that UK territory is populated is not an assumption specific to the *Eurobarometer*). The 'covert' assumptions are transmuted into the blatantly obvious simply because Law must employ those very assumptions in his reading of his illustrative text and he relies upon his readers to recognise these assumptions about the European Union being a multilingual organisation, interviews as oral transactions done in some national language(s), by persons who have commonplace elementary numerical skills (an assumption which, of course goes unremarked when Law repeats the interview findings in terms of numerical percentages) without Law needing to explain to his readers how he has managed to find these assumptions in his source materials even though they are 'hidden' and 'under the radar'.

That these 'obvious' matters are so is not something established or asserted in addition to reporting that the *Eurobarometer* is a product of multi-national interviewing (of what are, after all, identified as 'citizens' of the EU and its constituent nations), but something which is included in it. These things characteristically go without saying in the sense that they don't need to be announced to be present or to be specified in 'so many words' (one doesn't necessarily have to be told something to understand that it is relevant). Law declares 'No one noticed or commented on the fact that the collectivity is being created in this way' and that is 'what's interesting' about this 'doing of reality'. It is this which 'surely, is precisely the art of the whole mechanism' (2011: 9). It appears that what is being done by stealth, then, is the creation of a trans-European political collection of individuals whose views are set out in the report. The trouble for Law's stealth argument is that the authors of the report are quite clear that this is what they are doing. They state what the objectives and procedures of their report are (in their descriptions of the nature of the *Eurobarometer* as an EU-sponsored operation and in their presentation of the latest round of findings) and make a rather extensive series of comments on the fact that the collectivity – at least, cross-national and national levels of public opinion within the collectivity – are constructed in this way.

Let's be charitable and assume Law's point is not the enunciation of the obvious. What, then, could it be? Mike Lynch describes what Mel Pollner has called 'the ontologically fatal insight' (Lynch 2013, citing Pollner 1987: 88) as follows:

an insight sometimes arrived at in a moment of heady delight, but often as a horrifying realization – that the world we take for granted as an independent environment of action is not what it seems; instead, it is a product of our own constitutive practices and 'it could be otherwise'.

(Lynch 2013: 449)

Perhaps what Law wants to identify is what he imagines those who read the *Eurobarometer* reports, both the politicians in Brussels and the odd commuter on the bus from Didsbury, will find to be a destabilising revelation, namely that our cultural practices and the way we view the world might have been different – indeed, they have been different in that 'other people' have lived on the basis of different assumptions to those 'we' live by, with us being, perhaps, entirely oblivious to their assumptions. The trouble is they are the least likely people to read his description and his actual readership will find the suggestion hardly surprising, let alone horrifying. They well enough know that the emergence and dominance of modern natural science was a deeply contingent historical matter. It is not the interests of the readers of the *Eurobarometer*, the politicians in Brussels or even our Didsbury commuter that Law has in mind, but those of his fellow sociologists. What he does is replace what, for the sake of simplicity, we will call the practical relevances of the readers of the survey with sociological ones. In so doing, the phenomena found in the survey report are transformed. It is not the 'facts' presented in the findings nor even the one world metaphysical reality which those facts might be said to depict, but the role of practices – the practices of carrying out and reporting a survey – in constituting that reality which he wants us to attend to. The point he is stressing is not that realities could have been different, but that practices are. And if practices embed, convey and instil realities then won't the empirical existence of multiple practices mean the existence of multiple realities? This is the ontological horror Law is waving in front of us. If we accept that distinct multiple practices produce distinct multiple realities, how do we choose among practices and their realities? Since, as a society we don't have any sort of open and democratic procedure for schema selection, the chaos of relativism must only be being held at bay by the stealthy enforcement of a uniform acceptance of the one world metaphysics. It turns out Law isn't really interested in the *Eurobarometer* at all. What he is interested in is the possibility of metaphysical implosion and where that might leave the politics of knowledge in science and, by extension, Sociology as well.[4]

## Conclusion

The line we have taken in this chapter has been deliberately simple. When sociologists take an interest in representations of any kind, what happens is the substitution of extrinsic sociological interests for the intrinsic concerns of users of those representations. We have shown how this often leads to sociological critique by deconstruction wherein the 'immediate', 'surface', or 'obvious' characteristics of the representation are interpreted as conveying subliminal, hidden, or otherwise covert systems of 'social' meanings. For the sociologist, the purpose seems revelatory; to show that users, Bucciarelli's engineers, or Law's readers of the survey 'know not what they do'. They think they are learning the basics of Engineering or the opinions of a sample of people across Europe, whereas 'in reality' they are acquiring a particular 'object world' or a 'one world metaphysics'.

This substitution effect is one of the features (or even symptoms) of deep problems in Sociology's mode of reasoning, especially about other modes of reasoning. We are well aware we have done no more than touch on the most superficial aspects of these problems and have by no means given sufficient space and consideration to all the ramifying entanglements in this conceptual and methodological mare's nest. We have used the substitution effect as a way of marking difference (especially with respect to the casual treatment given to the use that documents have for their users), no more. We have no space here to do otherwise. In future discussions, though, we intend to return to the broader, more fundamental questions. For the moment, our marking of difference does all the work we need it to do. We have shown what we mean by it, that's all. We now need to show what we mean by doing things differently.

## Notes

1 The length of tooth of this phrase (it was the theme around which Don Zimmerman and Mel Pollner arranged their (1971) introduction to ethnomethodology's sociological reasoning) hints at just how late on the scene Prior was. As we will shortly see, the interest in documents he was pressing on colleagues was already well under way in some parts of the sociological world.
2 The history of 'sociological studies of science and technology' suggests that applying such ideas causes confusion and conflict amongst social scientists.
3 'Assumed' in this case does not mean 'absent from the text' but, rather, manifested in the text without being specified as assumptions – for example, the assumption that people are at least basically numerate is manifested in the fact that they are being asked to give numerical rankings on a scale.
4 There is a much tighter double bind here, of which Law is well aware (Law 2004). Law takes the work of Anne Marie Mohl to show multiple practices across disciplines produce multiple realities. This is the original stimulus for the *Eurobarometer* example. But so do multiple practices within disciplines. Steve Woolgar (1998) once called reflexivity a 'methodological horror' to which, since it could not be resisted, Science and Sociology must succumb. Law's worry is that the problem of multiple ontologies looks like the reincarnation of reflexivity. As with Woolgar, it seems for him all we can do is acquiesce.

## References

Anderson, R.J. and Sharrock, W.W. 2012. *PostModernism, Social Science & Technology*. www.sharrockandanderson.co.uk/the-archive/1990-present/post-2010.
Beer, F.P., Johnston, E.R. and De Wolf, J.T. 2006. *Mechanics of Materials (4th Edition)*. New York: McGraw-Hill.
Bucciarelli, L. 1994. *Designing Engineers*. Boston, MA: MIT Press.

—— and Kroes, P. 2014. "Values in Engineering: From object worlds to sociotechnical systems." In *Sciences After the Practice Turn in the Philosophy, History and Social Studies of Science*, by L. Soler, S. Zwart, M. Lynch and V. Israel-Jost (eds), 200–214. London: Routledge.

Hull, M. 2012. "Documents and Bureaucracy." *The Annual Review of Anthropology* 251–267.

Latour, B. 1992. "Where are the Missing Masses? The Sociology of a Few Mundane Artifacts." In *Shaping Technology/Building Society: Studies in Sociotechnical Change*, by W. Bijker and J. Law (eds), 225–258. Cambridge, MA: MIT Press.

Law, J. 2004. *After Method: Mess in Social Science Research*. London: Routledge.

——. 2011. *What's Wrong with a One-World World?* www.heterogeneities.net/publications/Law2011WhatsWrongWithAOneWorldWorld.pdf.

Lynch, M.E. 2013. "Ontography: Inventing the Production of Things, Deflating Ontology." *Social Studies of Science*, vol. 43, no. 3 444–462.

Prior, L. 2008. "Repositioning Documents in Social Research." *Sociology*, vol. 42, no. 5 821–836.

Woolgar, S. 1998. *Science: The Very Idea*. Chichester: Ellis Horwood.

Zimmerman, D. and Pollner, M. 1971. "The Everyday World as Phenomenon." In *Understanding Everyday Life*, by J.D. Douglas (ed.), 80–103. London: Routledge and Kegan Paul.

# 4 Representations without metaphysics

## Introduction

In the previous chapter, we examined two examples of the kind of investigations which might result from Lindsey Prior's call for a repositioning of the document in sociological studies. Neither was motivated by Prior's recommendation, but both display the sort of concerns which are typically raised when documents and other 'representations' are examined by sociologists. A common theme in these analyses is the assumption that, no matter where they are found – in science, religion, art, literature, or ordinary life – when formalised propositions, myths or other narratives, pieces of conventional wisdom, or taken for granted understandings (as well as their homologies in images, diagrams, pictures, icons and the like) state how things are and what is and is not 'real', 'existent', 'factual' and so on, they serve the key social function of cultural reproduction and integration. This being Sociology, interpretations of the integrative function are myriad. As we saw, Louis Bucciarelli felt the reproduction of the 'engineering mentality' in Engineering texts and diagrams leads to the acceptance of an 'object world as defined by Engineering'. John Law found a *EuroBarometer* report to evidence the domination of a not unrelated 'one world' metaphysics which he associated with the 'scientism' of advanced Western societies.

In both cases, the main pre-occupation was in delineating what might be implied or tacit in the documents rather than what was actually visible or explicit. The documents were treated as expressions of an unarticulated subtext. In the phrase which Prior borrowed from Zimmerman and Pollner, the documents were resources, not the sustained topic of the accounts given. This outcome was precisely the reason we doubted the likelihood that the proposals Prior himself made for re-beginning the sociology of documents would lead to the kind of radical break with pre-existing work he was seeking. Without changing the grounds of the investigations (i.e. the assumptions and pre-suppositions which frame it), we cannot see how Prior's call can lead to anything other than the same form of analysis which has always been produced, one which involves the 'substitution' move. In this chapter, we suggest a way of changing those assumptions, one that is rooted in third person phenomenology. In the jargon much favoured among some ethnomethodologists, we want to *re-specify* the sociology of the documents and similar artefacts in ways that are *indifferent* to sociology's concern with the metaphysics of representations. This chapter, then, is a bridge between our discussion of 'foundations' and the studies we present.

## Re-positioning documents

### Ethnography of documents

One of the studies Prior might have cited as an exemplar of the shift he had in mind is Richard Harper's (1998) investigation of the IMF. This is quite explicitly an 'ethnography of documents'. What Harper does very successfully is to use documents, and particularly a document type called a 'Mission Report', as a lens to focus and refract the organisation. The distinctive culture of the IMF and the meaning of the Mission Report are entwined and mutually explicative. These inter-relationships provide the basis on which the 'moral career' of the Mission Report is made visible and hence investigable, while the trajectory of that career throws the reflexive character of the surrounding organisational culture into relief. The Report passes through a number of formal stages and, at each, its organisational character changes with consequent change in its authoritativeness, the definition of who can make what amendments, as well what the Report is used to do. As Harper suggests, the moral career of the Mission Report is a socially constructed trajectory of plausibility and definitiveness, its format being a consequence of the organisation's preference for standardised procedures for standard processes.

In positioning his analysis, Harper underscores insights he found in Dorothy Smith's even earlier discussions (see Smith 1990). Taking her inspiration from Garfinkel's (1967) classic studies, Smith stressed the 'cargo of background knowledge' (Harper's phrase) which users of any document have to bring to bear to understand what they are reading. With this background knowledge, they can see at a glance what the document is about. Seeing its character allows them to shape their response. In her classic essay, *K in Mentally Ill*, Smith (1978) demonstrated how background knowledge is 'brought forth' by means of the recipient design of structures which facilitate a reading of a text as 'definitely saying this', 'providing an adequate description', 'making a reasonable case', 'stating a plausible proposal', 'drawing justified conclusions through sound logical inference' and the like.

Harper's study is, then, both a description of the functions and interpretive character of documents at the IMF and, following Smith's pointers, the beginnings of an account of the work of constructing their moral careers as the documents they so obviously are for those who work there. This second aspect is one element of the kernel of the re-specification we suggest. Asking what makes some document recognisably what it 'obviously' is means treating that document as an observable, a constructed object with a tactile, visual and other embodied materiality which acts as the occasion or site of the organisational work required to produce its meaningful character. On this view, the document as social object displays the work needed to find its meaning.

## Documents as worksites

Focusing on documents as material objects rather than simply as organisationally constructed sources of information, points to the ways their physical properties facilitate their use as coordination devices. Interactional and organisational processes can be brought into conjunction by treating the document as a 'work site'. Borrowing the term 'affordance' (and very little else) from J.J. Gibson's (1979) ecological approach to perception, we once suggested documents and other objects could be analysed as displays of organisational knowledge (Anderson and Sharrock 1993). The marking up of invoices, for example, allows someone who knows their way around a company's 'document system' to ascertain at a glance the current state and progress of any particular item through the relevant invoice processing division of labour. What we were pointing to was the ways organisations make their systems and processes available to and hence analysable by members and sociologists alike.

Others such as Hartsfield et al. (2011) and Rooksby (2011) have picked up this idea and described the detailed ways in which patient records and other types of information summaries are used both to create shared resources for determining the current position regarding a patient or an investigation, as well as for carrying out whatever tasks are in hand. The layout and formatting of a form provides mechanisms for it to act as a nexus of communication, thereby allowing the conjunction of organisationally and temporally separated activities and processes. As with Harper, the emphasis is on interactional and organisational practices as evidenced in and through documents-in-use.

## Documents as displays of professional practice

Ball's study (2011) of annual company accounts takes a slightly different line. Here the concern is the use of a type of document to display professional competence through the visual production of authoritative descriptions of a company's financial position. Ball draws out how features such as formatted structures of numbers, sequentially positioned logos, and the interdigitating of numbers, text and images all allow the professionally competent reader to determine both what financial state is being claimed for the company and the degree of trust to be placed in that claim. From the visual arrangement of the Annual Report, the veridical financial *gestalt* of the company can be constructed.

# Re-specifying documents

## The observability of lebenswelt pairs

In his analysis, what Ball is after is the relationship between the composition of the Annual Report and the understanding or interpretation of the accounts contained in the schedules. How do competent readers arrive at their own accounting of the company from the account in the Annual Report? In clarifying what he means by this relationship, Ball makes reference to Garfinkel's somewhat inscrutable notion of the '*lebenswelt pair*'.[1] To see what Garfinkel means by this, go back to Bucciarelli and the engineering drawings. Bucciarelli focuses on what was not being learned through the use of the drawings, namely that Engineering is a social activity. What he did not draw attention to was what *was* being learned through the continued and repeated used of textbook drawings, blueprints, mock-ups, models and all the other representations engineering students encounter. As they learn to engineer, engineering students are learning how to read, analyse, interrogate and use these things (and, of course, lots of other skills as well). Once they are experienced engineers, these skills become part of the 'cargo of background knowledge' Harper refers to. The same holds for accountants. In reading a company's Annual Report, experienced accountants draw on a similar cargo. Because it is taken for granted, this commonly known background knowledge is in the background. It is not explained, itemised, called out, or referred to in the drawings or the accounts themselves. It is unarticulated and, for those using the document, largely unarticulatable. Moreover, many drawings and accounts contain no commentary on how they are to be read and used. Sociology's enthusiasm for spelling out the tacit by focusing on sociological obsessions rather than the concerns of the document's users themselves also leads to a disregarding of whether those who use those documents need to spell out the unsaid (as we showed with the *EuroBarometer*, the tacit doesn't necessarily need to be explicit to be understood). However, this tacit knowledge is vital to the proficient, normal, routine, ordinary use of these artefacts and so the sociological challenge is to make it visible and hence available for analysis.

Working with a number of students, Garfinkel encountered the same question in the context of scientific practice. How could the bench skills of biologists, the proving skills of mathematicians, the data analytic skills of astrophysicists be made visible and available? The solution adopted was to apply the same logic as was applied in the 'breaching experiments'. Using the praxeological rule, the postulates of conceptual play and intersubjectively achieved recipient design, the written-up and publicly available formal account of the experiments, proofs and discoveries were rendered as instructions for doing the experiment, doing the proving, or finding the discovery. This rendering takes the form of interrogating the formal account as if one is using it to learn to do the science. In one example, Garfinkel and his students tried to undertake Galileo's famous inclined plane experiment using only the original written account. In going back and forth between the set-up and the account, seeing what had to be done to and with the set-up (what he calls 'the shop floor work') to reproduce Galileo's experiment successfully and thereby learning how to read the account to see what must have been done to make it work in the way Galileo says it worked, eventually Garfinkel and his students managed *somehow* to close the praxeological gap between the formal experimental account and the doing of the experiment. That pair – the account and the lived-work of performing the action the account is an account of – is a *lebenswelt pair*. In closing the gap, they made the lived-work of doing the inclined plane experiment visible, observable and analysable. What they made analysable, of course, was what every competent seventeenth-century (and most twenty-first-century) experimental physicists knew Galileo must have done to get the results he did.

Perhaps the most well-known example of the analysis of a lebenswelt pair is Eric Livingston's description of the work of proving Gödel's Theorem (Livingston 1986). As with the Galileo case, Livingston distinguishes between the activity of proving the theorem which Gödel and any subsequent professional mathematician has to accomplish and the 'proof account' of the proving set out in the published text. To accomplish the proving, the mathematician has to perform the proof. But performing the proof entails far, far more than is encapsulated in the proof account. To complete the proof, a whole body of taken-for-granted mathematical knowledge and skills is required allowing the prover 'to see' how each step naturally and necessarily follows from the last and what is needed to allow the projected sequence of steps to go on. Working through the published proof *for the first time* is the work of using the proof account as instruction for performing the proof and so achieving the followability of the text. With novel proofs on the frontiers of mathematics, such working-through-for-the-first-time may be challenging even for highly accomplished mathematicians.

The application of the concept of the lebenswelt pair offers a cogent demonstration of the distinctiveness of the ethnomethodological gaze, compared to the 'constructive' accounts given by conventional Sociology. The relationship embodied in the concept captures the essence of what Lynch and others describe in their investigations (Lynch 1988, 1993; Garfinkel et al. 1981). Whilst the study of the sciences provided the attention-grabbing demonstration of the phenomenon of lebenswelt pairs, they are not exclusive to science. Others, such as Stacey Burns (2001), George Psathas (1989) and Garfinkel himself, have demonstrated that legal cases, occasioned maps and flat-pack instructions could all be subjected to the same mode of analysis. More recently, Livingston (2008) has undertaken studies of such humdrum activities as origami, checkers and jigsaw puzzles.

'Lebenswelt pair' is one of an array of "strange phrases" (a term Mike Lynch (in press) finds particularly apposite) used to mark the distinctive approach which Ethnomethodology takes to phenomena made familiar by more conventional Sociology. In conventional sociological accounts, they are denoted by contrast pairs like product and process, reconstructed logic and logic-in-use, formal and tacit knowledge, know-how and know-what, cultural knowledge and cultural practices and so on. Each in its own way sidles up to the 'praxeological gap' between the formal, general purpose, abstract depiction of some activity and the engaged, *in situ*, working through and working out of the *doing* of that action. 'Lebenswelt pair' encapsulates the achieved unification of depiction and action, the finding of how to do the action in the depiction. Ethnomethodology's approach is to construe the gap as filled with the plena of the lived-work, the occasioned experience of the moment-by-moment, observable/reportable, step-by-step, quotidian performance of the action.

Garfinkel's strategy of discombobulation was designed to force ethnomethodological studies into a different mould from those of more conventional 'constructivist' social science. They are not just another theoretical reinterpretation of Sociology's standard formulations nor are they just another investigative technique to be used as part of the multi-method armoury used in empirical investigations. The strange phrases point to the extent to which Ethnomethodology seeks a complete methodological re-specification of Sociology's foundations and hence of its topics.

However, the term 'lebenswelt pair' itself has been felt to have an unfortunate degree of inscrutability. The familiarity of the phenomenon was lost in the unfamiliarity of the term, so much so that it was hard to see just what Garfinkel was actually claiming about the gap and its locally produced resolution. This was made all the more difficult because the leading examples were mathematical theorem proving and scientific discovery. For most readers, the lived-work of proving Gödel's theorem (or even any of Euclid's theorems) or of discovering the optical pulsar or reading micro-biological slides is beyond their reach. The technical specifics of the work are unremittingly arcane, and so while they could understand the claims being made (the gap and its evident traversal), making the traversal themselves was well-nigh impossible.[2] Most sociologists are not professional mathematicians, astronomers and biologists. On the other hand, the lived-work being pointed to was no news to mathematicians and scientists in exactly the same way that the lived-work of tying one's shoes or riding a bike is no news at all to the child that learns how to do them. Since they know what to do, they can see how the depiction relates to the performance of the activity though, of course, articulating what that means in ways that make it sociologically analysable may be a challenge.

## *What do managers know about documents?*

In our studies, we use the notion of lebenswelt pairs to render the use of ordinary, routine management objects as a topic for analysis. As we mentioned just now, Eric Livingston and others have already begun to extend the range of the term's application. In our analyses of spreadsheets, plans, organisation charts, sensitivity analyses and computational models, we extricate and explicate the socially organised practices by which the gap between the documentary action and its summary formal depiction is traversed, as these objects are competently, standardly, *effortlessly* used. We realise practical management is almost as unfamiliar to many sociologists as practical mathematics, practical astronomy and practical law-practice. This means some level of ancillary detail will be necessary to make the lived-work visible. This detail is not essential to the analysis but is, we think, *advisable* lest it tend to inscrutability in its own right. The formal analysis does not depend on the background detail, but the communication of that analysis well might. Naturally, readers being the motley they are, not everyone will need the same level of ground clearing, detailing and linkage making. We crave the indulgence of those for whom what is given is either too much or too little. Our hope is the Goldilocks among them will be sufficient in number to justify the balance we have tried to set.

One final preliminary point is probably worth making. We have made documents and 'document-like' objects the centrepiece of our analysis. Inevitably, then, we will be laying stress of 'managerial ways' of reading and writing. However, we do not want to be heard as claiming either (a) writing and reading documents is all or nearly all that managers do, or that (b) managers are all alike in what they do and how they do it. We have already pointed to the variegated nature of managers' lives. This holds true across the range of those managing organisations as well as for any manager in their own daily life. Our claim is simply this: given the types of objects we analyse can be found in many organisations, these are some of the ways they are written, read and used.

The final arch in our bridge from foundations to studies is a list of common sense facts managers know about the documents and document-like artefacts they use. This list is not a set of findings. It is not the outcome of sociological investigations. On the one hand, it is simply some of the things all of us, as ordinary members of society, know about documents and, on the other, some of the things members of organisations know. In that sense, it comprises part the common sense knowledge of both categories. We do not want to set up a contrast between these *corpora* of knowledge. Rather, we assume specialist management knowledge rests upon and takes for granted common sense knowledge. We take these facts as *the departure point* for our analysis. The descriptions we provide show how, oriented to the shared knowledge we identify and using the objects we attend to, managers define, describe and resolve the managerial problems they encounter through the application of the common sense methods of interpretation we describe.

Below, then, is our list. For ease of presentation, we speak only of 'documents', but the points can be extended to all document-like artefacts. The objects we are concerned with are 'formal' in that they have their place in explicit and formulated organisational processes. We have excluded others equally prominent and important for the routine running of organisations devices such as notes to colleagues, post-its, to-do lists and the myriad of similarly informal inscriptions one can find everywhere:

> Formal organisations are constructed around documents. They are one, if not the, primary 'medium of exchange' for transactions within organisations. As such, documents are trusted objects and this trustworthiness is taken for granted.
>
> The routine use of documents testifies to their trustworthiness. They are produced everywhere and circulate everywhere. Their recognisability as organisational objects allows them to be used 'thoughtlessly'.
>
> The meaning of any document is discoverable. In large measure, this meaning can be 'read at a glance'. Sometimes, however, meaning may have to be excavated through detailed work of tracking and cross-referencing. Even when such work is required, documents are not expected to be indecipherable.[3]

Documents are constructed for distinct uses but may be re-purposed for ends not envisaged by their creators. Their organisational historicity can be multi-purposed and multi-threaded. When documents circulate beyond their original domain of use, this can result in lines of organisational continuity as well as points of disconnect. Such migration may provoke issues of provenance, status and legitimacy.

The variety of purposes to which any document might be put complements the variety of users for a document. Given the permanent possibility of creator-user disjunction, document constructors have methods to circumscribe the 'open possibilities' of use.

Documents have a normative trajectory. This is what Harper meant by their 'moral career'. They pass through distinct identifiable phases, have proper places in each of these phases and should contain the structures and components appropriate to each. They are, therefore, 'accountable objects'.

Documents are organised into types or classes. The moral careers of different types are different. More particularly, different types of document can have very different organisational half-lives and hence very different associated structures of relevance.

Documents are socialised. They are found together and form proper collections (including collections of one). Such collections may comprise several different types of document, the appropriate conjunction of which constitutes a proper collection. Membership of a collection is organised in relation to specific organisationally given relevances.

Being shared allows documents to act as palimpsests for action. Layers of annotation, cross-referencing and explanation can build up across members of a collection. Equally, the collection so built can act as a palimpsest for its own constructed history. Documents singly and in collections tell their own historiography.

In contemporary organisations, document reproduction is trivial and largely unconstrainable. The resulting myriad versions create problems of tracking, provenance, ownership and control. Who owns a document, where it came from and how 'live' it is are frequently matters for investigation.

This list tells us some of what managers know/have learned about documents in organisations. It is part of the orientation they bring to any document with which they are dealing. Finding just how the considerations listed are exhibited in the particularities of any individual document is the use of locally and organisationally specific (hence endogenously shaped) documentary methods of interpretation. Once armed with organisationally contextualised instantiations of these methods, we can find our way around the document ordered world of any organisation.

## Notes

1 The most extended explanation of lebenswelt pairs is contained in *Ethnomethodology's Program* (Garfinkel 2002). This work also contains the attempt to repeat Galileo's inclined plane experiment and the discussion of flat-pack instructions mentioned below. By far the most friction-free introduction to the concept is Eric Livingston's (1987).
2 That all of this was bound up with the imagined promise of 'hybrid disciplines' didn't help.
3 The familiar attributions of 'meaningless jargon' and 'management-speak' attest to the supposition of decipherability.

## References

Anderson, R.J. and Sharrock, W.W. 1993. "Can Organisations Afford Knowledge?" *Computer Support for Cooperative Work*, vol. *1* 143–161.
Ball, M. 2011. "Images, Language and Numbers in Company Reports." *Qualitative Research*, vol. *11, no. 2* 115–139.
Burns, S. 2001. "'Think your darkest thoughts and blacken them': Judicial Mediation of Large Money Damage Disputes." *Human Studies*, vol. *24* 227–249.
Garfinkel, H. 1967. *Studies in Ethnomethodology*. Englewood Cliffs, NJ: Prentice Hall.
——. 2002. *Ethnomethodology's Program*. New York: Roman and Littlefield.
——, Lynch, M. and Livingston, E. 1981. "The Work of a Discovering Science Construed with Materials from the Optically Discovered Pulsar." *Philosophy of the Social Sciences*, vol. *11, no. 2* 131–158.
Gibson, J. J. 1979. *The Ecological Approach to Visual Perception*. Boston, MA: Houghton Mifflin.
Harper, R. 1998. *Inside the IMF*. San Diego, CA: Academic Press.
Hartsfield, M., Rouncefield, M. and Carlin, A. 2011. "Documents." In *Ethnomethodology at Work*, by M. Rouncefield and P. Tolmie (eds), 151–172. Farnham: Ashgate.
Livingston, E. 1986. *The Ethnomethodological Foundations of Mathematics*. London: Routledge and Kegan Paul.
——. 1987. *Making Sense of Ethnomethodology*. London: Routledge and Kegan Paul.
——. 2008. *Ethnographies of Reason*. Farnham: Ashgate.
Lynch, M.E. 1993. *Scientific Practice and Ordinary Action*. Cambridge: Cambridge University Press.
——. 1988. "The Externalised Retina." *Human Studies*, vol. *11, nos 2–3* 201–234.
——. In Press. "Garfinkel's Studies of Work." In *Harold Garfinkel: Praxis, Social Order and the Ethnomethodology Movement*, by J. Heritage and D. Maynard (eds), Oxford: Oxford University Press.
Psathas, G. 1989. *Phenomenology and Sociology*. Boston, MA: University Press of America.
Rooksby, J. 2011. "Text at Work." In *Ethnomethodology at Work*, by M. Rouncefield and P. Tolmie (eds), 173–190. Farnham: Ashgate.
Smith, D. 1978. "K is Mentally Ill." *Sociology*, vol. *12, no. 1* 25–53.
——. 1990. *Texts, Facts and Femininity*. London: Routledge.

# 5 Intersubjectivity and the arts of financial management

This chapter looks at a meeting document and its role in enabling consociation as the outcome of members' interpretive methods. Because our aims are limited, so are our claims. We will not suggest our analysis applies to all the ways meeting documents are used in organisations. Neither will we claim it applies to all organisational reasoning in regard to any meeting. We simply claim meeting documents can be used in the ways we describe and when they are, they provide an organisational solution to a structural problem. Although the materials we use are drawn from the daily life of senior executives, the methods we describe are general. They are of interest in their own right as *written-read* lebenswelt pairs. Our interest in the objects we analyse is simple. What practices, what managerial documentary methods of interpretation, make the coordination of writing and reading possible for individuals who are not co-present? How are the interest and relevance-shaped meanings of the writer and the interest and relevance-shaped understandings of the reader brought together through, in this case, a written-read document?

To help concretise the problem we have our eye on, here is a simple example:

> Alma is to take a proposal for her department's upcoming budget to a meeting of senior managers. She writes a briefing paper (or backgrounder) setting out her group's current achievements and proposed objectives for the following year. She lays them out in what she thinks is their order of priority. Attached to the briefing is a spreadsheet containing the proposed budget allocations. The two documents are drafted to be read *prior* to the meeting and to 'inform' the discussion. The meeting is held and the budget discussed without any procedural difficulties.

Our question is simply this. Given it is done, how is it done? How are the writing and reading of meeting documents organised so that their coordination is both possible and successful? And, in addition, how is this done when the normal array of methods for ensuring shared understanding in face-to-face interaction is not available? What features of meeting documents like those circulated by Alma provide for and sustain this kind of organisational hermeneutics?

Our explication will rest on the symmetry of two key notions – formatted courses of action and format-constructed documents – and on the practices which allow the one to project the other. Jointly they *order* social action and so together they enable the lebenswelt pair 'the written-read document' to become what we call *an ordering device*.[1] Clearly, formatted courses of action and format-constructed documents are not only found in organisations. Nor are the former only produced in virtue of the latter. Format-constructed documents may be sufficient for formatted courses of action but they are not necessary. However, we believe the pairing is of particular importance in organisations and may even be characteristic of them. For the moment, we merely speculate that if we want to set out the defining characteristics of organisations as contextures of intersubjective reasoning, rather than looking to forms of authority or types of management organisation, the pairing of format-constructed documents and their associated formatted courses of action might just be the key.

## Some key concepts and practices

### Document types

The taxonomy of organisational documents is multi-dimensional. It includes 'formal documents' which can be typed according to their function. More interesting though are the natural kinds. Two of these are the 'carry around document' and the 'throw away document'. Both may be instances of formal types on which a manager happens to be working. Because of their largely peripatetic work style, senior managers work on carry around documents in the interstices of their meeting structured day. Throw away documents, on the other hand, are used for a specific purpose (usually in just one meeting) and then dispensed with. They are not kept with the record of the meeting. 'Files' are another natural kind. Files are interesting because they exhibit the zonal structure of the social distribution of documents and a related division of document management labour. Most managers, and certainly senior executives, do not exercise control over their files. This is in the hands of someone else (their PA, secretary, assistant, or whoever). The distribution of control is commonly explained as 'They always lose things', 'I don't know where anything is', or 'I have my routine ways of managing them and they would mess them up.' All this is condensed into the universal (and telling) joke about where 'real' power in an office is to be found. Although it is easy to make too much of this, it remains true that managers, especially senior executives, live lives organised for them. Their lives are ordered and their 'support' provides that order for them. The 'support' role in co-producing the managerial division of labour is to prepare the schedule of activities the manager has to undertake and to ensure the manager is sufficiently prepared for that schedule. The normativity and normality of this orderliness emerges in the degree of trust executives have that the 'right' documents will be to hand when needed and that the right information is being given during the detailed 'going through the next day (or week)' sessions to prepare for the upcoming sequence of meetings.[2]

Looked at from the perspective of what managers spend a lot of their time doing, management is talking in meetings. Management is a talking discipline. If you ask managers what all this talk is about, they will tell you it is about getting people (the three S's – staff, stakeholders and superiors) to do what they want them to do. There are various and manifold connected ways in which this 'getting them to do what I want them to do' takes place. The two most prominent are meetings and processes (and most commonly working through processes in meetings). Managerial life consists largely in going to meetings, preparing for meetings and picking up the pieces after meetings. Managers manage by managing meetings and meeting documents (yet another natural kind) are the pre-eminent means of doing that. They are the tools, the artefacts, the devices of management and constitute one of its materialisations. Meeting documents encompass many different types. Briefings, backgrounders, reports (which may be occasioned or regular), memos, notes, statements, updates, etc. can all be meeting documents. What makes any document a meeting document is its association with a meeting. Other documents may be referred to, even introduced, but are not thereby meeting documents for that meeting. As we will see in Chapter 10, one way of construing (and hence fixing or disrupting) the agenda of an Agenda (and hence the management of a meeting) is through its meeting documents.

## *Format-constructed documents*

We start by distinguishing document parts and document formats. By the former we mean broad narrative components and sections with titles like 'background', 'proposal', 'recommendation', 'current state', 'objectives', 'strategy', 'operational plan', 'financial projections' and 'risks'. Narrative elements are normative for the successful performance of whatever outcome the document is seeking, and their presence or absence is both noticeable and accountable. By document format, we mean the standardised modes for organising the detail of reasoning within and between these narrative structures, as well as in relation to those of other documents. Obviously, document parts are resources for formatting. In addition, though, there are methods like paragraph colligation, column/row organisation of spreadsheets and tables, cell-to-cell linkages between spreadsheets and tables, ordered lists of activity types and their description, and the serial structure of individual documents making up a multi-part document. Both parts and formats carry documentary narrative; they are narrative constructors in that the 'meaning', 'message', or 'outcome' intended by the writer is both built and found in and through them. Written-read documents which use parts and formats to guide the reasoning of readers are 'format-constructed documents'. A simple example of written-read format construction we are all familiar with is the humble cookery book recipe with its components lists of ingredients and method. This guided reading is, then, a collaborative format-constructed activity. Format-constructed activities are an important mechanism for organising social order, especially in the context of non-co-present, consociate interaction. Devices which can produce format-constructed activities are a powerful way of solving the problem of social order. Format-constructed documents are one such a mechanism.

## The context

Here is a summary of the organisational and institutional context of our first example. Knowledge of this context was an important shared resource for its success as a written-read document:

> CU has just undergone its first HESES reconciliation. The HESES reconciliation is a comparison of the number of Student Full Time Equivalents (FTEs) active (aka 'live') in the institution on a defined date and the number of FTEs for which the institution has been funded. This was the first time CU had returned a HESES reconciliation and, for various reasons, it was disastrous. The agreed number of live FTEs was significantly below the level for which the institution was funded. Apart from the problem of how this had happened and what to do about it, the key issues were:
>
> 1  The institution would be liable to clawback of the funding for the 'missing' students.
> 2  CU's strategic development plan was based on a predicted level of students and a projected growth rate. This dictated the associated capital plan. Student number growth was through the provision of Additional Student Numbers (ASNs) by the Funding Council. The implications of the HESES reconciliation were (a) that CU had a lower base from which to grow and (b) would be hard pressed to achieve its predicted growth profile.
>
> Both the above threatened the agreed Capital Plan. A reduction in revenue implied it would be a struggle to raise and service the planned capital borrowing. A reduced base implied the capital development would not be needed on the scale or at the points originally envisaged.
>   The HESES reconciliation generated an organisational problem of the first magnitude. The challenge to senior managers was develop a revised strategy and capital plan which would solve the problem. If it could do that, the strategy and plan could be approved.

The problems posed by the HESES reconciliation became an item at a regular meeting of CU's Board. The workbook we examine was circulated in advance, along with other documents, to support discussion of the item at that meeting.

## Written-read format-constructed documents

### *The problem-solution document pair: a members' accomplishment*

No matter how they describe it, lay and professional sociologists regularly concern themselves with the causes and consequences of what we have called 'organisational entropy'. Medium and large-scale organisations are constructed to be stable, self-replicating patterns of concerted activities extended over space, time and scale. However, the elaborated division of labour they require, the emergence of rationalisation drift and other processes can cause their perceived integrating, centripetal forces to dissipate. The consequence is organisational entropy and increasing disorganisation. Collectively, the role of senior managers is to ensure the concerted character of organisational actions and consequently a preoccupying concern is the identification and management of the troubles, issues and problems thrown up by the permanent threat of organisational entropy. For the manager, the organisation is a world of troubles and things to be done to fix them. The contexture of this gestalt is experienced differently as the manager moves through the daily flow of managerial work. Problems come singly, in groups, or in swarms and are experienced as a highly diverse mosaic. For the manager, the world of work is shaped by an endless flow of entropy-threatening troubles and their actions. If there were no such troubles, there would be no need for management and managers.[3]

In dealing with entropy, managers focus on solving problems. We will conceive this as achieving a pairing: problem-solution. The pairing is achieved through the binding of solution to problem. An achieved pairing creates the possibility of an appropriate and feasible management course of action. For the binding to be successful and the pairing to be accomplished, the fit of problem to solution and the actions implied thereby must be brought within the legitimate order of the organisation. In all relevant senses, the problem-solution pairing is an accountable phenomenon. It is important to understand the point of view being adopted here. In line with our adoption of a third person phenomenology, these descriptions are of first person experience. Thus they could all be prefaced with 'From the senior manager's perspective', or some similar formulation. We are not offering an abstracted, decontextualised view from an organisational nowhere, but a view rooted in the point of view of the senior manager in the midst of doing the shop floor work of management.

Among the many different types of problem-solution pairs are those where the binding is achieved through a formal decision process. Central to such processes is the bureaucracy of documentation.[4] In formal settings, solutions are bound to problems as types of problem-solution pairs. Among the types of formalised organisational pairs are those which are 'defensible in a court or tribunal', those which have 'gone through proper consultation', those which have a 'full and auditable paperwork', and the type we will look at: 'those which have received proper organisational approval'. The problem-solution document pairing we analyse is a set of financial forecasts. These forecasts were constructed to bind a solution to the problem posed by the HESES reconciliation. We will show how the written-read set of spreadsheets which were circulated for the meeting in question achieved the locally managed and socially organised consociate binding of the devised solution to the identified problem.

We have talked about financial forecasts as achievements before (Anderson et al. 1988). There we were interested in how a run of numbers was constituted as a financial forecast within the flow of decision making regarding a particular contract.[5] How were the numbers which were used, produced? And how were they found to be a credible basis for a significant business decision? This time our topic is somewhat different. Whereas the array of numbers we looked at before was a heuristic balance sheet whose meaning emerged in the flow of the immediate discussion, the set of spreadsheets discussed here is the result of extensive and routinised data collection, collation and amalgamation whose meaning is designed to be found prior to the discussion for which they are relevant. The workbook was produced and distributed for a regular Board Meeting which had been scheduled for some considerable time. It was expected it will have been perused and interpreted before the meeting occurs. As a consequence, these financial forecasts have none of the ad hoc appearance of our previous example. The orderliness of that example was achieved there and then in the meeting.

The binding of any solution to a problem is an occasioned accomplishment. A defining feature of meeting documents is their association with a specific item on a specific agenda in a specific meeting. The agenda provides a way of reading the document, and the document provides a way of reading the agenda. In addition, in the case of spreadsheets, workbook work is needed to 'drill down into the numbers' to find crucial links, values and issues. Everyone will have to do some workbook work, but not everyone will have to do the same workbook work. What they have to do to find *their* meaning in the workbook will depend on what *they* know about the context, *their* relevances and motivations in reading the document, as well as *their* familiarity with the technical production of financial forecasts such as this. As such, reading is structured around the point of view which the reader brings to the document. In addition, whoever is involved and however it goes, the problem-solution document pairing is an intersubjective, reciprocally achieved structure. What anyone finds in a document depends as much on what they bring to it as what is provided in it for them to find. Of course, the variant readings which ensue are embedded in a management world which is known in common. Thus readers are attentive both to the sense which they make of the document *and* the sense which others will likely make of it.

## *Methods for co-producing 5.C.II._5 Year Projections and Cash Flow*

We will talk of the characteristics of the workbook labelled '5.C.II._5 Year Projections and Cash Flow' as 'design features'. This is more than the simple (though very important) fact that individually and collectively the spreadsheets in the workbook have recognisable standard components such as columns of revenues and costs and make up a standard set of expected reports on income and expenditure, asset and debit balances and cash flow. In addition, the interpretive methods used on the document turn on reciprocal assumptions about the availability of these characteristics.

*Assume the workbook is a condensate of local knowledge*

Spreadsheets are transducers. They convey information about things other than themselves. Unless the meaning of 'the numbers' itself becomes thematised, managers have no technical interest in them as the product of purely accounting techniques of summarisation and comparison. Instead, spreadsheets are interrogated for what they say about relevant organisational matters; in this case, the re-shaping of revenues and costs within the revised capital and strategic plan. This thematisation is organizationally given by the formulation of the agenda item.

The workbook is part of a package of documents each of which focuses on the strategic implications of the HESES reconciliation. The order of the agenda in Table 5.1 formulates the order of the discussion and thus its logic. The initials identify the owner of each document. The owners hold particular management roles and associated responsibilities. The combination of title, ordinal position and owner provides initial resources to situate the content of the workbook in the context of the proposed discussion. The columns laid out in the spreadsheets provide a transduced representation of CU over time. The example cited below is taken from the Income and Expenditure (I&E) account and shows the organisation as projected by the revised strategic and capital plans. We say more about the meaning of the time frame in a moment.

The financial evaluation is provided by an array of spreadsheets. This set of management accounts has five (Figure 5.1). They are interrelated and the set is a 'proper' collection for the financial projections of a Capital Plan. If any item is missing, it is both noticeable and a legitimate basis for enquiry. Raising such an enquiry indicates a possible weakness in the planning.

Each worksheet describes the organisation's activities in different ways. The array presents different facets of how the organisation's activities would evolve under the revised plans. The narrative contained in the workbook is clear. The key objectives can be retained but only by significant revision of the strategic and capital plans. This narrative is carried by the relationships between and within the spreadsheets.

The solution offered in the workbook gears into the social distribution of local organisational knowledge in a number of ways. First, the form the solution takes

*Table 5.1* CU Board HESA agenda item

| 5.C. | HESES/HESA 07/08 Reconciliation & Implications | |
|---|---|---|
| I | HESA Reconciliation and Student Projections (AB) *Paper attached* | Information & Discussion |
| II | Capital Implications (CD) *Paper attached* | Information & Discussion |
| III | 5 Year Projections and Cash Flow (EF) *Paper attached* | Information & Discussion |
| IV | CU Academic and Business Restructure (CD) *Paper attached* | Information & Discussion |
| V | Executive Summary (CD) *Paper attached* | Information & Discussion |

60  *The practicalities of executive management*

*Table 5.2* HFSA financial evaluation

| CU | | | | | | |
|---|---|---|---|---|---|---|
| *Financial Forecast 2007/08 to 2011/12* | | | | | | |
| Income and Expenditure Account | 2008/09 (£'000) | 2009/10 (£'000) | 2010/11 (£'000) | 2011/12 (£'000) | 2012/13 (£'000) | 2013/14 (£'000) |
| Income | | | | | | |
| 1 Funding council grants | 11,588.7 | 12,390.6 | 13,630.1 | 14,611.2 | 15,744.5 | 17,153.6 |
| 2 Academic fees and support grants | 13,872.1 | 14,752.9 | 15,954.5 | 16,988.1 | 18,150.7 | 19,659.2 |
| 3 Research grants and contracts | – | – | – | – | – | – |
| 4 Other operating income | 3,643.7 | 3,931.2 | 4,301.7 | 3,903.2 | 4,324.3 | 4,034.8 |
| 5 Endowment income and interest receivable | – | – | – | | | |
| 6 Total income: group and share of joint venture(s) | 29,104.5 | 31,074.7 | 33,886.3 | 35,502.5 | 38,219.5 | 40,847.6 |
| 7 Less: share of income in joint venture(s) | | | | | | |
| **8 Total income** | **29,104.5** | **31,074.7** | **33,886.3** | **35,502.5** | **38,219.5** | **40,847.6** |
| Expenditure | | | | | | |
| 9 Staff costs | 13,704.2 | 14,318.7 | 15,013.1 | 15,538.7 | 16,287.9 | 17,070.9 |
| 10 Other operating expenses | 12,308.8 | 12,644.4 | 13,783.6 | 14,773.6 | 16,356.1 | 17,469.1 |
| 11 Depreciation | 2,663.8 | 3,061.3 | 3,436.3 | 2,921.3 | 3,523.1 | 3,125.6 |
| 12 Interest payable | 667.5 | 667.5 | 738.8 | 873.1 | 1,005.7 | 982.8 |
| **13 Total expenditure** | **29,344.3** | **30,691.9** | **32,971.8** | **34,106.7** | **37,172.8** | **38,648.4** |

*Figure 5.1* Complete set of worksheets

is oriented to the known set of interests and relevances of the meeting attendees. The readers are a defined group of managers and Board members. Some members have 'been close to' the planning process. They have been briefed as the plans have been developing. They will have known 'HESES is causing problems' and have some idea of what those problems might be. Others have not. Thus, for some, there are no surprises in the spreadsheets. For others, there are. Part of securing the required binding will be through providing a set of reasoned steps by which these surprises become just the right thing to do.

In addition, some members are juggling perspectives. Everyone looks at the forecasts for what they mean for them as the members of the Board, but a few have other relevant but more tangential, interests. To take an obvious case, the sponsoring universities will be concerned with the impact on their relationship with HEFCE. They know that significant re-profiling of ASNs and capital build will mean they will have to do more lobbying, more explaining and more favour-seeking. In addition, to prevent recourse to HEFCE for extra funding, will they have to provide resources to see the organisation over the bumps and humps visible in the forecasts?[6] This is an important consideration. The universities know that HEFCE has celebrated CU as an example of its – HEFCE's – own innovativeness and willingness to explore new models. However, that doesn't mean that HEFCE will expect to intervene itself to prevent it failing. Rather, it would probably expect the universities to step in first. The universities know this. Thus members of the Board will not just be concerned with what in a moment we will call the 'shape' and 'fit' of the solution, they will have their eyes on possible implications for their own organisations and responsibilities.

A second way the social distribution of knowledge appears is the detail behind several of the spreadsheets. Here is the sheet marked 'Loan Covenants'.

The calculated values are tests of financial health the bank will use to track the organisation should it loan CU part of the capital to build another building. All the participants know broadly this is what the sheet means, but only three or four (those who negotiated with the bank) know just how the numbers were actually arrived at. The PASS comments look to be reassuring checks on the numbers (and they are) but for those who did the negotiation such reassurance is somewhat hedged! The comments hide the considerable 're-working' of the numbers

*Table 5.3* CU loan covenants

| CU | | | | | | |
|---|---|---|---|---|---|---|
| *Financial Forecast 2007/08 to 2011/12* | | | | | | |
| *Loan Covenants* | | | | | | |
| | 2008/09 | 2009/10 | 2010/11 | 2011/12 | 2012/13 | 2013/14 |
| Total operating profit before interest and tax | 427.7 | 1,050.3 | 1,653.3 | 2,268.9 | 2,052.4 | 3,182.0 |
| Gross financing costs | 667.5 | 667.5 | 738.8 | 873.1 | 1,005.7 | 982.8 |
| **Ratio of operating profit to gross financing costs** | **0.64** | **1.57** | **2.24** | **2.60** | **2.04** | **3.24** |
| Bank target | 0.10 | 1.10 | 1.10 | 2.00 | 2.00 | 2.00 |
| | PASS | PASS | PASS | PASS | PASS | PASS |
| Operating cash flow | (572.3) | 1,050.3 | 1,653.3 | 2,268.9 | 2,331.3 | 3,460.9 |
| Debt servicing costs | 667.5 | 667.5 | 738.8 | 873.1 | 1367.8 | 1414.9 |
| **Operating cash flow as percentage of debt servicing cost** | **−86%** | **157%** | **224%** | **260%** | **170%** | **245%** |
| Bank target | n/a | n/a | n/a | 140% | 140% | 140% |
| | | | | PASS | PASS | PASS |

which has gone on in the background to get them to their current values. This massaging is not an exercise in deceit. Rather, it is out-of-cycle mix of obvious and not-so-obvious changes achieved by re-organising activities, re-shaping and paring costs as well as moving them around (for example, between years), accepting best estimates for income the detail of which is not included in the sheet and so can't be interrogated, and so on. The readers for whom this spreadsheet was created, both those on the Board and others who will review the plans later, know this practical work guided by organisational acumen must have gone on to get the numbers to come out as favourably as they have, but only the managers closely involved know or care exactly what is entailed. The question for the Board is how far the risks resulting from the recruitment shortfall have been reduced or, to use the manager's phrase, 'managed out' and what other new risks might have been introduced in so doing.

The spreadsheets in the workbook look to be all at the same level of importance, but they are not. The availability of 'arbitrage opportunities' across year boundaries provides a profile of opportunities for managerial action. For example, the accounting of activities could be changed to take advantage of pools of unused funding, to smooth out cost profiles, and so on. These use of these opportunities is visible differentially across the sheets. For the manager, Cash Flow is by far the most important of the spreadsheets. The I&E and Balance Sheet statements are year-on-year projected summaries of each individual year's activity – that is, all up and all in, what is it projected to come to? The Cash Flow sheet shows the liquidity of the organisation across the six years. It shows not what the organisation has made and spent, not what it is worth, but how much cash it has in hand. Cash is vital for organisational flexibility. So Cash Flow is where everyone will look first. Looking at the I&E sheet, we see that after a small deficit in the first year, the organisation is projected to grow at a healthy rate.

At the same time, though, the Cash Flow Statement shows two years of negative cash flow.

Anyone who knows how to read the tables can immediately see that if these projections are off by just a small percentage, there could be major impact on the ability to fund activities. The organisation will be relatively 'rich' in assets and earnings but 'cash strapped'. The bank loan has already been factored into the cash flow and so, if the projections are out, who is going to provide the cash required to run the organisation? Securing cash flow is always a major consideration and is especially so for the binding of this solution to this problem.

*Table 5.4* Projected out-turns 2007–12

|  | 2008/09 (£'000) | 2009/10 (£'000) | 2010/11 (£'000) | 2011/12 (£'000) | 2012/13 (£'000) | 2013/14 (£'000) |
|---|---|---|---|---|---|---|
| 22 Surplus/(deficit) retained within general reserves | (239.8) | 382.8 | 914.5 | 1,395.8 | 1,046.7 | 2,199.2 |

*Table 5.5* Cash flow statement

| Cash Flow Statement | | | | | | |
|---|---|---|---|---|---|---|
| | 2008/09 (£'000) | 2009/10 (£'000) | 2010/11 (£'000) | 2011/12 (£'000) | 2012/13 (£'000) | 2013/14 (£'000) |
| 1 Cash flow from operating activities | (572.3) | 1,050.3 | 1,653.3 | 2,268.9 | 2,331.3 | 3,460.9 |
| 9 Increase/(decrease) in cash in the period | 2,715.1 | (1,087.2) | (586.0) | 3,577.8 | 802.0 | 2,046.0 |
| Closing cash balance | 7,090.1 | 6,002.9 | 5,416.9 | 8,994.7 | 9,796.7 | 11,842.7 |
| Cash days in hand | 88.2 | 71.4 | 60.0 | 96.3 | 96.2 | 111.8 |

The fragility of cash (in the sense that CU is neither 'cash rich' nor has major assets which can be easily turned into cash) is both known and evidenced in the profile of the spreadsheets. It is the key to binding the solution to the problem.

The spreadsheets are also a projected history of the organisation – or if you like, a future perfect history. They show what it will have come to over the designated period. However, this is not just any slice of the future. The end date coincides with a commonly known critical juncture. The workbook evaluates the revised plan up to a point at which major constraints will change. From now until then, all the things that matter today can be assumed to matter tomorrow, next year and the year after and, moreover, to be roughly in the same shape. After 2015, significant changes could occur. 'What will it mean for where we will be in 2015?' is a massive, almost omni-relevant, question for managers and the Board. To show why, we will give one example of the change in constraints. As their contribution to the funding of CU, the City[7] gifted a tranche of compulsorily purchased derelict land. Because of the regulations covering donations of this kind, the City placed a covenant on the gift. Over 50% of the land had to be built on by 2015 or it could exercise its right to claw back (some of) the funding. At the point of transfer, the value of the gift was set at £10m. If CU doesn't continue to implement its capital plan by building out its campus, in 2015 there is a chance it would have to pay back some or all the value of the gift. Just under 50% of the land in question had been used for student accommodation constructed under lease by a private provider. This means failing to continue the campus development might mean having to find £5m in 2015. No easy task!

Here we see the contingent nature of organisational problems. Not to solve one might generate others. Not being able to afford the capital programme creates another problem.[8] Equally, though, solving problems often has the effect of creating others! Agreement on the revised plan will generate the problem of selling the approach to the academic groups involved. They have had high expectations of the new organisation and the opportunities for new facilities it represents. In addition, their enthusiasm is critical to generating growth in student numbers to fund whatever growth is attained. When looking to see what the plan will mean for where they will be in 2015, readers will be scaling not just the problems solved but the problems created because of the solution.

*Table 5.6* Income and expenditure structure

**Income**

1 Funding council grants
2 Academic fees and support grants
3 Research grants and contracts
4 Other operating income
5 Endowment income and interest receivable
6 Total income: group and share of joint venture(s)
7 Less: share of income in joint venture(s)
**8 Total income**

**Expenditure**

9 Staff costs
10 Other operating expenses
11 Depreciation
12 Interest payable
**13 Total expenditure**

Finally, the workbook pre-supposes an understanding of the causal model of the organisation. That understanding is required to see the relationships across the main 'lines' in the spreadsheets.

The categories identified in the first columns of the main spreadsheets (Table 5.6 is taken from the I&E account) are proxies for operational activities. They are formulations of those activities and allow the scheme to stand in for the organisation while the elements of the scheme do the same for particular features of the organisation. The glosses are 'filled in' by the level of detail the reader has. If you know more, you can see more in the numbers. In this respect, as we describe below, lines of empty cells are especially interesting. What is not being done and what is envisaged will not be done over the plan period provides a depiction of CU's strategy as an HE institution. An obvious example here is academic research and correlated 'Third Stream' income. CU has very little externally funded research of any kind and does not have a diversified income base. Potential shifts in either the demand or the financial provision for teaching constitute major risks which cannot be assuaged by reliance on alternative income sources. The more you know about the ways HE institutions work, the more the workbook can be found to evidence the actual working of *this* organisation. Of course, any reader can always ask questions, but only if you know where to look and what you are looking at will you know which questions to ask – or, perhaps better, which questions are really worth asking.

*Assume the workbook is the residue of typical practices*

The organisation of numbers in the workbook is not plan determined. The spreadsheets and their components are the standard ones which will be used for most purposes of financial reporting and tracking. The drivers are such things as student numbers, staff levels, loans, etc. The values are all plan derived, but the form of spreadsheet construction is not plan specific. It is standardised. Only the Financial Director has any detailed knowledge of just how the numbers were gathered, collated and summarised. Other participants will have a differential understanding (or 'best guess') of some of them. No matter what the level of understanding, the assumption is that they are derived according to standardised protocols. So, in reading the spreadsheets, readers trust the numbers. They are numbers anyone who followed the relevant procedures would come up with. This assumption of standardisation is what guarantees the workbook's global veridicality. It is taken on trust as a whole. As we have just seen, this does not mean readers assume the numbers have not been 'massaged' in various ways. They certainly do assume this and one task in reading the workbook is to see where this might be obvious and potentially dangerous. But massaging is a well-understood and expected management activity. Managers provide the assumptions, ratios and constraints, and the accountants compile and run the numbers according to their standard procedures. Assuming readers assume this means that the writers of the workbook do not have to explicate how the numbers were arrived at. How they were put together is a writer's problem, not a reader's problem.

That assumption does not hold for the cash flow though. A specific commentary (Table 5.7) lays out how these were arrived at and why what looks to be straightforward on one sheet looks risky on another. In providing this commentary, the intention is to pre-empt some questions (for example, concerning the drivers of the cash flow) and direct attention to others such as the scale of the re-organisation.

This commentary marks a key difference between the Cash Flow and the other sheets. Although 'How did you get that number?' is an entirely proper management question, it doesn't mean 'Take me through all the steps by which the numbers were extracted, collated and summarised.' It means 'What were the original assumptions feeding through to that number?' To use the technical term: the chart of accounts (i.e. the architecture of CU's accounting objects) is massively taken for granted and known to be so.

*Assume the workbook provides necessary and sufficient accounts*

We have said that the written-read workbook proposes a binding of the solution to the problem. Given its association with the agenda item, the workbook's relevance to the binding problem is assumed (but, as always, *until further notice*). Moreover, even though everyone knows more and different numbers could have been provided and, if the discussion goes awry, might well be called for (and then an *until further notice* point will have been reached), the working assumption for readers is that what has been provided is all that is needed. The numbers provide the necessary and sufficient conditions for a binding.

These numbers provide *a* binding. The question is how *good* a binding is it? This has two aspects. How good a fit is the solution to the problem? We'll call this

*Table 5.7* Calculation of net cash flow

*Reconciliation of Surplus / Deficit for Year to Net Cash Flow*

|  | 2008/09 (£'000) | 2009/10 (£'000) | 2010/11 (£'000) | 2011/12 (£'000) | 2012/13 (£'000) | 2013/14 (£'000) |
| --- | --- | --- | --- | --- | --- | --- |
| 1 Surplus/(deficit) after depreciation of assets at valuation and before tax | (239.8) | 382.8 | 914.5 | 1,395.8 | 1,046.7 | 2,199.2 |
| 2 Depreciation (from Table 1 head 11) | 2,663.8 | 3,061.3 | 3,436.3 | 2,921.3 | 3,523.1 | 3,125.6 |
| 3 Deferred capital grants released to income | (2,663.8) | (3,061.3) | (3,436.3) | (2,921.3) | (3,244.2) | (2,846.7) |
| 4 (Increase)/decrease stocks | – | – | – | – | – | – |
| 5 (Increase)/decrease in debtors | (500.0) | – | – | – | – | – |
| 6 Increase/(decrease) in creditors | (500.0) | – | – | – | – | – |
| 7 Increase/(decrease) in provisions | – | – | – | – | – | – |
| 8 Interest payable (from Table 1 head 12) | 667.5 | 667.5 | 738.8 | 873.1 | 1,005.7 | 982.8 |
| 9 Investment income | – | – | – | – | – | – |
| 10 Profit on sale of endowment assets | – | – | – | – | – | – |
| 15 **Net cash flow from operating activities** | (572.3) | 1,050.3 | 1,653.3 | 2,268.9 | 2,331.3 | 3,460.9 |

the shapeliness of the fit. How tight is the binding? We'll call this the robustness of the fit.[9] The combination of shapeliness and robustness determines the binding. Until found to be otherwise, readers assume all the evidence required to make both evaluations has been provided. The workbook is assumed to contain all the information needed to track the relationships between income, cost, cash and capital expenditure. The alignment of the I&E account with the Cash Flow is not found by readers but assumed by them. Although other numbers could have been provided (for example, raw student FTEs), readers assume these numbers do what they are supposed to do. It is how well they do it that is the issue.

The workbook provides a path through the open space of discussion possibilities. Since it structures those possibilities, it is an ordering device.[10] The combination of the sequential presentation of the documents-for-discussion and the assumption of the workbook as necessary and sufficient financial evaluation projects the trajectory of the discussion and thus gives an order and prioritisation to its topics.

*Intersubjectivity and financial management* 67

*Assume the workbook is a locus of motivation and relevance*

The interests and motivations of readers circumscribe the relevance of the workbook for them. Reciprocally, in constructing the workbook, its writers assume sets of interests and motivations. This writing and reading in the context of actual and assumed motivations and relevances is central to determining the character of *this* document for *this* meeting. The notion of 'ownership' of documents is important as a relevancy organising construct here. Who owns the document provides a way of determining which relevances it attends to and hence how it should be read. In our case, the package of documents is presented by different owners who can be assumed to have coordinated relevances and motivations. This is not a point about governance and collective responsibility. Because the set of documents is a set, each individual written-read document is read against the others and from the others. Assuming integrated motivations and relevances facilitates this reading. The set is designed display its construction as an integrated set.

A document's structure can be read for the types of readership it is oriented to. In our case, these are institutional types (such as universities, local authorities, members of the Learning Network); personal types (the VCs, the university court members; partner college CEOs); course of action types (whoever is preparing a meeting pack for a participant, whoever is writing the minutes of the meeting). For all these types, the assumption is that sufficient and necessary information is provided for them to find what they need in the documents. Let's take the writer of the minutes. This is actually a team; a person who takes notes during the meeting and who writes up 'the first draft' and the Secretary to the Board who amends the draft for circulation to the CEO and then to the Chair. To be able to make 'notable sense' of what is going on, the person writing the notes has to be able to track the discussion back to the workbook's spreadsheets. The Secretary to the Board has to be able to see the sense of the spreadsheets in the produced draft minutes. The spreadsheet sheet titles, structure and column-row clustering provide appropriate tracking devices. When, in the discussion, numbers are pointed to, compared and picked out in whatever ways they are, these items can be referenced by sheet title and the column-row matrix. For the minute takers, the spreadsheet structure is a minute-relevant tracking system.

*Assume the workbook is self-explicating*

The workbook and its spreadsheets are designed to be self-evident. They have to be, or else discussion would thematise its structure rather than the binding of the problem and solution. We will pick out just three methods for achieving this self-explicating character: the use of a formatted structure, the provision of cell linkage, and reading by 'skimming' and 'eyeballing'.

We have said the structure of the workbook and its spreadsheets is standardised. Some of this is given by professional practice and some by the software which produced them. A standardised presentational format is not necessarily a standardised reading format. The key sheets are I&E and Cash flow and, as we have said, knowledgeable readers read Cash Flow first. The Balance Sheet summarises the value of the organisation which, in turn, reflects the value of the tangible assets. This sheet only becomes critical if the overall value declines or *in extremis* turns negative. In such circumstances, assets will have to be sold or liabilities paid down to 're-balance' the Balance Sheet. For CU, this is irrelevant. It is included simply because a Balance Sheet is part of the proper set. In effect, we have a structure of two linked sheets (I&E and Cash Flow) and the rest.

The format of all sheets is the same: top-down and left to right. Implications 'fall to the bottom line'. The standard format of bold and regular typeface is designed to allow 'skimmability', the quick filtering of the critical numbers from among the array presented. Using it, one can 'eyeball' the totals to get a sense of what it all comes to. Reading by use of the format moves back to front.[11] From bottom right leftwards and upwards. Actually, it is more by jumping to the bottom line and them skimming the totals backwards to see how that array of outcomes was arrived at. The format of bold/not bold is designed to facilitate this and used to do it. Equally important is the format of numbers. These are rounded to £10,000. It is just harder to compare at a glance an array of 8, 9 or 10-digit numbers. Since seeing at a glance what the numbers say is what the sheet is for, this cell formatting is vital.

Income inflow appears before cost outflow. This has the obvious advantage of not cluttering the top portion of the sheet with negatives (no matter how cluttered it gets with them lower down!). Each bundle is standardly itemised (see Table 5.2, the I&E sheet above). This structure (and the same holds for the Balance Sheet and Cash Flow) is taken from HEFCE's SORP[12] for financial reporting. Anyone used to spreadsheets of this kind can see all they need to know about CU as an HE institution from the I&E account. From the sparseness of the matrix, you can see it is a teaching institution, with all that follows from that. If you know what universities are generally like (what categories there are), you can see CU is a 'teaching only' institution rather than a 'mixed' or 'research-led' one. From that, you can see the 'Manhattan' of cost drivers determining the operational viability. You can also see some 'heroic' assumptions must be being made about either income growth or cost management (or both) to drive 1st line profitability from about 1% in 2009/10 to 4% in 2011/12 and 5% in 2013/14. Those two (income and expenditure) are all you need simply because the rest of the matrix is so sparse.

With all this in hand, readers can interrogate the Cash Flow. First there is the Commentary (Table 5.8) linking the I&E account to Cash Flow. It contains one 'new number', deferred capital grants. This is the draw-down profile of funding provided by HEFCE and the other stakeholders and matches the expenditure on capital development. This is 'money-in/money-out'. With these numbers picked up, the net position in terms of the flow of cash moves from (572.3) in 2008/09 to 3460.0 in 2013/14. What is driving this is the forced 'virtual saving' through the depreciation programme, zero increase in debtors and creditors and the increase in interest (though this too is really money in and out since it is deducted in the cash flow analysis). The summary annual inflow of cash appears as the top line in the Cash Flow Statement.

*Table 5.8* Calculation of cash flow

*Cash Flow Statement*

|  |  | 2008/09 (£'000) | 2009/10 (£'000) | 2010/11 (£'000) | 2011/12 (£'000) | 2012/13 (£'000) | 2013/14 (£'000) |
|---|---|---|---|---|---|---|---|
| 1 | Cash flow from operating activities | (572.3) | 1,050.3 | 1,653.3 | 2,268.9 | 2,331.3 | 3,460.9 |
| 2 | Returns on investments and servicing of finance | | | | | | |
| 2a | Income from endowments | – | – | – | – | – | – |
| 2b | Income from short-term investments | – | – | – | – | – | – |
| 2c | Other interest received | – | – | – | – | – | – |
| 2d | Interest paid | (667.5) | (667.5) | (738.8) | (873.1) | (1,005.7) | (982.8) |
| 2e | Other items | | | | | | |
| 2f | Net cash flow from returns on investments and servicing of finance | (667.5) | (667.5) | (738.8) | (873.1) | (1,005.7) | (982.8) |
| 3 | Taxation | – | – | – | – | – | – |
| 4 | Capital expenditure and financial investment | | | | | | |
| 4a | Payments to acquire tangible assets | (8,245.1) | (2,190.0) | (4,310.0) | (12,410.0) | (340.0) | – |
| 4b | Payments to acquire endowment asset investments | – | – | – | – | – | – |
| 4c | Total payments to acquire fixed/ endowment assets | (8,245.1) | (2,190.0) | (4,310.0) | (12,410.0) | (340.0) | – |
| 4d | Receipts from sale of tangible assets | – | – | – | – | – | – |
| 4e | Receipts from sale of endowment assets | – | – | – | – | – | – |
| 4f | Deferred capital grants received | 7,700.0 | 720.0 | 1,809.5 | 10,013.0 | 178.5 | – |
| 4g | Endowments received | – | – | – | – | – | – |
| 4h | Other items | | | | | | |
| 4i | Net cash flow from capital expenditure and financial investment | (545.1) | (1,470.0) | (2,500.5) | (2,397.0) | (161.5) | – |

*(continued)*

Table 5.8 (continued)

Cash Flow Statement

|  |  | 2008/09 (£'000) | 2009/10 (£'000) | 2010/11 (£'000) | 2011/12 (£'000) | 2012/13 (£'000) | 2013/14 (£'000) |
|---|---|---|---|---|---|---|---|
| 5 | Acquisitions and disposals | | | | | | |
| 6 | Cash flow before use of liquid resources and financing | (1,784.9) | (1,087.2) | (1,586.0) | (1,001.2) | 1,164.1 | 2,478.1 |
| 7 | Management of liquid resources | – | – | – | – | – | – |
| 8 | Financing | | | | | | |
| 8a | Capital element of finance lease repayments | – | – | – | – | – | – |
| 8b | Mortgages and loans acquired | 4,500.0 | – | 1,000.0 | 4,579.0 | – | – |
| 8c | Mortgage and loan capital repayments | – | – | – | – | (362.1) | (432.1) |
| 8d | Other items | – | – | – | – | – | – |
| 8e | Net cash flow from financing | 4,500.0 | – | 1,000.0 | 4,579.0 | (362.1) | (432.1) |
| 9 | Increase/(decrease) in cash in the period | 2,715.1 | (1,087.2) | (586.0) | 3,577.8 | 802.0 | 2,046.0 |
| | Closing Cash Balance | 7,090.1 | 6,002.9 | 5,416.9 | 8,994.7 | 9,796.7 | 11,842.7 |
| | Cash days in hand | 88.2 | 71.4 | 60.0 | 96.3 | 96.2 | 111.8 |

The cash flow account simply tracks the lines of cash in and out over the year. This is a 12 monthly picture. The 'puts' and 'takes' from income and financing appear at line 6. In 2008/09 a (572) cash deficit turns into a (1,784) one. In 2013/14 a 3460 cash pool is reduced to 2478. It is the ins and outs of loan acquisition and payment which then produce the net inflow/outflow of flow of cash. So CU's cash pool increases and decreases at different points in the period. The cash balances are the prior year cash balance plus the net inflow/outflow. As long as the reduction in cash is not continuous, the organisation can trade its way through the periods of outflow. What is critical, though, is the number of days the organisation can operate with that cash in hand. This both, metaphorically and actually, is the 'bottom line' measure of solvency. The normal minimum is 60 days. CU would prefer a great deal more.

What is on display in the workbook is the work which has been undertaken to revise assumptions about growth, to re-schedule capital expenditure, re-shape activities and manage cost and income flows so that a new financial model of the organisation can be bound onto the problems posed by the HESES return.

The model is a whole new set of financial arrangements. The question is: can they be delivered and are they enough?

For an experienced reader of this type of workbook, the issues surrounding the binding are all there to be seen. Assumptions about ASN growth, saving, debtors, and so on, together with the structure of the capital programme, are driving cash flow. If any combination of these, or any one of them, is off, even marginally, the ability to trade through the period of the revised capital programme will be compromised. What the meeting had to decide was whether the risk of any or all of these events happening was too great, and if so what alternative action should be taken. That is, were the shapeliness and robustness of the solution sufficient to conclude the binding was tight enough to take the risk? Could it be made tighter? If so, how? And what risks would follow from doing that? In bringing the item to the Board with the proposal that they have, the management team clearly believe the binding to be 'good enough'. This belief and its rationale are displayed in the workbook and made available to Board members. In that sense, the set of spreadsheets and workbook provides a shared locally organised course of reasoning as a material solution to a management problem. Whether it was an acceptable solution is what had to be determined.

## Conclusion

In this discussion, we have looked at one version of a very general problem, namely ensuring the coordination of laying out and following of a course of reasoning.[13] The example we have examined is drawn from a case where that consociate coordination is asynchronously accomplished in both co-present and non-co-present achievement of written-read documents. We have argued organisations (but, of course, not only organisations) use a specific solution to the problem of accomplishing this achievement: the pairing of written-read format-constructed documents and formatted courses of action.

The written-read workbook of financial forecasts showed how a revision of strategic and capital plans could be bound onto a critical problem. This binding was proposed as a 'good enough' workable solution to the problems faced providing some managerially obvious risks were accepted. The example is an instance of managerial or organisational hermeneutics. The capacity to carry out such hermeneutics on a routine basis, framing and re-framing it as they move from meeting to meeting and document to document is one of the 'core competences' of managers. But, of course, in different ways with different forms, it is one of the 'core competences' of normal social life as well. Being able to pass unremarked as an ordinary, capable practising manager at home in the documentary world of an organisation means no more and no less than being able to deploy common sense documentary methods of interpretation in that organisational context. The forms this deployment takes are locally shaped for the setting in which they are used but the deployment is a general phenomenon. As with science, medicine, truck driving and farming, the managerial attitude is imbricated with the natural attitude. A commonality of methods threads them together. Providing a description of how achieving that threading is experienced, a taxonomy of the ordering devices so used and the rules that underpin them is what third person phenomenology as a First Sociology of managerial action comes to.

## Notes

1 We follow Harvey Sacks in our use of this term. It is a distant cousin many times removed of the subsequent usage popularised by John Law and other proponents of Actor Network Theory (see Law 1994).
2 There is massively important work yet to be done analysing this and other 'coordination of a working life' practices.
3 Those who speak earnestly of self-managed work teams and dispensing with the need for 'management' only shift the work of management downwards to the team. It doesn't go away. The teams have to do it all for themselves.
4 An orientation to the auditability of the pairing is a significant feature of these processes.
5 There is an accounting discipline called Management Accounting. And there are schedules called 'management accounts' produced by management accountants (the workbook we discuss is one such). But management accountancy as we described in our earlier study is done on the hoof by managers in and for meetings and is distinctively different. It does use some of the same artefacts but the accountant's work produces a standardised and regulated formulation of the organisation: a 'this is how it is'. The manager's work produces a formulation of 'this is what it means', where 'this' is to be taken as a gloss for whatever policies, procedures, strategies and plans are being discussed. For the manager, spreadsheets and workbooks are the ground of action. Their significance lies in what they tell you to do.
6 Cash flow is an important consideration here. The universities provide services to CU for which they charge. However, re-scheduling invoicing, allowing year-end runovers, 'eating' some costs themselves can all have material effects on cash flow. The numbers in the spreadsheets are big, but so too are the flows in and out. As with many organisations, and probably more than most, CU operates on the margin.
7 The identities of CU's partners are discussed in the organisational setting section of the Preface.
8 No doubt the very first thing CU would try to do is get the City to commit not to claw back. The City could do this but it does not have to. Given the usual turnover of senior staff in Government Agencies, you don't know who you might be dealing with in 2015, so better to get the current leaders to make the commitment. They, of course, would be reluctant to do that.
9 For managers, these two aspects are distinct and equally important. To take an obvious pair of examples, if CU wants to bear down on its costs, it could ration the volume of reprographics allocated to each member of staff. This would cut costs (fit) but is unlikely to stick (loose binding) because two leading terms of the strategy to grow the business are student-centred teaching and student satisfaction. In the markets CU is in, students are support hungry. Extending the life cycle of the rolling capital maintenance programme or the central IT infrastructure will have the same effect (fit) and (at least until disaster strikes) the binding will hold.
10 This throws up a familiar meeting trouble managers have. The document ordered agenda item is shaped for its own rationality. These are Brentano-intentional objects composing a phenomenal field. Chairmen who, without notice, insist on re-ordering the agenda give managers the unenviable challenge of re-constructing the rationality of decision flow in flight.

11 This is quite a common feature in reading meeting and other organisational documents. The linearity of the narrative is inside-out or back to front rather than the beginning-to-end form of the novel. For other examples of this, see Harper (1998).
12 Statement of Recommended Practice.
13 We would be tempted to call our studies an 'ethnography of reason' if doing so didn't require us to mark them off from Eric Livingston's 'ethnographies of reason' (2008). We feel we could only do that by pointing to the different kinds of sociality involved in each. For us, that would make Livingston's studies more 'ethnographies of ratiocination' – which is a bit of a mouthful.

## References

Anderson, R., Hughes, J. and Sharrock, W. 1988. *Working for Profit*. Aldershot: Gower.
Harper, R. 1998. *Inside the IMF*. San Diego, CA: Academic Press.
Law, J. 1994. *Organising Modernity*. Oxford: Blackwell.
Livingston, E. 2008. *Ethnographies of Reason*. Farnham: Ashgate.

# 6 The contingencies of due process

## Introduction

Managers don't need social and management scientists to tell them the activities they are endeavouring to orchestrate have a diversity of goals, objectives and ends, or that the means for obtaining them are equally diverse. They also know the diversity is divergent, often at odds and more than occasionally contradictory. Such mismatch is but one of the forces creating the entropy they struggle to contain. They may not classify that diversity in terms of Meyer and Rowan's (1977) trichotomy of ceremonial, technical and institutional structures, but they are well aware that its sources lie both in the contingencies of implementing the strategies they are pursuing and the constraints laid upon them by groups, agencies and bodies beyond their organisation and over which they have little or no control. Working through the daily round involves, in part at least, finding a way of weaving together some or all of the array of ends and means, objectives and activities operational in the surrounding environment. Of course, the rationalisations produced by this plying and patterning are a hopefully adequate mix of the purposive, the principled and the ad hoc.

In this chapter, we will look how this reasoning is applied to the construction of organisation charts, a class of objects whose purpose is to provide a publicly available global definition of some activity structure, management hierarchy or organisational process. We will do so through the examination of a single case: the Governance6 chart given in the Appendix to this chapter. The aim will be similar to that of the previous chapter. The purpose of the chart is to show how CU's critical decision processes conform sufficiently to governance good practice. Facilitating a reader to make such an assessment is the work of the chart. It displays a lebenswelt pairing of chart and judgement. We will propose the chart displays instructions for its own use and its success as an operationalised representation of CU's organisational world relies upon following these recipient-designed instructions to close the praxeological gap between reading the chart and making the judgement. By recognising and following its instructed actions, users can find governance good practice at work in the chart. Those who constructed the chart designed it to be used in this way.

One of the features of all representations is that they are typically purposive – that is, they are constructed for a purpose. In this case, we have a background document provided as input to the Quality Audit to be carried out at CU. They are also designed to be used for a purpose, a display of the degree to which governance of key organisational processes at CU complied with 'good practice' as defined by the Quality Assurance Agency (QAA). However, managers are well aware that such objects, having been used for the purpose for which they were constructed, are not necessarily confined within those bounds. Documents in organisations are quintessential boundary objects (Starr and Greisemer 1989). They travel through the organisation and beyond, and are used for purposes for which they were not envisaged, let alone designed. Very often, of course, they are useful resources. Equally often they simply add to the flux and entropy that managers face. This being so, although they might be designed for a specific course of action type to use (in our case, someone who is on a QAA panel), organisational representations are also shaped by consideration of who else might use them and what else they might reasonably and not-so-reasonably be expected to be used for.[1] These two, the presumed intended and likely unintended uses, are the contingencies of our title.

Organisational governance is not as familiar a topic as other aspects of organisations, such as forms of management structure or the division of labour. Indeed, until recently, concern for governance was largely confined to the fiduciary aspects of financial management. However, over the last 25 years or so, we have witnessed the emergence of what some have called an 'audit culture' (see Strathern 2000; Shore and Wright 2015), where principles of normativity, efficiency and effectiveness have been invoked by both managers within organisations and other outside institutions to justify the measurement of conformity to standards of good practice with regard to decision making and operational routines in both private and public bodies. In academia, to take an example which is close to home, we find these measures used to assess the 'impact' of groups of academics within an institution (and, by extension, the disciplinary areas to which such academics belong) upon economic, social and policy arenas in wider society. Apart from 'impact' itself – a term whose meaning is not so much polymorphous as endlessly mutable – the key associated concepts are 'traceability', 'transparency' and 'accountability' within a 'governance framework'. In the ideal case, the framework of specified values (means and ends) is derived from the formally stated and endorsed strategic objectives of the organisation. The audit of governance is concerned with the traceability, transparency and accountability of decision making within the organisation. Are decisions made in conformity with the requirements of the formally endorsed sets of objectives specified for the organisation and the documented statement of strategies (means) to attain them? In other words, does the 'paper trail' show the organisation actually does what it says it does?

The governance chart's function was to provide members of a QAA[2] panel with a synoptic view of the relevant key decision processes in the management of learning, teaching and assessment (LTA). It was to be used in conjunction with exercises in 'case chasing' by panel members to assess conformity to good practice. This determination was not to be arrived at simply by perusing the chart. Rather, it was to be done by examining audit trails of documents through the lens of the chart. For such an audit, good practice largely concerns two things: the interdependency of the management of learning and teaching and the managing of operations; and the sequential coordination of key decision points in both decision flows. According to the prescriptions of the QAA, high quality in teaching and learning outcomes are achieved when the priorities set for learning, teaching and assessment drive operational priorities. It follows that operational decisions should not have processual precedence over LTA ones. In displaying CU's arrangements for these two, Governance6 is intended to display conformity to good practice.

The chart encompasses two management models: those of LTA and operations. For most HE institutions, this poses few problems. They are mature organisations and the structural relationships among their major systems have (or should be) bedded in. CU was different in three critical ways. It was a new organisation and its systems were only just being created. They were certainly neither complete nor bedded in. Second, it was facing a major set of growth challenges which its senior managers and Board believed would require the exercise of strong central management control if they were to be achieved. Finally, it was set up as a Limited Company and so its corporate governance was regulated by the provisions of Company Law. Although QAA audits are often moments of tension in all institutions, the relative goodness of fit of LTA management and operations management can largely be taken for granted. With CU, this was not the case. Each of the lines of difference in things like the ordering of short-term priorities and the immediate foci of management attention carried possible misalignments between the management models. Because it was known to be a developing institution, the QAA panel would not expect complete conformity with its standards of good practice. However, conformity should be significant. For senior managers, audit represented the challenge of moving their operational model towards conformity whilst at the same time not prejudicing the priorities they had set for growth, culture change and activity initiation. To fulfil its task, the chart has to represent both LTA and operational management models by depicting the organisational reality of governance as close enough to the good practice model to satisfy the auditors whilst not, at the same time, giving too many hostages to fortune with regard to the ability of managers to set the goals and drive the growth of the institution by appearing to emphasise areas of activity the senior management team did not, at this point, wish to invest in.

Process charts are often referred to as 'maps'. As with direction finding and other maps, this term captures the character of the depiction as a normative or conventionalised projection of features of the process being described. The relevances determining such norms are not, though, primarily concerned with 'wayfinding' or 'step following'. The use of the chart was not to work out what to do, what steps are to be followed and in what order. Rather, as we have just indicated, what the map projects are the managerial considerations prioritised in a QAA audit – namely the coordinated sequencing and step-wise due process being followed within distinct lines of decision making. Governance maps provide the topography of decision making as proper sequences of legitimated and authorised decision steps. Reading the chart is finding that topography represents management operating in the ways required.

In this discussion we will do two things. First, we will use Governance6 to illustrate the general design principles for constructing governance and similar charts as analogues of what George Psathas (1989) called 'independently readable maps'. It is their independently readable features which enables them to function as management devices for achieving the outcome sought. Second, we will show how consideration of possible known and unknown uses of the map led to less than optimal transparency and traceability of 'proper decision making'. These considerations provide good managerial reasons for more than a little obfuscating synoptic representation.

## Common sense organisational cartography

Using the framework set out in the first four chapters, we will draw out some of the ways Governance6 displays the operation of the managed resolution of the tensions between operational and LTA management at this point in CU's development.

### *Idealised formalisation*

#### *Modalities of material form*

Governance6 is a 'one pager', a widely used class of organisational documents used to provide ready-to-hand, easily surveyed and assimilated high-level summaries of background information. One pagers are designed as guides to be used alongside other documents and as prompts in discussion of relevant issues. They are, then, a re-usable, carry around document whose precise deployment cannot be anticipated but whose general application is given by their contents. Governance6 is about what it says it is about – namely the management of curriculum planning and academic standards and the management of operational processes. What such management consists in is *not* thereby specified but the components (that is, the ordered sequence of decision steps) of its management decision making are. Whatever goes on in the management of these processes at CU is not to be discovered by reviewing Governance6 but by using it as part of the audit process. This use is not adventitious. It involves the deployment of reciprocal and complementary skills to bring off the chart's essential characteristics.

#### *The hermeneutics of spatial distributions*

No matter the format of the page (portrait or landscape), the orientation of the chart is read-off from the orientation of the title. The orientation of the title text is the orientation of the process landscape. From that orientation, the geography of placing is determined. This geography has two interpretive coordinates: level of authorisation and degree of coordination. These two produce a matrix fixing placement on the chart. As one moves up the page, coordination by authorisation is exhibited as a stratified succession of coarse-grained blocs. These blocs are unnamed but display associations of relatively similar authority levels. Thus, where some decision forum stands in the 'authorisation chain', and its relationship to other authorisation chains, can be seen at a glance. Entities aligned in blocs at the same broad level on the page have the same broad level of authority. Processual synchrony of decision is somewhat more fine grained. Here, there is a banding within and between blocs. Alignment in a band stands for procedural synchronisation of decision making where the parameters of temporal synchrony scale according to type of decision and flow.

### Recognisable relevant completeness

The set of decision nodes and interrelationships depicted on the page are all that is needed for due process in the coordinated governance of learning and teaching and operational management. Whilst it is known that there will be other groups, fora and relationships involved in the making of relevant decisions, what is on the page is all the necessary and sufficient detail required to find conformity to good practice. What is off the map and what is invisible in the map (both topics we return to below) are not necessary for the purposeful reading of the map. The whole decision chain, from formal initiation to formal completion, is contained in that detail. While lots cannot be seen, nothing is missing. What the map provides, then, is the world of relevant governance. As we discussed in Chapter 3, much of what a document says cannot be spelled out if it is to maintain its function as a high-level schematisation. These are its implicatures. In addition, there are those things which, whilst not spelled out, could be if needed. In advance of the chart's use in earnest, it was impossible to say what they might be.

### Universal locatability

Any element, component, or point in a decision flow can be allocated to an appropriate place on the page. Decisions are always on the map somewhere and the determination of just where is carried out by triangulation of what has been done, what is yet to be done and who is known to have authority to take the relevant decisions and actions. Finding where an issue is in the processes is a matter of interpreting the choreography of events. Being on the map is not the same as being at a node. Decisions may be 'pending', that is, waiting to enter a node, 'in flight' from one node to another as well as being 'under consideration' or even 'stalled'. No matter what their status, they can be placed on the map somewhere.

### Local relativities and absolutes

The material mode of the one pager determines the need for recognisable relative and absolute scaling. Organisational space is not two-dimensional, but has to be represented as such. In order to produce the representation, some relationships have to be fixed whilst others are allowed to float. This produces chart-projected warpings analogous to the Mercator distortions we are familiar with on maps of the world. The result is 'organisational distance' which does not necessarily equal 'distance on the chart'. Some differences, such as with linkages and labels, are significant but not metrical. Differences in font scale or line thickness matter but only as indicators of centrality to the main purpose of the chart. Distance on the page is also neither metrical nor arbitrary. There are no conclusions to be drawn from the relative spatial distance of the Curriculum Planning node from the Academic Board, compared to its distance from the Executive. But equally, distortions which push key decision points to the periphery of the chart are avoided. Comparison is a matter of 'scanning' the blocs, not measuring coordinates.

The significance of co-location is just as variable. Placing Academic Communities within 'easy reach' of the Planning Processes and the Executive allows an interpretation of their importance (see below). In the same manner, distance on the page and temporality of decision making are not commensurate. It is not supposed to take 'longer' to get to the Academic Board from Planning than to the Executive, and such distancing cannot be used to represent decision flow. However, the known calendrical periodicity of both does give rise to the possibility of tension regarding the *durée* of decision making, with 'Quality Processes' often being felt to be slow and ponderous compared to the fast turn-over of decisions along the operational flow. As we will see below, the meaning of experienced elapsed time – how long it seems to take for decisions to be made – is one of the known stress points of good practice. Firmly held views on decision velocity often cause disagreements among those responsible for the two decision paths. At root, this comes down to differing interpretations of what 'good enough' due process might be. That there will be such differences is a given for the audit. They are a well-known consequence of different managerial relevances. The audit's concern is with how they are managed and one of its tasks will be to try to surface them – something which is also well known.

In addition, specification of detail is *relatively material* – that is, material relative to the purpose of the diagram or the status of the node. Thus the listing of the sub-Committees of the Board and the lack of detail on the sub-Committees of the Academic Board relates to the formal legal requirements for governance of a Board of Directors, not the integration of quality and operational management. Key committees of the Board of Directors have to be displayed on public documents. But that display does not speak to process good practice as the QAA defines it. On the other hand, the explosion of the box marked as Curriculum Planning does. This is one of the central quality practices in the QAA framework and a lack of detail here would be a noticeable and notable absence.

## Recognisable investigative relevances

The map is purposeful in two distinct but related ways. It has been constructed for a purpose (providing guidance for the audit team) and to be used for a purpose (the display of due process). Users are presumed to be interested in both and to have sufficient relevant knowledge of the organisational structures of Higher Education to see in the detail just what is needed for them to carry out their task. They need what they have been given – though, naturally, it is not all they will need. To make the judgements, cases, instances and issues will have to be chased through the structure by following the 'document audit trail'. Given instances of just what *they* are interested in, with Governance6 in hand, the panel will be able to interrogate governance due process at CU. Process surveyability is a design feature of the chart.

## *Closed configurations*

The map identifies two pathways through the decision maze. These have common initiation and termination points. The pathways are not loops (decision flow is all one way); nonetheless, there is process closing at the common points. Under the idealisation of the chart, any policy, initiative, or innovation can be found to have originated at a recognisably proper point (that is, proper, from the point of view of LTA good practice) and to have progressed though the decision flow to an equally recognisable proper final decision point. At the same time, the chart makes it clear there is no single, universally applicable final decision point.

## *Co-selection of inclusion*

The pathways comprise a proper set of steps. Each passes through a number of decision nodes whose relevance is derived from the nature of the pathway. They are co-selected for their 'quality' or 'operational' character and represent what, in the idealised world being depicted, would be a complete, serially constructed hierarchy of authoritativeness. The elements within each band and bloc together with the 'coattails' of groups they imply, all have a place. Tracing through the paths from Curriculum Planning to University Senates and University Councils, each band and bloc has its appropriate representation.

## *Demonstrable proper sequencing*

In as much as the depicted flows are known to be what 'normally' rather than what 'always' happens, the chart portrays a flexible ordering. On occasion, decisions get 'fast tracked' and sometimes skip steps. But the idealised state is a flow through the full complement of correlated and coordinated sequenced steps. Some of these steps are known to be key process anchor points (for example, Academic Board and CU Executive). These are the most important internal management loci for each flow. Their alignment on the page provides a display of synchrony in decision flow. The link between the two (we discuss the codification of links below) provides an on-the-page (that is, formally accountable) correlation and calibration mechanism. That linkage is one of the hitches holding the two processes together. In other cases (for example, JAC and the CU Board), such co-anchoring is missing, thereby indicating these are not to be seen as anchor points of the same order.

## The grammar of symbols

The notation of organograms is one of lines and labelled boxes. The position and concatenation of the boxes acts as a vocabulary for determining the existence of due process. In Weider's (1974) phrase, the contextual syntax and semantics of the organogram together tell the code of these relationships. We will bring out this character of the diagram by examining just two aspects.

### *Only connect*

The Key provides the set of linkages which structure the chart. Two of these refer to decision flows and two designate types of membership. This distinction is important. According to quality prescriptions, for proper decision making, not only must the decision be considered in an appropriate order but those doing the considering must be appropriate for the level of authority concerned. Membership linkages are within blocs. Scanning the decision lines in conjunction with the membership lines indicates who is taking what decisions at what point – the core due process question. Considered as a network, the chart clearly displays that the single point of decision initiation lies where it should, within the Curriculum Planning node. From that point on, the decision lines diverge and are connected by the membership linkages. Thus the chart displays the social organisation of the required shared planning knowledge across the different operational groups. This gives a clear sense of the integration of academic and operational decision making which is central to the QAA model. If exercises in case chasing show that the reality belies the formal structure, then breaches in standards of good practice in the operation of the decision structure will have been found.

### *Reading the runes*

At one level, the 'vocabulary of connection' captures the 'formality' of the relationship. Thick solid lines represent standard formal decision making and approval processes. Thinner solid lines are the quasi-formal relationships of consultation and recommendation. These connect nodes outside the formal control loops with nodes in those loops. In that they find a place for these nodes but not on the central decision making pathway, we might say they are *inclusive but excluding*. Third, there are the *ex officio* common membership connections between key nodes in different control loops (broken lines). The claim to common membership is, of course, a limited one. Not every member of the Executive is a member of the Academic Board. Nonetheless, marking commonality of membership provides a further demonstration of the connections between the two decision flows. The fourth linkage is the dotted one of representation. CU was a tightly managed environment. It had to be if it was to achieve its immediate goals. To conform to the model of democratic academic governance promoted by the QAA, the chart has to show formal representational connections for academic staff within the institution.

Parsing the syntax and semantics of boxes and lines allows the user of the chart to find a due process topology in the complex topography of the map. The vocabulary has no codes for 'important', 'necessary but less important', 'required for good practice sake', and so on, yet such differentiation is discoverable and captures the pragmatics of governance. This pragmatic logic can be construed from the constructed logic of the lines and boxes.

## The contingencies of achieving correspondence by Fiat

At the start of this chapter, we suggested that managers are well aware that formal documents are boundary objects and so attempt to include features in their design which militate against uses which will cause obvious problems. In this last section, we will pick out a few examples of such contingency management in Governance6 and discuss how their meaning is shaped.

### *Modified flow closure and its problems*

When considered as abstract, formalised structures, the boundaries of most organisations whether in education or elsewhere are the operational boundaries of all its key decision processes. At this stage of its development, this was not the case with CU. The management of learning (that is, learning, teaching and assessment) passed outside the organisation to a Joint Academic Committee of the Universities and on to their Senates. This clear diffusion of decision processes into partner institutions threatens the internal closed-flow principle for good governance. Operational decision authority passes through management teams and terminates with the Board. On this line, governance is internal. The line of quality governance passes outside CU because at this point its qualifications were being 'guaranteed' by the partner Universities. It is the standards of the universities' degrees which the QAA is approving (they are guaranteeing CU's standards by permitting it to award its students with their degrees) and so QAA requires that the decision flows for LTA terminate within the universities. But, as we indicated at the start, that provides an opportunity for misalignment between the two management models. Proper closed flow governance, means *both* academic quality and operational management should terminate in a single place. The chosen locus was the University Councils. However, given the formal constitution of CU as a not-for-profit company, this might imply that the Councils were acting as 'shadow' Directors since it would make it appear the Board does not have final authority over all its own operational decisions. To have 'shadow' Directorships in place is a violation of corporate (but not LTA) good governance. To obviate this, the linkage is defined as 'representational' rather than 'approval'. Of course, that designation can only refer to the Directors who are actually members of one of the University Councils. This form of modified flow closure creates enough ambiguity to avoid drawing attention to the central tension in the decision making of the institution, namely that between the necessary *independence* of CU as an operating business and its equally necessary *subordination* to quality decision processes within the Universities. The way this tension was actually being managed was through interpersonal relationships. Interpersonal relationship management is not a formalised governance process. In other words, depending on which model (LTA or operational) was being examined, the ambiguity of the device either revealed or hid the tensions at the heart of this aspect of governance.

## *Organisational fictions and their consequences*

A similar order of contingency is represented by the inclusion of three boundary spanning groups: Stakeholder Group, Reference Groups and Academic Communities. Their inclusion rests in different kinds of organisational gestures. The first two were informal bodies of 'political supporters' whose continued support was required for local opinion formation, funding, promotion and policy alignment. In return for this support, the groups felt they could and should offer comments and suggestions on academic and operational matters. They were not, however, formal decision-making bodies. Their inclusion on the chart was a matter of public acknowledgement of their place and 'managing the politics' which resulted, rather than recording the authorising or supervising of decisions.

A different kind of fiction applies to Academic Communities. These did not actually exist. Those advising on quality development insisted they be included since the QAA model assumed the coincidence of the organisation of learning, teaching and research and the structure of academic communities within any HE institution. Not to be marking the contribution of academic communities to the management of LTA would be a very noticeable omission. The cross-centre delivery model of academic content which CU was using made the formation and support of such disciplinary-based communities a hugely resource-hungry challenge, one which the management team felt was definitely subordinate to the plethora of other resource-hungry challenges they faced. The presence of Academic Communities on the chart is ambiguous. They are nominated but since financial and other resources are not allocated to them, they are not being managed. From the perspective of the model of operational management, if it is not being managed, it is not key.

## *Underspecified calibration of ideal and operational topologies*

The chart lays out the formal decision flows for the management decisions it covers. It is an idealised depiction. This is something everyone knows. What the chart does not provide is a fixed model of the flow of actual decisions. As we have already said, the exigencies of practical management will inevitably mean that some decisions are 'fast tracked' through the processes. In such cases, decisions

84 *The practicalities of executive management*

are 'taken as read', approved by 'Chair's action', or some other formally constituted way not listed on the chart. Other decisions will short circuit the flows by 'node jumping' or by being initiated in anchor nodes such as the Executive or Academic Board themselves. The importance of underspecifying the 'bridging mechanisms' by which the representation might be made to correspond with the realities of actual day-to-day management lies, of course, in the management flexibility the lack of detail provides. Conforming to the spirit of due process whilst violating it in practice is what practical management often requires and which the chart allows. It is precisely what in Chapter 2 we saw Bittner meant by 'organisational acumen'; knowing what needs to be done in accord with the formal scheme as well as knowing what should not be done so the scheme can be preserved.

## *Alternative readings of symbols*

Earlier, we described the process flows emerging from the node labelled 'Curriculum Planning'. The name clearly designates this as a 'quality' process. However, it is also a business critical operational process. At the point at which the chart was drawn, senior managers had run 'a very quick and dirty' review of the course 'offer' being made and were determined to 'refresh' its provision as a matter of urgency. To enable this, academic development proposals were to be taken through the CU central planning process controlled by the Executive as well as through the usual 'quality loop'. This was to allow the senior team to control the content and rate of change of curriculum revision. The duality demonstrates the required process coordination for quality good practice. It also signals senior managers' desire to drive rapid top-down development and the tension this creates. Those responsible for quality want to embed the QAA mature model in the organisation and see developments emerge from the (as yet unformed) Academic Communities. The code being told is different depending which perspective one holds and when. From the senior managers' perspective, the chart's purpose is to enable the institution to 'get through' the upcoming audit. At some future date, CU would be audited again, so a placeholder had to be left to accommodate active Academic Communities (should they develop) without committing any managerial resource now to support them. For those managers, designed ambiguity is a virtue rather than a defect.[3]

## *Managed representation*

Our final example is the display of conformity to the good practice principle of representative democracy in academic planning. This is clearly displayed in the chart. However, the nodes where such representation is demonstrated are also those which are tightly managed by senior management. The content of agendas, the periodicity of meetings, the composition of other membership are all controlled by the Executive. The nodes where representation is found are not free form but severely constrained. The inclusion of representative democracy is not a fiction but rather a gesture. It provides what is needed but preserves the capacity of senior management to control the formation of policy objectives.

## Conclusion

Principles of good practice are idealisations. The danger of over-conformity to the ideal is managerial and operation inflexibility. The danger of too little conformity is the taking of inconsistent and ad hoc decisions, as well as decisions taken in pursuit of objectives not endorsed by the relevant authorised bodies. Every organisation tries to set an appropriate balance between these two. Anyone (such as a member of a QAA panel) who knows how to read and use a chart such as Governancev6 knows how to find the balance being struck. Audits are about tolerance limits. Much of the indeterminacy and designed ambiguity of Governancev6 provides for soft tolerance boundaries where enough conformity to the idealisation can be found whilst permitting enough departure from it to allow management flexibility. The work of working with the chart is the work of determining for any actual case just where that balance is being set. The work of designing the chart is the work of ensuring the balance satisfies the audit principles whilst at the same time allowing managerial room for manoeuvre and avoiding setting constraints on any future initiatives senior management might want to take. Reading the organisation's governance through the chart is seeing the dynamics of 'the space of balancing' within which actual management practice works.

## Notes

1 We are back with Donald Rumsfeld's classification!
2 The Quality Assurance Agency is the public body charged with ensuring and monitoring standards of teaching quality in UK universities. 'Assurance' is provided by the use of mandated 'quality processes' adapted from business. Monitoring takes the form of cross-university comparisons of adherence to 'best practice' with regard to these processes.
3 Those who relish the nuances of these things are invited to consider the relationship between the CU Board of Directors and the Academic Board where similar orders of designed ambiguity are on view.

## References

Meyer, J. and Rowan, B. 1977. "Institutionalized Organizations: Formal Structure as Myth and Ceremony." *American Journal of Sociology*, vol. 83, no. 2 340–363.
Psathas, G. 1989. *Phenomenology and Sociology*. Boston, MA: University Press of America.
Shore, C. and Wright, S. 2015. "Governing by Numbers: Audit Culture, Rankings and the New World Order." *Social Anthropology*, vol. 23, issue 1 22–28.
Starr, S.L. and Greisemer, J. 1989. "Institutional Ecology, 'Translations' and Boundary Objects." *Social Studies of Science*, vol. 19, issue 3 387–420.
Strathern, M. (ed.). 2000. *Audit Cultures*. London: Routledge.
Weider, D.L. 1974. *Language and Social Reality*. The Hague: Mouton.

# Appendix

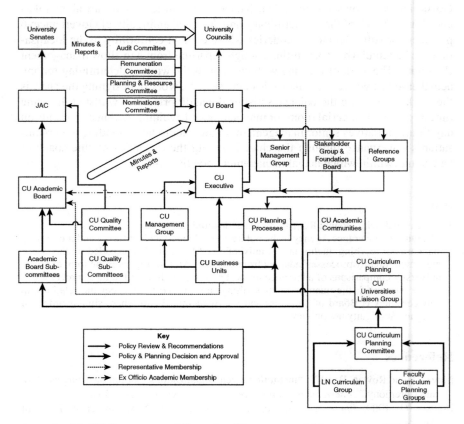

*Appendix 6.1* CU Governance of Operational Processes and Management of Curriculum Planning and Academic Standards

# 7 Sensitivity analysis as practical modal realism

## Introduction

A constant theme of this book is that the routine, daily work of management is overwhelmingly given over to managing and where possible reducing the threat of organisational entropy. In this chapter, the example is a 'Sensitivity Analysis', a widely used management tool which addresses the possibility, given certain outcomes, of a major increase of organisational entropy. The disorganisation in question would occur if there was significant variance between the way events actually turn out and the current provisions within the approved strategic, financial and operational plans of the organisation. Part of the work of addressing the possibility of such variance is the construction of counterfactual possible worlds and the assessment of their likely correspondence to current projections. On the basis of that assessment, management actions are formulated to address the issues which would arise should any of these possible worlds turn out to be the actual world. What senior managers are doing when they do this is grappling with the problems posed by what might be called the 'modal logic' of organisational possibility.[1]

## Possible worlds

The example we have chosen was prepared by the senior management team for a task group set up by the Board of Directors and is relatively straightforward.[2] This has the significant advantage of not requiring us to provide extensive contextual detail when describing how it works and hence allows us to concentrate on the *reasoning* which is going on.

### *Some distinctions*

We start by marking a distinction between what we will term the 'attitudinal' and 'possible' worlds of the manager. The attitudinal world is the configuration of courses of action, social actors, institutionalised norms and values, material resources, external forces and whatnot with which the daily life of the manager is taken up and in the management of which he or she is immersed.

The attitudinal world is the *gestalt* of daily management which constitutes the reality of management experience. This gestalt is constituted by the matters which they take seriously as offering grounds for inference and action. A possible world is a narrowly constructed configuration of the attitudinal world – a configuration to which the manager turns for the specific management purpose of plan evaluation. As we keep stressing, the attitudinal world is permanently subject to the emergence of the unforeseen. This is precisely not the case in the construction of possible worlds. They are entirely foreseen and circumscribed worlds.[3]

It is important to be clear about the character of the reality we are examining. These worlds are 'real' not simply in W.I. Thomas's sense that if management believes they are real and acts on their belief then they will be real in their consequences. Within the managerial attitude, they are both doxastically real and metaphysically real in that each of them is a way the actual world could turn out to be. Indeed, it is stronger than that. One of them, or something akin to it, is what they are assuming the actual world will turn out to be. The point of constructing these worlds is to estimate the risk and degree of entropy likely to be present at any of them and what could or should be done to manage that risk. The reality of the risk is a direct derivative of the reality of the possible world. Each possible world has its risks. The question for managers is not whether these risks are real, for they all are, but how likely they are to eventuate. Just as David Lewis (1986), a leading figure in developing the logic of possible worlds, claimed his possible worlds were not fakes, fictions, or fantasies but real worlds constructed for important philosophical purposes, these possible worlds are possible real worlds constructed for important management purposes.

Because the possible worlds we will discuss are financial, we need to make a further distinction, namely between management-constructed financial possible worlds and management-constructed financial descriptions of activities in the attitudinal world.[4] In Chapter 5, we described how a financial account provided projections of the state of an operational organisation at particular points in time (the Income & Expenditure account) and over a defined period (the Cash Flow). The numbers in the account represent the activities being carried out. Managers know the representational nature of these numbers, and considerable time and effort is spent evaluating the degree of verisimilitude between the reality of organisation as experienced and its reality as depicted in the financial description. Of course, since the conventional management mantra is to 'manage by the numbers', precisely what the numbers are telling you about the actual state of the organisation when they are at variance with experience, takes on considerable importance. In a Sensitivity Analysis, because all the representations are of possible future states, there is no possibility of divergence between experience and representation. For the purposes of the exercise, what the counterfactual numbers come to is what the possible organisation is to be. They are not abstractions from the actual world but constructions of very likely 'possible actual worlds'. Just like other financial descriptions, they are co-produced using formatted schedules as ordering devices designed to allow the assessment of the degree of organisational entropy associated with them.

## Possible world pairings and their constitution

A Sensitivity Analysis is a planning support document, a familiar class of management objects. We treat the Sensitivity Analysis as a 'lebenswelt pair' which requires the closing of the praxeological gap between the documentary account and the grasping of the management implications of that account. This gap is closed by finding and following the instructions provided in the documentary account.

Planning support documents provide supplementary material, offer further explication and analysis, or try to head off particular counter-arguments raised within the course of a plan's development and approval process. The analysis itself consists of a number of pairings, the most obvious of which are the schedule and its text. These two are designed to be read together. In addition, jointly they are paired with and designed to be read against the set of formally approved strategic plans. In both pairings, the documents are mutually explicative. The analysis makes sense in the context of the plans; and the schedule makes sense in the context of the text. What the plans come to as plans (that is, their strategic robustness) and what the text is glossing are determined reciprocally. The familiar processes of mutual elaboration and specification are at work here. This is not to say each component could not be interrogated individually, but the elements of the analysis, and the analysis and the plans, are designed to be taken together.

The worlds of a Sensitivity Analysis are entirely financial.[5] The elements making them up (what in the jargon are called 'the drivers') are set out in the strategic plans. They consist in financial structures and their outcomes. These are:

> A working operation defined as a bundle of costs (within the financial model) entailed by the 'delivery model' in the plan. In universities, elements of such models have become increasingly formalised as emphasis has been given to ensuring maintenance of standards in learning, teaching and assessment by the stipulation of activities to be carried out. Alongside the specified LTA activities are 'support' and 'infrastructure' activities which are included in the delivery model (and hence the financial model).

> A set of revenues (again within the financial model) generated by the delivery model through the organisation's interaction with its surrounding environment. The range of possible interactions is limited to the financial.

> A set of financial consequences (surplus/deficit and cash flow) resulting from the balance of costs and revenues associated with the operation of the delivery model.

The Sensitivity Analysis traces the effect of variations in the drivers upon the outputs. It attempts to estimate how sensitive the current objectives and targets might be (that is, what level of change would follow) to the variations in the drivers. Each world is a specifically constructed and worked through analysis of those effects.

90  *The practicalities of executive management*

There is a fourth pairing. The Sensitivity Analysis is also paired with a set of management actions elaborated in the text. The purpose of the analysis is to act as a stimulus for and rationalisation of management action in the conditional future tense. Should any of the actual possible worlds be realised, given what is known now, this is what would be done then. Plan, Sensitivity Analysis and putative actions make up an integrated architecture of management modal logic in the face of the contingent unfolding of possibilities.

## The construction of possible worlds

Like the other management objects we have discussed, the Sensitivity Analysis was designed for a particular set of users undertaking a particular activity. It is purposeful in two senses. It is designed for a purpose, and to be used for a purpose. The envisaged users are the Board of Directors and Senior Managers. These groups are presumed to have a working knowledge of CU's objectives, values and motivations and how these are articulated in the strategic plans. This knowledge is what makes the mapping of the financial schedules and the text visible. Seeing the mapping involves tracking an array of reciprocal adjustments across both the financial model and the management model of the institution. The document glosses these adjustments and what they will entail. The financial model is the approved composition of revenues and delivery costs (revenue model and delivery model) required to achieve the current targets. The management model is the framework of operational arrangements needed to support the financial model. The financial model and the management model are taken as given background for the analysis. The pairings we just described provide a determination of the gap between possible future variance in costs and revenues on the one hand, and currently envisaged targets for future revenue on the other, and what will need to be put in place to manage the consequences of that variance. In some 'worlds', small adjustments will allow targets broadly to be retained. In others, targets will have to be re-fashioned or dispensed with entirely.

So far, we have identified two required sets of background knowledge: the plan and the financial and operational models. In addition, an understanding of and trust in the normal operation of financial procedures is taken for granted. To enable real planning, these have to be trusted because they are already deeply embedded in the routines of the organisation's affairs. To change them would involve large-scale changes in the way the financial administration was carried out. This is not simply a matter of assuming the probity of the financial team or that nefarious financial practices are not and will not be used by managers. In management discussions these two possibilities are always set aside (unless . . .). Rather, what we are pointing to here is trust in the robustness of the accounting processes generating the numbers upon which the analysis is based. Despite the fact that the institution is not yet in operation, despite the fact that the numbers used are derived from procedures which are not all that transparent, despite the fact that some of the numbers have had to be extrapolated because no relevant values are available, despite all these things, to interrogate the accounting infrastructure would have meant sacrificing the analysis. This was an outcome no one wanted. In addition, given the information which was available and usable, it was assumed that running the exercise in any other way would result in much the same outcomes. The aim was not to test the method or the financial processes, but the robustness of the projections which were embodied in the extant plans.

A third set of required background assumptions, perhaps as important as the others, is about the significance of what is not in the schedule. We have said each 'scenario' is not an exhaustive description of all the features of the possible world it describes. It is the world as defined for the analysis. The list of 'scenarios' is not exhaustive either. This is the set deemed managerially relevant for the presumed users. The horizon of managerial relevance is given by the filters set out in the top right-hand corner of the financial analysis. The filters act as an Occam's razor for possible worlds. The worlds excluded are those where CU produces a deficit significantly more than £1.5m together with a negative cash flow for more than three years. The Board and Senior Managers know such conditions would render CU financially unviable. Response to a world in which the institution was unviable would not be redirection and redesign but dissolution. At this point, planning for dissolution was not on anyone's agenda!

The filters provide the logic for the variances in the drivers. Holding all other revenues to target but reducing HEFCE income below 90% of target will make the institution unviable. There is no point in working through the case where HEFCE income falls to 85%. There will be no managed response other than 'exit'. The filter logic works for the other scenarios too. Holding other incomes at target and reducing the Strategic Health Authority income below 90% makes the institution marginally viable after three years. Once again, the effect of further reduction in the health contract is excluded. In all but three of the 'scenarios', cash flow is negative for more than three years. Whilst on its own this does not indicate 'unviability', it would pose serious management challenges. The logic of the 'scenarios' described expresses the boundaries of management manoeuvre in the face of its known risks. What no one can plan for, of course, are the unknown risks.

Just what is it everyone is assumed to know but disregards about these worlds? Take, for example, the composition of the 'Baseline'. When the analysis was constructed, CU was not fully operational. It had no functioning processes through which the elements of the model were delivered. Its operation was largely given over to planning in 'shadow mode' and so the figures used were reasoned and reasonable predictions, since there were no current inputs and output values to feed into the financial model. Everyone knows these numbers are projections. The documented Strategic Plan contains a sketch of the delivery model to be used, a sketch derived from the ratios of revenues to delivery costs contained in the financial plan within that strategy document. This sketch represents the outline of how it is hoped the organisation will run. The numbers in the Strategic Plan are assumptions about how resources and their associated costs in the predecessor organisations will translate into the CU operating model. Never mind the other scenarios, even the 'Baseline' is composed of future perfect numbers.

The text of CEO087 provided alongside the Sensitivity Analysis sets out revisions in the numbers in response to events which have happened since the financial plan was initially constructed. These revisions imply correlated changes to the 'best guess' estimations for revenues. They too are revised versions of the targets set out in the plan and originally derived from information provided by the predecessor institutions.[6] These revisions reconfigure the management gestalt of the institution. The CU of the Sensitivity Analysis is not the CU of the Strategic Plan. It is different, but not entirely different. The work of doing the analysis is the discovery of what that difference is and what it means.

Here is the summary of the revisions set out in the circulated document CEO087.

In reviewing the revenue projections, it was decided:

1 To retain HEFCE FTE growth targets at the levels set out in previous projections. These targets formed the basis of the bids to the various funding partners.
2 To include HEFCE Moderating Teaching and Widening Participation additional formula driven funds but only at current levels held by The College. Other formula-driven funds for CU will be identified in the Funding Letter from HEFCE to the universities.
3 To set the SHA contract at the level offered in the initial negotiations with the Health Authority. This represents a 20% reduction on the 2005/06 contract value. We fully expect this position to ease considerably. If the contract returns to the 2005/06 levels of recruitment, this will lift the SHA contract value by £400k in 2007/08, £800k in 2008/09, and £1.2m in 2009/10.
4 To assume that The College will achieve approval of its build programme before the deadline set in the contingency arrangements. If they do not, up to £10.2m may be released at the end of Phase 1 which could be used either to reduce CU's debt or to reduce future borrowing requirement.

The following revisions were made to the modelling of costs:

1 Staffing levels and costs for 2007/08 were set by the requirements of the agreed TUPE transfer arrangements and full year costs for planned incremental posts.
2 Academic staff payroll costs were set to increase at 15% of incremental revenue.
3 Central services staff payroll costs were set to decrease year on year from 26% to 22% of income.
4 Central services non-pay costs were set at 6% of income.
5 Charges for services provided by partner Universities were set at 1.5% of income for 2008/09 onwards. The projection for 2007/08 is 1.3%.
6 Internal capital investment was set at 2.5% of income.
7 A two-year long-term loan repayment holiday was assumed.

Each of the eleven points above is a header for a complex blend of sound information, plausible inferences, and tested and untested assumptions and aspirations. Given the institution's current status, there is no remedy for this. The users of the analysis know this though *without further detailed enquiry*, they do not know and cannot know precisely which bits of information are sound and which not, the bounds of plausibility on the inferences, which assumptions are tested and just how much of a gap there is between the resulting calculations and what could be defended. There and then, the only way of closing the gaps was by aspiration.

This does not mean the numbers are entirely mysterious. On the basis of their own experience, the Board and Senior Managers can make judgements about them. Take the first point: the growth in HEFCE FTE targets (ASNs). This is the main driver for growth in HEFCE revenue, and, as we have seen, is the central component of the financial plan. It was accepted that a combination of a drop in base HEFCE income and a drop in HEFCE FTE growth would be catastrophic.[7] The analysis does not have to say what everyone knows, and so assessment is only the impact of a shortfall on recruiting ASNs – that is, failing to grow at the rate proposed, not an actual reduction of the projected base for 2007/08. Achieving 90% of ASNs would leave the institution just about viable in terms of the balance of its costs and revenues. Eighty-five per cent would tip it over into unviability. Without significant cash injection, the institution would be insolvent and so, if it were to have a future, this would have to be completely different to the one currently envisaged. Equally, it was well known that there could be no clear definition of the costs of the TUPE transfer of staff. Some general principles had been agreed but the full cost would be understood only when the transfer actually occurred. What was known, though, was that there would be a significant increase in running costs. The figure of 15% functions as a conventional managerially reasonable number; not too low to raise eyebrows and not too high to raise concerns. Knowing where to pitch such estimations, especially in the face of a complete lack of experience of similar circumstances, is a delicate exercise in organisational acumen.

The revised positions together with those costs which have been left as they were in the Strategic Plan, make up the financial and delivery model underpinning the analysis and expressed in the 'Baseline' surplus/deficit figure for 2007/08. This constructed actual is then projected for the following four years. This is the 'Baseline' possible world.

The 'Baseline' is a vector of financial consequences. So are the other 'scenarios'. Each is a counterfactual of the Baseline where one or more of the inputs has been varied. The worlds are ordered cumulatively as the variation in key revenues accumulate. Each world is what, as a financial entity, CU will turn out to be 'If HFCE income is 95% of target' or 'If HEFCE income is 95% of target and SHA income is 95% of target', etc. With these changes in inputs, the projected CU worlds are tracked as they evolve through the planning period.

There is one final feature of the schedule worth bringing out. The analysis tracks 'downside risk' only. This is unusual. Just as much as shortfalls, managers usually want to understand the risk of a 'success-disaster' consequent upon over-achievement of targets or goals. If CU recruited more students than could be accommodated by its delivery model, this might imply significant increases in costs for space, teaching staff and other resources. Given this, excluding 'over-recruitment' to target is unsurprising though. No-one expected it to happen. The targets defined in the plan were exceedingly 'stretching' and were known to be so. Indeed, the Sensitivity Analysis was a response to the suggestion in some quarters they were too ambitious and hence the whole project was unlikely to be successful. Serious overachievement was not a world anyone wanted to devote time and energy planning for. Second, one of the premises of the plan is that what is currently felt to be a highly inefficient delivery model in the predecessor institutions will be significantly re-shaped as CU 'goes live'. At the global plan level, then, any marginal over-achievement is be used to 'mop up' resources that were currently under-utilised.[8]

## Managing at possible worlds

The calculative logic of the Sensitivity Analysis produces ten possible CU worlds. In CEO087, these worlds are sifted and clumped to produce a deployable set of management responses. Those which the filter criteria render borderline or below are gathered into one set. The rest are grouped into four bundles 'similar enough' to enable coherent sets of management responses.

The borderline-and-below bundle is labelled 're-design', a term which implies the jettisoning of the current strategy and plan. Though it is a possible world, it is effectively set aside. Since they would almost certainly be the first casualties of any such outcome, the egological character of the management team's relevances means they are not going to 'waste time' thinking about what *someone else* would have to do if CU had to abandon its strategy. Some 'exit strategies' are gestured at, but that is all. The management team attends to what *its* problems will be.

> **CU Re-design** (HEFCE or SHA below 90%)
> On this scenario, CU has major deficits in its first three years and negative cash flow extends into Phase 3. In short, the current CU strategy becomes unviable and would have to be completely re-designed. The most obvious way forward might be to integrate with one of the University partners, with The College, or even with another partner. Provided they were carried out in a carefully managed way, all would offer opportunities for significant reduction in support and overhead costs. Alternatively, the Board may seek an exit from HE altogether, though this may create major issues for stakeholders. Any disposal of the facilities on the Waterfront and College South site would have to be negotiated with funding partners.

The cumulative structure of the possible worlds is replicated in the cumulative logic of the responses to the scenarios. Actions to be taken build incrementally as the differences from the baseline increase. Since no one expects the divergence from the baseline to be exactly as laid out in any of the scenarios, showing a 'tuneable set' of responses reinforces the visibility of a rational and controlled management strategy capable of responding effectively to an array of possible outcomes. At each world, actions are taken to manage revenues and costs. Managed Start Up is the least divergent from 'Baseline'. Here priority is given to getting as close to target revenues as possible and to making compensating cuts to the delivery costs:

**Managed Start Up** (Base Line; ASNs above 85% of target)

As indicated above, on this, CU posts deficits in 2007/09 and 2008/09. Cash flow remains negative for the first three years. However, the assumed SHA contract and HEFCE formula-driven revenues are conservative/pessimistic. Nonetheless, the central goals of the 2007/08 and 2008/09 operational planning and implementation will be to focus energy and attention on, first, securing the revenue growth set out in the plans and, second, reducing and controlling costs in order to reduce the negative impact of any initial deficits.

Four lines of action are underway to ensure that the *revenue targets* are achieved or improved upon:

1. As explained above, we expect to close the SHA contract at base levels closer to the 2005/06 levels than currently assumed in the planning numbers.
2. To ensure targets are met, significant emphasis is being placed upon curriculum development, extensive marketing and public relations development, as well as proactive student recruitment. In the past, there has been very little emphasis on explicit market development of this kind.
3. Faculty and network partner plans and resulting performance will be monitored for delivery of improved retention rates. At present, The College does not monitor cohort progression and so no historical information is available. Informal indications are that in some areas this offers a major opportunity.
4. We will seek accelerated value release from The Quay through earlier than planned student residence development.

The immediate actions to be taken regarding *costs* are:

1. To profile staff ramp up over 2007/08 to ensure a break even position is achieved.
2. To reduce the planned staffing ramp up for 2007/09 with particular emphasis on central services staff.
3. To review other cost categories with a view to minimizing the deficit in 2008/09. Key tools in this will be the introduction of a cost allocation model as part of annual planning, the use of course costing processes in curriculum planning, extensive provision of fully costed campus services for The College, extensive use of the VLE for curriculum management and course delivery, and cost sharing of network points of presence with regional partners.

4 The Board is aware that CU's start-up costs are currently planned to be significantly greater than originally envisaged. Examples of such costs are: the TPS pensions transfer, dual validation and accreditation, and VAT on partner-provided services. The last of these has led to the need to minimise rather than maximise the use of back office and IT services from the universities, and to plan carefully the provision of common campus services with The College. As part of planning for 2007/08, ways are being sought to ameliorate the impact of such unforeseen costs.

From this platform, the remaining three scenarios gradually pare out more and more cost as the world realises greater variation from the Baseline targets, goals and levels of activity. Here is what the team call 'Managed Re-Direction'.

**Managed Re-direction** (HEFCE 95% or SHA 95%)

Without major corrective management action, recruiting to 95% of the HEFCE or SHA targets over the 2007/10 period will pose significant challenges to the achievement of the CU strategy. Major deficits will be returned in the first two years and for the HEFCE stream in 2009/10 as well. Both produce an extended negative cash flow.

In addition to the actions outlined for the Managed Start Up scenario, further significant cost reduction will be required as well as growth in alternative revenue streams. The most obvious is CPD. Capital planning for Phase 2 could be scaled back considerably and the development of The Quay for academic activity could be postponed. This would allow early release of greater value from The Quay. With these actions implemented, CU could continue to grow but on a much lower trajectory.

In providing these sketches of actions-to-be-taken, CU's senior management team is demonstrating to the members of the task group that it has understood the significance of the variations in its financial drivers and can offer an array of plausible responses which could be implemented. Such responses would allow the organisation to keep 'broadly' to its current strategy. Here 'broadly' can be taken to mean something between 'somewhat close to original plan' to 'heading in approximately the same direction but at a much slower pace'.

The financial schedule articulates a logic of incremental disparity between envisaged possible worlds and the constructed actual world of the Baseline. The management responses follow that logic. The text and the numbers go together. In the text, the logic operates at two distinct levels: successively stronger ameliorating responses across the bundles, and reciprocal emphasis on revenue model and delivery model. Each response is designed as a balancing of feasible management actions in the face of greater and greater challenges. Key here is the recognisability of 'feasible'. Across the set of 'scenarios', what we have called the 'management gestalt' of CU undergoes significant transformations. The analysis is designed to ensure the Board is convinced that faced with any or even all of these transformations, the senior management team would have envisaged, planned and implementable compensating lines of action. No miracles are required, no white knights, no *deus ex machina*. Given the premises of the Sensitivity Analysis, and in particular the application of Occam's razor on possible worlds, the logic of the management proposals maps onto the logic of the possible worlds. Building the analysis so that the Board could see the mapping is all the senior management team could hope to achieve. Merely to have claimed that a modified strategy could be delivered would not have been as convincing as the demonstration of what actions would need to be taken for it to be done. Finding that demonstration in the schedule and the text is the work of understanding the Sensitivity Analysis.

## Conclusion

In a discussion of philosophical questions regarding the 'reality' of sub-atomic particles, Ian Hacking tells the following story. Talking with a friend about the measurement of changes of a charge on a niobium ball used to detect quarks, he was told if, as the charge changed in strength, it flips from positive to negative, that is an indication of the presence of free quarks. 'So,' asked Hacking, 'how do you change the charge?'

> 'Well, at that stage,' said my friend, 'we spray it with positrons to increase the charge or with electrons to decrease the charge.' From that day forth I've been a scientific realist. *So far as I'm concerned, if you can spray them then they are real.*
>
> (Hacking 1983: 23; emphasis in original)

In this discussion, we have shown how managers at CU created a number of real possible worlds and designed responses to them No doubt some will query this, suggesting 'what-if' exercises generate nothing more than envisionments, speculations, or even phantasmagoria. That is not what they represent for the management team. For them, securing the plausibility of the analysis and their responses to it was a test of their managerial competence. Paraphrasing Hacking, we are inclined to say: 'If you think the future of the organisation (and hence your job) is on the line if you can't show you can manage them, then possible worlds are real!' Showing that if they had to, they could manage the relevant possible worlds they had constructed was all the management team could do, and exactly what it did do.

## Notes

1 That there might be structural similarities between the social organisation of this engaged managerial grappling and the social organisation of the engaged grapplings of professional philosophers struggling with the logical problems of possible world semantics (e.g. Lewis 1973, 1986, 2001) would be one interesting consequence of reversing the usual order of dependency and treating philosophising as itself a practical activity. See Liberman (2007).

2 The whole analysis is given in a document labelled 'CEO087'. The core financial section is set out in the Appendix to this chapter. Relevant excepts from the interpretations of the financials and the planned interventions contained in CEO087 are cited in the text.
3 Let's be clear here. We are not suggesting they are exhaustive (i.e. denumerably infinite) inventories of what will be the case. Rather, whatever properties the possible world is defined as exhibiting are all the properties that world needs to have. They constitute the-world-for-all-the-practical-purposes of planning.
4 This distinction, along with many such, brings out the ramified nature of the manager's attitudinal world.
5 This makes Sensitivity Analysis different to scenario analysis. In the latter, it is common to vary political, economic, social and technological conditions, as well as the financial aspects.
6 The extent to which the management team had or could get a good grip on the verisimilitude of all these figures was a constant concern for both the Board and the team itself – a problem of practical epistemics if ever there was one!
7 In Chapter 5, we discuss activities set in train when it was discovered just such a catastrophe had occurred.
8 Saying this does not mean that should such a state of affairs come to pass, its management would be easy. Resources are rarely where growth is.

# References

Hacking, I. 1983. *Representing and Intervening*. Cambridge: Cambridge University Press.
Lewis, D.K. 1973. "Causation." *Journal of Philosophy*, vol. 70, no. 17 556–567.
——. 1986. *On the Plurality of Worlds*. Oxford: Blackwell.
——. 2001 (originally 1973). *Counterfactuals*. Oxford: Blackwell.
Liberman, K. 2007. *Dialectical Practice in Tibetan Philosophical Culture*. Lanham, MD: Rownman & Littlefield.

# Appendix

CU Strategic Plan: Financial sensitivity analysis

Filters deficit > £1.5m
Negative cash flow > 3 years

## Surplus/Deficit

| Scenario | | | | | | 2007/08 | 2008/09 | 2009/10 | 2010/11 | 2011/12 |
|---|---|---|---|---|---|---|---|---|---|---|
| Baseline | | | | | | -132.00 | -668.00 | 482.00 | 2066.00 | 3472.00 |
| HEFCE 95% | | | | | | -462.00 | -1141.00 | -325.00 | 853.00 | 1849.00 |
| HEFCE 90% | | | | | | -973.00 | -1594.00 | -1067.00 | 139.00 | 474.00 |
| HEFCE 100% | SHA 95% | | | | | -419.00 | -881.00 | 263.00 | 1842.00 | 3242.00 |
| | SHA 90% | | | | | -707.00 | -1093.00 | 44.00 | 1616.000 | 3012.00 |
| HEFCE 95% | SHA 95% | | | | | -749.00 | -1352.00 | -542.00 | 672.00 | 1618.00 |
| HEFCE 100% | SHA 100% | ASN 90% | | | | -307.00 | -947.00 | 144.00 | 1569.00 | 2824.00 |
| | | ASN 85% | | | | -395.00 | -1084.00 | -21.00 | 1322.00 | 2501.00 |
| HEFCE 100% | SHA 100% | ASN 100% | O/S 95% | | | -132.00 | -683.00 | 450.00 | 2017.00 | 3405.00 |
| | | | O/S 90% | | | -132.00 | -702.00 | 424.00 | 1975.00 | 3340.00 |
| HEFCE 100% | SHA 100% | ASN 100% | O/S 100% | R&E 75% | | -173.00 | -692.00 | 451.00 | 2024.00 | 3417.00 |

## Cash Flow

| Scenario | | | | | | 2007/08 | 2008/09 | 2009/10 | 2010/11 | 2011/12 |
|---|---|---|---|---|---|---|---|---|---|---|
| Baseline | | | | | | -32.00 | -650.00 | -622.00 | 262.00 | 2497.00 |
| HEFCE 95% | | | | | | -362.00 | -1453.00 | -2202.00 | -2456.00 | -1802.00 |
| HEFCE 90% | | | | | | -693.00 | -2237.00 | -3702.00 | -4956.00 | -5643.00 |
| HEFCE 100% | SHA 95% | | | | | -319.00 | -1150.00 | -1335.00 | -670.00 | 1339.00 |
| | SHA 90% | | | | | -607.00 | -1649.00 | -2046.00 | -1602.00 | 180.00 |
| HEFCE 95% | SHA 95% | | | | | -649.00 | -1951.00 | -2911.00 | -3380.00 | -2954.00 |
| HEFCE 100% | SHA 100% | ASN 90% | | | | -207.00 | -1104.00 | -1402.00 | -1001.00 | 602.00 |
| | | ASN 85% | | | | -295.00 | -1329.00 | -1786.00 | -1623.00 | -333.00 |
| HEFCE 100% | SHA 100% | ASN 100% | O/S 95% | | | -32.00 | -665.00 | -668.00 | 168.00 | 2338.00 |
| | | | O/S 90% | | | -32.00 | -684.00 | -712.00 | 84.00 | 2190.00 |
| HEFCE 100% | SHA 100% | ASN 100% | O/S 100% | R&E 75% | | -73.00 | -715.00 | -713.00 | 135.00 | 2322.00 |

# 8 Benchmarking as reality conjuncture

**'Where do we stand?' as a problem for management**

Although managers have deep and detailed knowledge of their own organisations and are usually very perceptive about the strengths and weaknesses of their performance, they often struggle to get a sense of where they stand relative to their competitors, or those whom they would like to be their competitors. Of course, if they ask (and they do), they can find out what their customers think; they can consult public documents such as financial accounts, and they can hold focus groups, run surveys, and so on. From the manager's point of view, all these are good mechanisms for ascertaining what others think of your performance. What customer surveys, focus groups and public accounts cannot tell you is anything about the effectiveness of your organisation as an organisation compared to that of others. Are they more efficient? Is their structure more complex? Is the balance of their resource distribution similar to yours? Answers to these questions will prompt management reflection and, depending on the estimation of the degree of variance from what 'the best' are doing and its import, a range of management action might be initiated.

Benchmarking is a standard way of generating this kind of 'global view'. As with all management action, carrying out a benchmarking exercise is motivated. The purpose in finding out where you stand is to see if there is anything you should do to improve your performance (and hence your place in the ordering). Gaining the global view is the means and the end is management action, which, naturally, is itself a means to getting closer and closer to 'the best' or even being 'the best'. The logic at work here is something like: 'The more we do what they do, the more we will achieve what they achieve.'

Benchmarking involves assembling a set of comparator organisations – the ones you think you are like and a few of the ones you would like to be like, and then compiling a list of descriptors of your own and those organisations on which comparisons can be made. For the most part, the descriptors are first and second order direct and indirect measures.[1] The assemblage of the measures provides a synoptic view of each organisation and hence an aggregated composite picture of where everyone stands. Of course, in unifying the descriptors into a single overarching picture, managers face the task of calibrating the measures as well as the pictures which emerge of each organisation. Only when measures and pictures are well calibrated can the composite *rendering* be taken to approximate to reality and so provide a reasoned basis for intervention in your own organisation. Or, at least, that is the working theory. The example we examine is contained in the document CEO216_Benchmarking_final, provided in the Appendix to this chapter.

## The provenance of CEO216_Benchmarking_final

The provenance of the benchmarking document will be examined as an 'analytic object' later in this chapter. Here we simply set out some background to enable the reader to follow the discussion with relative ease. This background is part of what was commonly known by the intended readers of the document. How that detail becomes visible in the document is the analytic issue:

> The document was written by the CEO as a 'backgrounder' for the 'kick off' meeting inaugurating an annual planning round. It was circulated to the management team and shared informally with the universities and HEFCE. It did not appear as a formal item at the Board. It was written following an email exchange between the CEO and the Regional Advisor for HEFCE in which concerns expressed by financial planners at HEFCE were shared. For some time prior to this event, HEFCE had been collecting data on various aspects of the institutions it funded (the annual HESA survey). The results of the survey are published. Given the difficulty of forming equivalence classes across HEIs (the usual apples and apricots problem), HESA data is not widely used by universities themselves. However, HEFCE does use the data to monitor the progress of institutions. A quick 'eyeballing' of CU's cost base compared to institutions thought to be very similar, revealed it to be out of line. The question was raised in an informal manner so the concern was not an 'issue' in the sense of a first step in a potential escalation process. All that was being offered was a 'heads up' on the surprise at HEFCE at the differences and all that was being asked for was (reassuring) feedback. The CEO responded with a high-level discussion of the 'distinctiveness of CU' (a localised version of the difficulty of comparing apples and apricots) and outlined the 'platform costs' (mostly to do with IT and expectations concerning the quality of 'the student experience') which a modern HEI no matter what size had to accept. Although the query and its response were known to the management team, they had not been party to the exchanges. The response appears to have been sufficient since, at least for the moment, the matter was dropped.

If the question was dealt with, why engage in a benchmarking exercise? There were two interrelated reasons. Both shape the way the exercise was framed. First, CU was now 'live'. It was a medium-sized organisation. Although the team's competence was not actually being questioned, nonetheless given the rapid growth and the continuing (indeed escalating) risky nature of the overall project, the management team felt the question of their performance was always open and hence there was a permanent need to reassure key players that the project was under control.[2]

102  *The practicalities of executive management*

Every opportunity was being taken to give that reassurance. The general view at HEFCE was that appropriate use of business practices was innovative in and positive for Higher Education institutions. Universities had to become more 'business-like' in their operations. In part, the CEO had been recruited because he had an industrial as well as academic background and was expected to introduce management practices used in business. Carrying out benchmarking would be just the sort of thing HEFCE and other stakeholders would be looking for.

The second reason was internal. The management team was new and some of its key figures came from one of the predecessor institutions. The CEO wanted to change some of the operational practices which had been transferred into CU when it became operational.[3] Because it is a well-known business practice, benchmarking would have credibility with stakeholders and be something the team would accept. This allowed it to be used to try to engineer change. Demonstrating the exercise could give a 'fair' and 'objective' view of the challenges facing the organisation, and would allow it to act as a lever for change. As well as reassuring key partners as to the competence of the management team, then, the benchmarking exercise would help initiate change – or so it was hoped.

## The problem

We have said that CEO216_Benchmarking_final is a motivated document. In writing it, the CEO wanted to achieve a set of outcomes. To achieve these outcomes, readers have to find the conclusions the CEO wants them to find in the document and those conclusions have to be credible — ones they will accept as necessary and appropriate. This is the recipient design problem of closing the praxeological gap between adopting the findings of benchmarking and the formal account presented in CEO216_Benchmarking_final. To do what the CEO wants it to do, the document has to be designed to achieve its intended effect. It is shaped for 'just these' readers and not, as are some of the other documents we examine, for some set of broadly designated readers and anyone else who happens to come across them. Philosophers such as H.P. Grice (1981) and Nelson Goodman (1974) have discussed the challenge of providing a philosophical account of the fixing of meaning or descriptions. The CEO's problem was its real-world practical complement – how to make it happen.

## The character of CEO216_Benchmarking_final

This analysis aims to show that the establishing of the authoritative character of the benchmarking exercise and the followability of benchmarking document are a lebenswelt pair. To bring this out, we make use of a term introduced by John Austin (1962) and talk of the CEO216_Benchmarking_final as a 'performative' document. That is, rather than treating it as a retrospective description of the exercise (a process description perhaps, or an action record, set of minutes, information report, or whatever), we treat CEO216_Benchmarking_final as the benchmarking exercise. We need to be careful here. Although undoubtedly the CEO talked with lots of people about the exercise, asked others to gather the numbers, called meetings to look at the numbers and argue about them, and from the records, we know the document passed through several drafts, we are not treating CEO216_ Benchmarking_final as a record of that process. Of course, it is an outcome of some process, and if we have some understanding of the organisation, it might tell us a lot about the way the organisation was operating at the time. But to do that, we would have to read back from the benchmarking-as-accomplished-in-the-document to the organisation-as-we-know-it. Our question is a prior one: how is the followability of benchmarking-in-the-document accomplished and how does that followability enable its authoritative status? CEO216_Benchmarking_final was written to be read as a lebenswelt pair, namely an authoritative benchmarking exercise. The corollary of this (and this is the point we are labouring) is that co-producing authoritative organisational descriptions is a practical management skill. Describing that skill is what we want to do here.

## *The social construction of authoritativeness*

Most routine problems are solved using standard solutions with standardised components. Standardisation is what makes them routine. Deploying the components properly and hence solving the problem is an ordinary competence. In the case in hand, the problem is a management one and the solutions are managerial, as are the competences. In 'bringing off' the authoritativeness of the benchmarking exercise, the CEO has to undertake a number of interrelated tasks. These can be summarised as the ensuring of authoritativeness of:

1   The objective;
2   The logical grammar of the narrative;
3   The evidence;
4   The transformations of form; and
5   The interpretation of the composite description.

## *The objective*

The ostensible reason for the benchmarking is the assessment of 'Where do we stand?' as step in the qualifying of the development plans. 'Qualifying' is a semi-technical term and in this instance does not mean 'expressing reservations about' but 'ensuring approximate fit for purpose'. Are the plans covering everything they need to? Are the elements in the plans realistic and likely to be effective? Is there evidence of over- or under-resourcing in any area? Are there actions that need to be taken now to put the plan back on track? If we ask about the reasons for choosing this mechanism as the device for framing some of these questions, light is shed on some of the other reasons for undertaking the exercise and how the management team is responding to them. These reasons are the commonly known but unremarked background to the exercise. They are what anyone who is an intended reader of this document will know and understand. In the rest of this discussion, we will spend a lot of time talking about how the document is designed for its readership. Right now we are highlighting how that readership is constituted through the knowledge at hand which readers are presumed to have.[4]

The motivated character of the exercise is thematised in the first paragraph and drawn out in the rest of the document.[5]

> **Rationale:**
> During the planning for (last year) and the early stages of this year's planning round, concern was expressed over the kinds of expectations it would be appropriate to have for UCS, and in particular the UCS Hub, as an operating organisation. Comparisons with the previous regime at the College would not be helpful because of both the relative sizes of the organisations and their educational mandates and mix. Equally, comparison to the sponsoring universities would not provide appropriate guidance.
>
> This paper offers an initial, and it must be stressed very preliminary, first pass at a benchmarking exercise. It seeks to raise a number of questions for consideration in the light of data for a number of comparator institutions. These questions are offered as prompts for the discussions to be carried forward from 15th April and into the next planning round. The ambition is to open discussion up not to close it down, and certainly not to provide a definitive set of answers to some of our planning dilemmas

Two important resources are used for thematisation. First, reference is made to a specific date (15th April) and the related discussions to be carried on. That is, these discussions are co-selected with discussions at a meeting on that date. As we have already discussed, this was to be the kick-off meeting for the planning round, a meeting which only the senior managers would attend. The two, then, are tied together. The pairing of date as proxy for the meeting and the binding of the discussions to that meeting and its participants, defines both the management team as the primary intended readership and the rationale of this document. The document is to be read against the planning process which starts then. However, the term 'expectations' plays a critical role here. Each manager would be bringing forward plans for their own groups constructed in terms of their expectations of what they would be doing and the resources needed to do it. It is conventional for these to be 'over-built'. Managers ask for more, knowing that whatever they ask for will be whittled down. The 'expectations' of CU could be read as raising questions about the expectations which CU has of its activities, as well as questions about the expectations others should have of it. The designed ambiguity introduces the possibility that the expectations managers hold for their organisations will be one of the things the benchmarking exercise will question. Managers should read the exercise not as a simple description of where things stand but as indicating implications for their own planning.

Second, reference is made to anonymous 'concern' being expressed about 'the CU Hub, as an operating organization'. Those who are the 'designed readership' of the document (that is, the managers going to the kick-off meeting) know who can properly express concern about CU and the core organisation – that is, who can express concerns which will require a response. Of course, the man in the street, the local press, students, staff, and many others can express 'concerns' about anything connected to CU, but these concerns would not be expected to surface as a background feature of the forthcoming planning exercise. They might be addressed but not through planning. So, who can express concerns which would need to be addressed through planning? The obvious answers are the Board, the partner universities and HEFCE. Why? Simply because these are the people who will see and approve the plans. Any and all of these groups can expect a clear response to concerns they might raise. If you know who these groups are and why they need a response, then you are a proper reader of the document.

Thematisation is achieved by a combination of a designed ambiguity in defining the 'rationale' and a binding of that rationale to the need to create a different management culture. If the benchmarking exercise is successful and provides sufficient grounds for a set of actions, then the binding will have been secured. At the same time, the structuring of the readership also tells us about the document's design intent. And the design intent tells us about who the readership is. The resulting combination of intent and readership is visible throughout the document in the mechanisms used to secure the authoritativeness of the exercise.

## *The logical grammar of the narrative*

Narratives have a logical grammar. That is, they have a set of conventionally defined proper parts and associated rules for their positioning and use. When telling a joke, for example, it is conventional to place 'the punch line' last. Placing it first would be inept, a misfire. Equally, a conventional biography begins with family background and childhood, traces the individual through adolescence and maturity and closes with old age and death. Lifetime phases provide the biographer with recognisable logical grammar. In both joke and biography, the use of the logical grammar make the narrative's trajectory recognisable.

In organisations, the various types of management document have their own narrative structures. Minutes follow the order of the agenda; Financial Statements have a recognisable structure of Balance Sheet, Income and Expenditure and Cash Flow sheets; Task and Finish Reports are usually set out as Problem Statement, Problem Description, Problem Resolution Options and Recommendations. When skimming through minutes, financial statements and reports from task and finish groups, a reader can use the conventional logical grammar – the parts and their ordering – to determine the completeness and the *prima facie* quality of what has been provided. Financial statements without cash flows, task and finish reports without recommendations are both incomplete and incompetent, or fishy in some other way.

With benchmarking, things are not quite so straightforward. Benchmarking is not a routine practice in HE and certainly was not routine in CU's predecessor institutions. In addition, apart from the CEO, none of the team had been involved in a benchmarking exercise before. Although they knew 'roughly' what such an exercise was about, they had only general expectations of how the exercise would be carried out and the outcomes presented. In addition, unlike the conventions of financial reporting, there is no standard process for undertaking and reporting benchmarking. Lots of consultancies and 'gurus' promote their own models, all of which include the obvious steps: defining the scope, choosing the methods, selecting the data, compiling the results, summarising the analysis, and setting out the actions. Constructing the document around these steps, or something like them, provides a recognisable 'common sense logical grammar' for the narrative. The format of CEO216_Benchmarking_final with its structure of rationale, data, comparator institutions, analysis, discussion and next steps follows this grammar. When 'eyeballing' the exercise, those reading the document will have to decide if the set of components is 'possibly complete'. Does the set appear complete? Are there obvious lacunae? If all the appropriate elements seem to be in place and in the right order, even those who have no prior experience of benchmarking can recognise the format as the sort of structure a benchmarking exercise should have. The format, then, has a clear self-explicating character. Using the format makes the exercise appear recognisable and authoritative, even for those who don't know what the format should actually be. If it looks right, it must be right.

The power of the format in constructing the plausibility or authoritativeness of the exercise is also evident within sections. This is particularly so in the analysis section. Here data are gathered under several heads: size and scale, sustainability, and efficiency. This selection and its ordering is not random. Selection and placement reinforce the theme. Can CU grow sufficiently to become sustainable? What would sustainability look like? Is its organisational structure is a barrier to this? All are interlinked key issues which CU's stakeholders have raised. They are the known unknowns of the organisation which, of course, doesn't make them any less critical nor any easier to answer. That *these* are the components of the analysis provides first designed reassurance that the management team is focused on them and understands how they are related. It also provides an indication that organisational structure and sustainability will be the focus of planning.

## *The evidence*

The thematisation of the document provides a first writing/reading interpretive problem for the construction of the document. What kind of evidence would bear upon the theme and provide authority for the set of actions to be undertaken in the planning process? Call this the 'data authority' problem. Somehow, whatever data was available and however good it might be, that data has to be shaped up to give authority to the actions. Its relevance and interpretation must be secured. A second interpretive problem is the selection of comparator institutions. Unless these are found to be reasonable, no matter what the data says, its relevance will be compromised. Call this the 'reasonableness of comparisons' problem. If solutions to these two problems are not found, then the whole exercise is in jeopardy. This is not a matter of plausibility, but of conviction. The data and the comparisons must be convincing to do the work that they do. The document provides an elegant solution to both these problems through *achieved representativeness*. The institutions and the data are representative of the Higher Education type which CU is to be a member of and the measures given for them provide good representations of likely sustainability.

Achieving representativeness involves a number of strategies by which the data is produced as relevant evidence. 'For all practical purposes', we might say, the resulting evidence is just the benchmarking data to be used. To bring out their character, we will cast these strategies as a set of preferences:

> Prefer data sets that have external authority. That is, use data someone else has collected and used for similar exercises. The data is drawn from HEFCE published sources. The data has not been collected for CU's purposes but is being *re-purposed* here. Re-purposing accomplishes representativeness.
>
> If at all possible, disregard the incompleteness of the sets. The data is derived from exercises HEFCE undertook for its own purposes and so whatever is in those published sources is all that can be used. Given HESA is a standardised process, the data published will be in the same 'output form'; that is, each measure for each institutions will be ostensibly 'the same'. But of course there are only very light controls over how the input data is selected and constructed. This is the usual problem of 'big data' exercises. That there will be incomplete data, missing data, or differentially compiled data, all of which might impact the reasonableness of the representations, is known and disregarded. The incompleteness of the comparator set is also disregarded. This is a list of 'new' institutions but by no means all the new institutions which could be said to be like CU. That list might have included another dozen or so institutions. Finally, the possibility that other measures might have been used is disregarded. There is no weighing of the advantage and disadvantage for each measure. These are the measures and these are the institutions to hand and so these are the ones to be used.
>
> Try to ensure the depictions are standardised. We have said the list of comparator institutions is potentially incomplete. It is also potentially highly differentiated. Many of the institutions are very different to CU on some key dimensions. A number were created out of pre-existing single independent institutions. Some were Church of England teacher training institutions. All have their own histories, subject mix, and so on. None of these characteristics is deemed relevant for the benchmarking. Standardisation of depiction by suppression of differentiation achieves a thematic unity for the comparator set. They are treated as the same 'for all practical benchmarking purposes'. The standardisation of depiction is achieved through infilling and shaping the data. None of the published data matches the data to be used for CU. The published data is therefore shaped so that a common base for the measures is achieved. The key criterion of reasonableness becomes visible here. The one piece of data for each institution which is not 'normalised' to the base year by the use of a set of inflators is enrolled student numbers. There are no

external guides for the relative growth of student numbers by type of institution. It would be possible to use the national mean (or some other measure of average growth), but to do so would have compromised reasonableness. The closeness to the average of any of the institutions in the set on that measure would be an obvious and important question. Acknowledging the limitation and underplaying its implications is an important mechanism by which the reasonableness of the set and the representativeness of the data is secured. The reasonableness of the forms of qualification reinforces the reasonableness of the exercise.

## *Analysis by transformation of form*

A number of devices are used to secure the authoritativeness of the analysis. All involve transformation of form. These transformations are used in conjunction with a self-explicating unfolding analytic logic: size and scale, sustainability, and efficiency. For managers, this is a natural causal chain. Size and scale make sustainability more likely through economies of scale, but can also lead to diseconomies with inefficiencies in resource distribution. Weighing the balance between the economies and diseconomies being gained by the comparator institutions and likely to be gained by CU is the core of the benchmarking exercise. The structure of the analysis and hence its followability as a narrative grammar turns on borrowing the format of the natural logic of organisational causation. Since sustainability and efficiency are omni-relevant categories of possible risks for managers (not only in CU and start-ups generally), and risk is what managers manage, then this is just the logic they would expect to see used and these, and not the subject spread, the course sizes, the TLA strategies, library spend, etc. etc., are the things they would expect to see included.

A cursory look at the analysis will reveal a number of writing/reading devices:

1    Modal transformation of measures: We have already seen modal transformation of data in the brigading of the comparators with reference to the baseline. In the analysis, it appears in the calculation of data on sustainability, the input and output measures for efficiency, and so on. What is interesting about these derived measures is that both the untransformed data and the logic of transformation are to be taken on trust. There is no explication of how the transformations occur. Third, the transformations are to be assumed to be 'methodical' and 'systematic' in the sense that one modality of transformation is not used on one institution and another on a second. An horizon of relevances for the reader is being assumed and the analysis is being written in the context of that horizon. The reader is assumed not to be interested in the mechanics of calculation but only in the output. Unless otherwise caused to do so (see the point about student numbers above), readers will take the methodicalness and systematicity of the calculations for granted.

2   Ad hoc generalisation: The data presented is recast as sets of discursive summary generalisations which can be derived from them. These generalisations provide readings of the data. There is an recursive interpretive reciprocity at work here. The meaning of the numbers is explicated by the generalisation and the meaning of the generalisation is explicated by the numbers. Together they provide the elements of the assembled kaleidoscopic colligation of data about the comparators and CU. This emerging pattern is critical to the provision of a composite picture or rendering.

3   Incongruity procedures: At several points in the analysis, but especially with regard to the measures of efficiency, the untypical or outlier character of CU is brought out only to be explained away by data adjustment on the basis of accounts of the reasonableness of the incongruities and hence their relative unimportance. This is most stark in the re-framing of the input and output measures for efficiency (income/member of staff). The run of data show CU underperforming, in some cases by a considerable margin. The text offers ways of reading some of this underperformance as perfectly expectable and perhaps even appropriate (academic staff costs) or as indicating deep-seated problems which will need to be solved through planning (for instance, the cost of central administration).

The devices used produce an assemblage, a pattern, from the colligation of direct and derived measures. As each run of data is introduced, it is fitted into the emerging pattern. This fitting of data into the pattern and constructing the pattern from the data (patterning the data) is a practical solution to the synecdoche problem. Without the whole picture, you cannot see where any particular part fits but without all the parts you cannot see what the picture is. The kaleidoscopic colligation of data as a self-explicating emergent pattern is the solution to achieving the written/ read acceptance of the benchmarking exercise.

## Conclusion: the authority of composite depiction

The section labelled 'Discussion' renders the emerging pattern in terms of the objective of the document, namely the upcoming planning process. The pattern is configured as a series of issues to be discussed and addressed through that process. To use a phrase we use elsewhere, this rendering is in terms of 'the agenda in the agenda' of planning. The resulting configuration provides the practical management solution to the praxeological gap closing problem we started with. The configured rendering takes what is *said* and fixes what is *implied*. These implications are the need to change in order to address the challenges faced and the need to undertake the series of next steps to ensure this happens. The picture of CU as presented in the benchmarking exercise is a picture which has been put there to be found and its interpretation is fixed through its emergent configuration. The authoritativeness of this configuration is what mandates the actions to be taken.

## Notes

1 Direct and indirect measures are as standardly conceived. So are first order measures. Second order measures are transformations of one or two first order (direct or indirect) measures of a set of processes or outcomes to give an indirect measure of a third. Measures of efficiency are classic second order indirect measures.
2 'Key players' here means the Board, the university partners and HEFCE.
3 You might ask why, given it was a new start, these practices had to be transferred. The simple answer is a practical one. You can't change everything at once. That is both a 'practical impossibility' and a good piece of management wisdom. Trying to change everything will severely threaten the integration of the organisation.
4 It is also constituted by the circulation list for the document. This was very restricted.
5 The complete document is presented in the Appendix to this chapter.

## References

Austin, J.L. 1962. *How to Do Things with Words*. Oxford: Oxford University Press.
Goodman, N. 1974. *Ways of World Making*. Indianapolis, IN: Hackett.
Grice, P. 1981. "Presuppositions and conversational implicature." In *Radical Pragmatics*, by P. Cole (ed.), 113–128. New York: Academic Press.

# Appendix

NB This document has been lightly edited to preserve anonymity.

**An initial benchmarking exercise for CU**

*Rationale*

During the planning for last year and the early stages of this year's planning round, concern was expressed over the kinds of expectations it would be appropriate to have for CU, and in particular the CU Hub, as an operating organisation. Comparisons with the previous regime under The College would not be helpful because of both the relative sizes of the organisations and their educational mandates and mix. Equally, comparison to the sponsoring universities would not provide appropriate guidance.

This paper offers an initial, and it must be stressed very preliminary, first pass at a benchmarking exercise. It seeks to raise a number of questions for consideration in the light of data for a number of comparator institutions. These questions are offered as prompts for the discussions to be carried forward from 15th April and into the next planning round. The ambition is to open discussion up not to close it down, and certainly not to provide a definitive set of answers to some of our planning dilemmas.

*Data*

The data used have been drawn from the HEIDI data base which is managed by HESA. The available data is for the academic year 2003/04. This data was supplemented by data for 2006/07 published by THES/Grant Thornton on 3/11/07. Where data was not available in the THES/Grant Thornton data set, the base HEIDI data have been inflated to bring them into line with CU 2007/08 data. The following inflators were used:

Income 1.4

Staffing costs 1.35

Other costs 1.17

Overall cost 1.3

It is recognised that these assumptions must be approximate. HR, in particular the staff cost data may be too low. Salaries, overall, have probably increased by more than 40% in the relevant time frame. However, the data do facilitate general comparisons. No attempt has been made to scale up student FTEs. Undoubtedly, this will impact on some of the ratios based upon student FTEs – however, this is likely to have made the comparisons more favourable to CU rather than less, overall.

*Comparator Institutions*

The following institutions have been chosen for this exercise:

Bishop Grosseteste University, Lincoln

Buckinghamshire New University

Canterbury Christ Church University

University of Chester

University of Chichester

University of Cumbria

University of Winchester

These institutions were chosen for a number of reasons. First, they are nearly all in their early stage of development and so might be expected to share some of the start-up challenges that CU has. Second, they are roughly of a similar size to CU now or are within our target growth range. Third, many are multi-campus. Fourth, they have similar regional backgrounds to CU, at least in general terms. That is, they are based in small or medium-sized towns and have a rural hinterland.

Two other institutions were considered: the University of Cornwall and the University of the Highland and Islands. The former was set aside as its operating model is very different to CU. Being a Scottish institution, it was felt the latter operated on too different a basis for useful operational comparison. Comparison on other dimensions of start-up has, of course, already taken place with these institutions.

*Analysis*

*Size and scale*

Table App.8.1 summarises some basic population data for each institution.

Clearly all the institutions except Bishop Grosseteste are bigger than CU, but they are of a scale which encompasses our growth targets. This implies first that CU is unlikely as yet to be gaining any economies of scale that should be returned to these other institutions for a number of central and corporate costs, and second that we should manage in order to capture these economies as the institution grows.

Table App.8.1 Population data (FTE)

| Institution | Student FTEs | Staffing | | |
|---|---|---|---|---|
| | | Academic staff | Total staff | Staffing ratio |
| Bishop Grosseteste | 1190 | 49 | 140 | 0.38 |
| Bucks New | 7424 | 343 | 841 | 0.41 |
| Canterbury | 10238 | 481 | 1108 | 0.43 |
| Chester | 7081 | 353 | 939 | 0.37 |
| Chichester | 3962 | 185 | 369 | 0.5 |
| Cumbria | 7097 | 358 | 904 | 0.39 |
| Winchester | 4214 | 223 | 514 | 0.43 |
| CU 2008/09 | 2456* | 166.8 | 318 | 0.52 |

* Marketing Targets

The staffing ratios are interesting and indicate, broadly, the smaller the institution, the greater the preponderance of academic staff to other staff, which is not surprising, although Bishop Grosseteste does appear to be an exception. A clear implication is that central and support services tend to be reinforced with growth in student numbers at a faster rate to academic delivery. This implies increases in staff/student ratios. (See below.) The reasons for this may be readily understandable (increased scale of demand) but nonetheless that tendency should not be without challenge – at least in the CU context.

On the assumptions built into the modelling, the comparator institutions are in surplus on operating costs, even those of an approximate scale to CU. However, a further 5% added to the staffing costs would eradicate this level of surplus. Second, given that a number have more 'other income' than CU, some of which might be from streams such as student accommodation and commercial operations which might be taxable, we might expect the actual 'bottom line figure' to be somewhat smaller. Even so, the consistency in financial performance (apart from Bishop Grosseteste which must be operating in exceptional conditions) is interesting and indicates what CU should strive for. The question to be resolved

Table App.8.2 Financial data (£k)

| Institution | Income | Expenditure | Surplus | Surplus as % of income |
|---|---|---|---|---|
| Bishop Grosseteste | 10815 | 86307 | 2184 | 20 |
| Bucks New | 64460 | 59478 | 4967 | 7.7 |
| Canterbury | 88942 | 82890 | 6051 | 6.8 |
| Chester | 56278 | 51851 | 4426 | 7.8 |
| Chichester | 29369 | 26353 | 3015 | 10.27 |
| Cumbria | 59932 | 53615 | 6316 | 10.5 |
| Winchester | 31707 | 28483 | 3224 | 10.1 |
| CU Hub 2008/09 | 21584 | 22059 | (475) | (2.21) |

## 114  The practicalities of executive management

here is how long we can continue to explain our deficits in terms of 'start-up' and similar costs on the one hand, and the legacy of The College on the other. A critical piece of comparative data might be the level of debt that each is servicing and the cost of awarding their own degrees. As we know, both debt and validation are quite a significant burden for CU.

### Sustainability

A single measure has been used in this context: ratio of Funding Council grant to total income. This measures diversification of income streams, and hence the relative dependency on a single customer.

The data demonstrate that many comparator institutions appear to have moved further toward diversification than CU. However, we must be careful. The data do not allow us to unpick the number of 'Other Income' contracts. It could be that some (or all) are simply more dependent of their SHA contract (or a similar arrangement) than CU. However, equal dependency on two sources rather than one *does* spread risk.

An alternative measure of risk or 'precariousness' would be 'Liquidity Days'. HEFCE has a good practice guideline of 40 days' cash burn held in reserves. CU intends to adhere to this guideline.

### Efficiency

#### Input factors

The ratios in Table 4 show relative levels of input factors in the delivery of provision.

The cost-based ratios offer a divergent set of signals. The total cost per student for CU is above the mid-range but not exceptionally so, indicating the CU provision processes students broadly in line with its comparator institutions.

Total cost per academic and total cost per member of staff are measures of economies of scale. In both, the larger the ratio the more efficient the organisation (i.e. fewer staff deployed relative to the cost base). Here, CU is clearly

*Table App.8.3* Sustainability

| Institution | Ratio of funding council grant to total income |
| --- | --- |
| Bishop Grosseteste | 0.64 |
| Bucks New | 0.44 |
| Canterbury | 0.42 |
| Chester | 0.47 |
| Chichester | 0.62 |
| Cumbria | 0.5 |
| CU Hub 2008/09 | 55.67 |

*Table App.8.4* Input measures I

| Institution | Total cost/ student | Total cost/ academic | Total cost/member of staff | Staff/student ratio |
|---|---|---|---|---|
| Bishop Grosseteste | 7.25 | 176.13 | 61.6 | 25.5 |
| Bucks New | 8.01 | 173.4 | 70.7 | 21.4 |
| Canterbury | 8.07 | 172.3 | 74.8 | 20.7 |
| Chester | 7.32 | 146.8 | 55.22 | 20.0 |
| Chichester | 6.65 | 142.4 | 71.42 | 21.6 |
| Cumbria | 7.55 | 149.7 | 59.31 | 21.9 |
| Winchester | 6.76 | 142.4 | 61.5 | 21.9 |
| CU (Hub)* 2008/09 | 7.73 | 129.48 | 67.66 | 14.72 |

* This is preliminary data from the initial financial plan.

failing to gain economies of scale, certainly with regard to academic staff and, to a lesser extent, all staff. This signal is reinforced by the staff/student ratios. The CU teaching and learning model consumes more academic resource than might be expected. However, in coming to conclusions about academic staffing and the efficiency of our use of this resource, we need to compare student progression, achievement and retention. We might feel the high resource input justified if the levels of these key outputs were also high.

A second set of input measures throws some light on the drivers of CU's heavy resource usage.

It is clear from the comparison of average academic staff costs that the CU total remuneration package is at the lower end of the spectrum. This data, though, is in advance of the JE Project which may have a significant impact on salary levels. Without access to comparative demographic and post-profile data, it is impossible to determine if this is the result of CU having a younger staff base (intuitively, this seems unlikely), a greater preponderance of senior academic posts in comparator institutions, or simply that CU pays less.

*Table App.8.5* Input measures II

| Institution | Staff cost/ total cost | Academic staff cost/ total cost | Central admin staff cost/total cost | Central admin cost/ total cost | Average academic cost |
|---|---|---|---|---|---|
| Bishop Grosseteste | 63.9 | 32.9 | 0 | 24 | 58 |
| Bucks New | 64.7 | 32.5 | 1.59 | 22.5 | 56.4 |
| Canterbury | 61.1 | 33.7 | 1.28 | 14.5 | 58.1 |
| Chester | 67.63 | 37.2 | 1.41 | 16.6 | 54.6 |
| Chichester | 60.62 | 34.9 | 0.68 | 17.39 | 49.8 |
| Cumbria | 67.92 | 37.6 | 0 | 17.01 | 56.3 |
| Winchester | 60.32 | 30.54 | 0.57 | 19.59 | 43.7 |
| CU Hub 2008/09 | 61.3 | 35.1 | 12.6 | 28.6 | 46.3 |

Not surprisingly, the proportion of cost devoted to academic staff shows a similar pattern, with CU at the low end of the spectrum. The same holds for all staff costs.

Where CU does appear to be out of line with comparators is in the cost of its central administration. (Here, comparisons will turn on precisely how senior academic managers are categorised. For the CU data, I have excluded Academic Development but included all other non-Faculty staff.) Progress on resolving this issue will have to await the CU HESA return and hence, the application of standard criteria to CU.

The whole issue of staff costs gains extra weight when we take into account the dynamics of the pension burden. This will only escalate, particularly if the requirement to show the share of deficit in multi-employer schemes on the balance sheet is implemented.

*Output measures*

In this preliminary analysis, a single output measure is used. For a complete analysis, reference would have to be made to student progression and achievement alongside pure income earned. However, acceptable retention data are not available either for CU or comparator institutions at this point.

This output measure confirms, in a somewhat startling way, the picture emerging from the input measures. In staffing terms, CU is relatively inefficient. A larger body of academic staff is employed than might be expected for the relative size of the institution. Or, to put it another way, the level of staff base is not generating the income streams which might be expected, be it through student numbers, research, consultancy, or any other income source.

## Discussion

We need to step carefully here. Further analysis is required before firm conclusions can be arrived at. However, three major messages do emerge from the data.

CU is slightly more 'risky' from a financial point of view than its comparators. It is planning deficits and is more dependent than most on the HEFCE contract.

*Table App.8.6* Output measures

| Institution | Income/member of academic staff (£k) |
| --- | --- |
| Bishop Grosseteste | 220.7 |
| Bucks New | 187.8 |
| Canterbury | 184.9 |
| Chester | 159.4 |
| Chichester | 158.7 |
| Cumbria | 158.5 |
| Winchester | 141.86 |
| CU Hub 2008/09 | 129.6 |

The CU staffing model seems to be over-resourced. That is, it requires a greater staffing input than other providers. This might be a scale problem; it might be a start-up problem, but that is unlikely; or, as is most likely, this may be a consequence of *an inefficient teaching and learning model.*

The academic staffing base is relatively under-rewarded. Whether this is simply a consequence of historical accident (and to be resolved by the JE Project) or a reflection of relative fitness for an HE environment is, perhaps, a question for debate.

CU appears to be spending more on central administration than might be expected. However, this can only be confirmed after the HESA survey. Should this be the case, one explanation might be the need to underwrite start-up 'platform costs' in the first few years.

For me, this all adds up to three major implications.

1 In planning for and resourcing growth, we have to build in drivers of increased efficiency in teaching and learning. This will force us to make some difficult choices and to ask questions about some of the fundamental propositions underlying our T&L strategy. We simply cannot afford to grow to the levels we need for academic sustainability with staff/student ratios at 15:1 or thereabouts.
2 In underpinning growth, we have got to expect and manage for economies of scale in our support services, both centrally and in the Faculties. There will be some significant challenges here. Both of our core non-administrative services (IT services and Estates) are below minimal levels for effective functioning. All administrative services could make good use of more resource. But unless we take cost out of non-staffing budgets in Estates and IT, we cannot grow the staffing bases without wholly unbalancing our business model. Such choices also will have an impact on that shibboleth 'the student experience'.
3 Finally, we have a key opportunity to start thinking through and addressing some of these issues when we consider the operation of our processes. Reducing process cost, either in human or cash terms, releases that resource to drive growth.

## Next steps

*Table App.8.7* Next steps

| | | |
|---|---|---|
| 1 | Define final list of comparator institutions | ASAP |
| 2 | Initiate institutional relationships with comparators to facilitate detailed data exchange | ASAP |
| 3 | Join HEIDI | ASAP |
| 4 | Complete HESA return | Autumn 2008 |
| 5 | Undertake full benchmarking exercise using HEIDI and other data | Spring 2009 |

# 9 Does it wash its face?

## Introduction

*Homo œconomicus* is one, albeit the most prominent, application of the general notion of 'the rational actor' used as the cornerstone of much of the Philosophy of the Social Sciences. Supplied with a suitable set of dispositional properties and the machinery of calculative rationality, *Homo œconomicus* is the idealisation of the basic unit of economic action (prototypically buyers and sellers) where exchange is the equally idealised relationship they stand in. The aggregate of such transactions is a market. Hence, for Economics, *a priori* rational markets are institutions displaying the operation of economic rationality.

Not surprisingly, there is a tradition as old as Economics itself which contests these idealisations (or at least, contests their use in undiluted form) as the description of what actually goes on in any 'real-world' market. 'Just how "economically rational" are real economic agents?' and 'How far do they actually deploy the machinery of calculative rationality in making their judgements?' are questions that have motivated much debate both within Economics and between Economics and the other social sciences (Sen 1977; Gintis 2000).[1]

We do not want to step into that debate here.[2] Instead, we want to turn away from idealisations of economic exchange, and of calculative rationality in particular, to ask what some of the work of doing the latter looks like for actual social actors operating under particular sets of market or market-like conditions. What are the organisational conditions which make calculative rationality possible and how is the operation of that rationality achieved as the repetitive, cohort-independent *institutionalised* feature of markets that Economics supposes it is? We come at this question, then, from the vantage point of making a market – the decisions by which buyers and suppliers determine price efficiency for a product. Our aim is to elucidate the interior configuration of 'market making' as a socially organised process. We do not want to banish the idealisation of the rational actor to the outer darkness but rather to ask how calculative rationality might work so it produces the characteristics of markets which Economics seeks to explain.

For Economics, markets exist to coordinate the needs of buyers and sellers. This much is uncontested. Moreover, in a perfect market, these needs will be so matched that the market will 'clear'. There will be no unfulfilled demand

and no residual supply. The perfect market of economic theory is, then, a miracle of social coordination. However, just how this coordination is achieved remains something of a mystery. Notions such as supply, demand and price remain obscure labels pointing to unknown processes. Even though markets exist all around us, and with a lot of effort we might be able to estimate the level of operational demand and supply as well as current 'market price' in any one of them, exactly how demand, supply and price are arrived at resists empirical description. How do suppliers in the market determine the scale of the opportunity which the market represents for them (that is, the level of demand accessible to them, the level of supply they should provide, and the price which they should charge)? In microeconomic theory, this puzzle is resolved by conceptualising the market as a melee of transacting buyers and sellers somewhat like an idealised bazaar or street market (or their apotheosis, the stock market) with, as we have said, coordination being taken care of by the application of a set of assumptions about individual rational choice under perfect information, nil transaction costs, no barriers to entry or exit, and so forth.

Of course, Economics doesn't much care if those in a market actually do coordinate their activities in the way it assumes they do, just as long as coordination is achieved. All it needs are the twin assumptions that the process is rational and based on valorisation of the kind it describes. These two are easily extended into markets where actors are 'collective individuals', such as organisations and companies. Yet what is being assumed away here is the central empirical problem of sustained economic action – namely how supply and demand are managed as a matter of large-scale, coordinated practical action across social time and space. If markets are coordination devices, how is supply matched to demand in the aggregate as a practical matter of economic life? For Sociology, this turns out to be just another instance of the general problem of social action. The institutionalisation of the market is of the same order as the institutionalisation of family life, religious practice, political competition, or organisational activity and is resolved by invoking the same explanatory device: normative compliance.

In this chapter, we try to disperse some of the miasma surrounding market coordination by treating it as a species of intersubjective consociation. Suppliers have, somehow, to ensure their 'product offering' remains aligned with what they perceive those in the market want. Buyers have to match their needs to what they perceive suppliers are willing to provide. Both have to ensure they do so without, to use a modern idiom, 'destroying value'. How both are done are intriguing questions. Our tack will be to focus on product selection and the assessment of market viability, and in particular on the use of a computational tool, a costing model, to calculate financial value return for products.[3] We accept financial value is not the only criterion determining whether a product is offered to the market, though it is an important one. Indeed, one of our aims is to outline some of the ways financial and other value judgements are meshed in making these decisions. In focusing on this one piece of the market coordination jigsaw, we are trying to open up the possibilities of analysis, not exhaust them. While not quite a first foray, this discussion is certainly not the last word.

## The context

### The rationale

Many of the courses which CU inherited had been in existence for a long time. In the view of those in charge of the marketing strategy, many were 'tired' and in need of 'refreshing'. Some were plainly very successful (at least in terms of recruitment numbers). Others, though, were struggling. Finally, there was a whole raft of courses for which the position was unclear. One of the tasks which had been agreed early on was a programme of 'course renewal' whereby the portfolio was to be sifted and, over time, 'low value' courses replaced by newer 'higher value' ones. What was to determine value here was not, of course, simply financial return. Courses such as Business Studies, English Literature, History, Art and Design were those which an institution like CU would be expected to offer. Others, such as Nursing and Midwifery, were part of a long-term regional contract. Even so, there remained a large number where the argument for continuation had been taken as 'given', but where removal would provide opportunities for course innovation. Course renewal was to be a central part of annual planning. Senior academic managers were expected to assess the value of courses as part of planning and, where necessary or desirable, retire those which were low value in order to introduce new ones.

The value of courses whether existing or new proposals, was to be assessed against four clusters of measures:

Market positioning – measured by applications and market data;

Quality positioning – measured by entry qualifications, levels of awards and retention;

Quality enhancement – measured by curriculum update status and External Examiner reports;

Efficiency – measured by financial parameters and staff/student ratio.

Given the mix and multi-dimensionality of these measures, managers would be expected to use their judgement when assessing course value. It was recognised the criteria above would not produce a linear ordering where a clear cut-off could be applied. Rather, they give bundles of associated courses which would be labelled 'high value', 'satisfactory', 'refresh and renew' and 'terminate'.[4]

### The model

A relatively simple course-costing model was developed for use in determining the economic efficiency of a course. An early prototype was deployed with senior managers. This 'Beta Release' was used primarily as an investigative tool. The present discussion concerns this version of the tool.

The model had three distinct intended uses. The first was within the major review of clusters of courses already underway. The second was as part of deciding whether a course had recruited enough students in its first year to be allowed to run. Here a 'quick and dirty' assessment would act as 'triage' to enable decisions to be made quickly. Once a course is being taught, an implied contract is in place between the institution and the student. The existence of this contract discourages terminating the course before it has run through its life cycle. Third, the model was to be used as part of planning new course provision. It would allow systematic setting of 'break-even' and other targets and aid decisions about the introduction of a new course. To do this, its results would be set alongside issues of brand, strategic importance, competition, market demand, and so on.

The model consists of four linked Excel worksheets.[5] The worksheets are structured as follows. The summary takes the user input (cells marked in blue) and presents the computed output. The income detail and cost detail sheets contain the calculations. The core data sheet is a data base of information about teaching contracts, course banding, space cost, and so on. The computations in the calculations call up this data as needed. It was expected the release version of the model would 'black box' the data base and computations so that all the user would see was the information input and the computations displayed on the summary sheet.

For the purposes of this exposition, the model has been populated with dummy data. In what follows, we will give a brief explanation of how the model works by walking through the sheets one by one. Detailed discussion of the reasoning needed to deploy the model's logic is presented later:

1 **Summary Sheet:** The user inputs data into the blue cells. The contract variables are HEFCE and SHA (Strategic Health Authority), the two teaching contracts held by CU. The faculty variables are ABS (Arts, Business and Social Science) and HWS (Health & Well-being and Science) which are the two Faculties. The course name is taken from the courses list held by SITS, the student information system. The table of annual teaching hours holds the timetabled annual hours for each member of staff teaching on the course. Course formats such as foundation years and post-graduate qualifying years for professional courses mean that some courses can take five years to complete. The norm, though, is three years. Three tables of outputs are presented. One table sets out year-by-year summary breakdowns of the income and costs associated with the course together with gross and net surplus positions. This table replicates at course level the kind of 'financials' which managers use to manage their teams. The next table summarises the total student number (in FTEs) and the equivalent staff resource associated with the course. In the example, year 1 has twenty student FTEs and requires 1.345 FTE of a member of staff. The SSR (staff student ratio) is computed as a ratio of these two FTEs. The final table presents a set of KPIs (Key Performance Indicators) for the course as a whole together with an (invented but not unlikely) set of targets. The variance of the KPI from the target would be one of the key issues when assessing the efficiency of the course.

2 **Core Data Sheet:** Data on this sheet comes from many different sources. Some tables are combinations of different data from different sources. The table containing the list of courses, for example, uses data published by HEFCE and the Strategic Health Authority regarding contract bands. It also holds measures of space usage. Both are held on SITS. The space charge table is derived from the Facilities Management Data Base and broken down by site and usage. The levels of Tuition Fees are also held on SITS. The overhead charges are taken from the financial breakdown in the Annual Plan. Student numbers are taken from SITS. The calculation of maximum working hours is derived from the standard academic contract. The data on this sheet are taken as given for the model.

3 **Income Detail Sheet:** The main table populates the contract process for the named course. The manager inputs the FTE numbers of students on each year or level of the course. A model which was fully integrated into the management systems would derive these numbers from SITS. In the version being analysed, the data has to be entered by hand. The same holds for grant and other forms of income. The table summarises the income by level/year. The results of the calculations are set out on the Summary Sheet.

4 **Cost Detail Sheet:** The first array labelled 'Academic Staff' translates the name and salary data given on the summary sheet into 'grossed-up costs' by adding in other costs of employment. For each member of staff, this grossed-up cost is then set out alongside the annual teaching hours on the course. The array labelled 'Direct Cost' allocates the total cost of employment of a member of staff to the course pro rata to their teaching commitment as a proportion of the total hours that could be worked. These allocations are aggregated as 'Total Staff Costs'. The 'Staffing Resource' is the sum of the FTE staff hours timetabled for the course. Looking at Year 1 for example, P. Picasso is timetabled for 10.9% of his time on the course. This is estimated to be a cost of £5195.45. The whole staffing commitment is 1.35 FTE member of staff and is estimated to cost £51105.95. Other Direct Costs are of two kinds. Bursaries are fixed corporately as a proportion of the student fee. Other values are free and input by the manager. Space usage and Overhead Costs for a course are picked up from the Core Data Sheet. The results of the calculations are set out on the Summary Sheet.

The model produces a set of computations derived from the data provided. These computations are standardised measures of financial and resource efficiency.[6]

## The work of course costing

One of the central problems in the theory of computation turns on its dualities. On the one hand, computation seems to be manifest in material objects *and* an abstract logical structure. On the other, this ontological dualism is closely related to the problem that the program itself (its logical structure) seems to be both a mathematical abstraction and a causal process. As a result, just how we should theorise computational objects and what they do remains a deeply puzzling affair. In fact, Brian Smith (1996) among others has argued the ways computation is currently theorised are deeply flawed and that a whole new way of thinking through the relationships is required.[7]

For the manager, the dualities appear as the distinction between computational and calculative order. This distinction does not present itself as a theoretical problem but as a practical one: how to make the computations work to produce the required calculations. This requires embedding the calculative order of managerial objects in and then extracting it from the structure of computational objects making up the model. The working model is the lebenswelt pairing of these two orders and the objects they structure. Without such integration, the model can do no managerially relevant work. Managers are not interested in what might be said about managing courses 'in the abstract', 'in principle', or 'in an idealised case'. They are interested in gaining 'as good a handle' as they possibly can on what is actually going on and in using as specific as possible information to make decisions. Making models work by integrating computational and calculative orders is one of the ways they do this.

In addition, to determine the significance of the eventual run of calculations, two orders have to be integrated and extricated: the calculative model and the organisational setting. This is not a matter of sampling, abstraction, or generalisation, but of achieving synecdoche. The calculations produced have to be usable proxies for the course they represent, even though they are derived from just some of its features. Only some 'financial parameters' for courses have been included in the model. If synecdoche is not achieved from *these* calculations, the process of evaluation would have to be replicated for all relevant aspects of the course. As we have seen in previous chapters, determining the materiality of 'relevance' is a practical matter of closing the praxeological information gap and deciding when what is to hand is 'good enough'. Without this, reaching a conclusion might well be unending (or 'run in open loop', as system designers like to say). To be useable, the model needs to be embedded in and extracted from the organisation it stands for. Achieving the embedding and extraction is the manager's practical problem of arriving at a costing for a course.

In what follows, we will treat costing as a lebenswelt pair and the model as embodying instructions for this process of embedding and extraction; both are 'designed for' and 'achieved by' the use of the model.[8] We will talk of the deployment of the model as involving both a *usable* device and as *intentional* device. What the device provides are 'for all practical purposes' solutions to the problems of embedding and extraction. The usable and intentional distinction does not imply using the model is not a matter of interpretation. Neither are we saying that the meaning and significance of the computations are entirely divorced from the way the model is used. The distinction is thematic, a way of framing different sets of practical management concerns – that is, getting results you can use and then working out what they mean. To get results you can use, you need to understand the device you are using. And when interpreting its results, you have to know how they were derived.

Our second objective is to bring out the recalcitrant character of computation. It takes work to make it work and much of this work involves bridging the gap between abstraction and application.[9] This work is the 'double fitting' of the structure of the organisational representations to the structure of the computational requirements. It is work that has to be carried out every time the model is run. Such specification and operation is an improvised production process of step-by-step model use.

In using the course-costing model, then, the manager has to accomplish the following tasks:

1   Determine the acceptable correctness of the working calculative order;
2   Determine the plausibility gap regarding empirical reference;
3   Resolve the synecdoche problem through the projection of the outputs as elements of a reasonable summary of the operational characteristics of the course.

Managers accomplish these tasks by interrogating the model to find its 'calculative accountability'. This accountability is rendered as the relative correctness and plausibility of the proxy calculations and their implications for the overall assessment.

## The intelligibility of correct calculative order

### *Materiality*

The correctness of the calculative order is a relative matter. Data assembled for input and data stored in the model are selections from the range of sets which could be utilised. In addition, their provenance is variegated. In principle, this raises the possibility of an endless search for an exhaustive list of descriptors and for certainty in the numbers. To pre-empt this possibility, managers deploy an Occam's razor for materiality: 'Don't seek data validity and verification beyond need.' This injunction is summarised in two widely used managerial aphorisms: '"Good enough" is good enough!' and 'Pareto's Rule rules!'[10] Beyond a certain point (though precisely which point is a locally determined judgement), expending more effort to 'get better numbers' will give incrementally reducing returns. Whenever they feel they have reached this point, managers will decide it is enough to go with the numbers they have. The invocation of materiality acts as a stopping rule on the quest for certainty.

The stopping rule on the quest for certainty is an important feature of management calculative rationality. But what exactly shapes it? How is the level of materiality determined, recognised and implemented?

First and foremost, the model lives in an ecology of data. That ecology is constituted by organisational processes, many of which are metered or measured, or else explicitly designed to collect and store such measures. For the manager, these process measures and stores are organisationally to hand or within reach but, for this exercise, placed beyond enquiry. For reasons we have discussed in several previous chapters, to be of practicable use they have to be taken on trust. Running the model means setting aside any possible scepticism with regard to any given measure and its values. Whilst in the midst of deciding if a course 'washes its face', a manager cannot question why the rate for grossing up salaries should be 27% and by what process that inflator was arrived at. Neither can he or she question how Facilities Management arrived at the share/single-use space charge apportionment. These numbers are taken as organisational givens for the course-costing process.

Trust in the numbers prevents the task dissolving into a recursive search for certainty. This is a result of the operation of horizons of relevance and structures of interest. If any manager wanted to interrogate those numbers, such a ramifying and open-ended process would rapidly become a practical impossibility.[11] Each of the processes which generated the data is itself the outcome of process algorithms and their working interpretation. Decisions will have been made by others (or this manager on some other occasion) about how to accommodate oddities, incompatibilities, outliers, exceptions and other unruly data in order to produce the results which are now being used. Even if managers wanted to chase all these decisions down, they could not. Their implementation lies buried in the intestines of the processes. They are known to be there, but very much ignored because it is not worth the effort of exhuming them.

Some of the information built into the model's use is corporate data collected and collated by others. This data is pre-defined and, as we have said, taken on trust (at least for the time being). There are also data which managers have to ensure is gathered and collated for themselves: student numbers, staff names, salaries, other income and costs, and so on. Assembling this data requires knowing one's way around the local ecology of organisational data as well as having enough 'organisational acumen' (Bittner 1965) to assess the state of any data set. Other data stores have to be interrogated and other data aggregation processes have to have been completed for the assembly process to begin. An obvious example is course and staff timetabling. Using the cost model during the course recruitment process requires the allocation of staff time to courses. But for this to be done, staff personal timetables have to have been completed and agreed. Without the list of names and numbers, direct costs cannot be estimated. Since course and staff timetabling is known to be a wicked problem,[12] the timing of the collection of data for staffing is an artful practice. It needs to be done late enough to have allowed the process to become relatively settled, but early enough to enable the consequential room allocation and similar decisions to be made, as well as to allow revisions in the whole process in order to adjust for over- or under-loading of staff, unanticipated course sizes, and so on.

Similar considerations surround student numbers. This is obviously tricky when using the model during recruitment since the 'number on SITS' and 'the bums on seats' may be very different.[13] However, it is equally germane when the model is used as part of a larger course review. As we discuss in Chapters 5 and 7, in its early years, the calculation of CU's student numbers was subject to a number of inaccuracies. These inaccuracies had implications for estimations for course viability. Assembling usable data is not simply a matter of knowing where to find the relevant numbers but also of understanding their provenance, making allowance for its variability and deciding if they are 'good enough' to use for the purpose in hand.

## Structure

*Format*

In previous chapters and elsewhere, we have explored how formalised devices are designed to provide for their own intelligibility.[14] One prominent method for achieving this is the use of structured formatting. The formal objects in the devices are structured in ways that reveal their computational order. In running code, statements and functions are laid out to reveal their interrelationships. Similarly in modelling languages, graphical and other 'tools' are used to design a lay-out such as a flow charts, pipelines, directed graphs, or other visual representation. As we have already seen a number of times, spreadsheets are no different. The grammar of their objects (sheets, columns, rows, cells) provides for the intelligibility of the computational order they represent. Finding the interplay of the defined grammar of the objects and the specification of their instantiation as the management objects of 'this case' (measures of 'space cost', tallies of 'income', calculations of staff/student ratios and 'surplus', for instance) is the work of discovering their intelligibility. It is the work of finding the calculative and computational logic in the model.

The presentational ordering of the worksheets is critical to the intelligibility of the calculations but irrelevant to the computation. Excel doesn't care how the sheets are arrayed, nor, indeed, what they are called. In the absence of a 'local' name, the code will use the default (sheet and cell #). From the point of view of intelligible calculation, the order has to be seen to represent and preserve the calculative logic in ways that are managerially recognisable. The naming and separation of income and cost sheets mirrors the familiar accounting balance sheet structure of summarisations and has its own distinct trailing paths of calculation. These calculations are 'behind' the summary sheets and separately presented. The cells of the table on the Summary Sheet 'pick up' or point to locations on the relevant sheets. Looking at the Summary Sheet is looking into the supporting sheets. Managers are very familiar with how to multi-task along these separate paths in the construction of summary balances. The sheet listing bar provides the logic of this pathway summarisation.

The format of each sheet is also important. Although each is different, its logic is 'skimmable'. The left-to-right, top-to-bottom tallies of income build cumulatively. The cell and column structure is the standard one. Ignoring, for the moment, where the numbers come from (some are input by the user on the Summary Sheet and some picked up from the Core Data Sheet), the logic of column addition makes itself visible. Whatever the labels mean (and we come to this below), the relationships between cells and columns is the vernacular one. Although the Cost

## Does it wash its face? 127

Detail Sheet has far more data, its logic is precisely the same. Even if you don't know the meaning of the references, the logic of the calculative order is recognisable. In this sense, the structured design of the sheet is domain independent. If you know nothing about Higher Education, course costing and CU, you could still find your way about. The same is true of the Core Data Sheet, though this logic is simply an inventory. Again, if you know nothing about the context, you can see the rows are discrete co-classed items set out in lists. In all cases, the format of the sheet carries the recognisable intelligibility of the calculative order.

### Names and numbers

Names and naming are important for the linking of the representational model and the computational model and hence their mutual intelligibility. The course-costing model uses a large number of standard or locally standardised accounting terms. Some of the more obvious are 'student', 'income', 'surplus', 'SSR' and 'space type'. Often, these have locally recognisable referents. On other occasions, the same term might be non-standard. Take, for example, the term 'student' at cells E44 and E46 on the Cost Detail Sheet. Here the reference is not to a count of individuals or even FTEs but to a ratio, the cost of space per student. The figure for Total Working Hours has a similarly specific local definition. Since the vast majority of staff are on full-time contracts, one might assume the total working hours would be 52 weeks × 37.5 hours per week minus the standard holiday allowance: in other words, 48 × 37.5 = 1800. However, the model discounts for a further 20 days of national and other paid holidays resulting in the total number of working weeks in a year being defined as 44. The working year is neither the calendrical year one is paid for, nor yet the working year, nor again the teaching year of 2 × 20 week semesters; it is a notional 'institutional operational year'. When the model was first deployed, this definition generated considerable consternation since managers interpreted the reference to Total Hours as an academic staff loading model. They pointed out staff worked far more than 37.5 hours a week and for more than 44 weeks a year *and* undertook research and other activities not accounted for in the way the model was designed. Learning the definitional lore of the model is essential to its use.[15]

Alongside the mix of standardised and non-standardised references for terms are standardised and non-standardised references for calculations. Travel costs, fee income and grant income might appear to be things subject to being calculated in obvious ways.[16] Space costing and overheads however are not obvious. Overheads are not the costs of delivering *this* course which have been absorbed by the overarching organisation, but the percentage of the institution's total income represented by the costs of Faculty and Corporate administration. Courses, then, are allocated a standard share of the global cost of administration based on their income, not the estimated cost of the demands they make.

A third set of idiosyncrasies can to be found in the mix of number types used for counts and costs. Numbers and costs might be actual, estimated, or assumed. Estimated and assumed figures may be organisationally determined functions (as in the case of the grossed-up salaries) or complex ad hoc derivations (as with space allocations). The range of types and their possible combination as mixes of measures, symbols and metaphors makes the use of these numbers an important issue in determining the meaning of the summary measures which they generate.

Managers usually adopt a variety of strategies to handle idiosyncrasies such as these. Some involve what Lindsey Churchill (no date) called 'everyday quantitative practices' whereby the materiality of possible misplaced precision, discrepancy, or lack of clarity can be managed. Projections of numbers such as 'students' will be treated as indifferently falling within groups of '5s' in the case of low numbers and '10s' with larger ones. Finding the precise count for an individual group is set aside. A similar rule is used for salaries. These are assumed to be 'correct' with a tolerance of £200 or so. In both cases, any imprecision is assumed to be washed out in the aggregations and summarisations. Other sets of numbers, though, will be aligned or triangulated to provide reality checks both on them and on the set itself. Staff number, cohort size and staff student ratio are obvious examples. Since the value for staff student ratio is calculated from staff number and cohort size, if these numbers are out of line with each other, further analysis will be required or a re-working of the calculation. Other numbers are known to be standardly 'iffy'. Projections of numbers and growth rates offered in new course proposals, for example, if not Churchill's 'WEGs' (Wild Eyed Guesses), they are certainly likely to be aspirational. The requirements of building a 'robust business case' often result in these numbers being inflated to make the case stand up. Managers expect this and regularly deflate these claims as a part of exercising 'budgetary realism'. In other cases, the 'strangeness' or 'opacity' of numbers is simply ignored unless or until the run of summary calculations fails a test of reasonability. Disregarding the status of these numbers is not a matter of trusting in the outcome of uninvestigable processes but of the organisationally known indeterminability-in-the-midst-of-calculating what the material impact of variation in such numbers might be.

*Traceability*

Two reasons for the use of Excel as a modelling platform were (a) the ability to exploit the natural management metaphor of linked worksheets and (b) the use of an 'English-like' programming language for specifying the arguments. In principle, this combination makes it possible to see the link between the computational and calculative logics in a relatively straightforward way. Although many arguments (for example, cells which invoke LOOKUP and SUM procedures) do precisely what you would think they would do, others do not. Take the argument which produces the number in cell G35 on the Cost Detail Sheet. This is a rate for bursaries and is:

=IF(G6= 'Health',0,0.35*'Income Detail'!D25)

The argument contains no reference to the actual course being assessed (which is Fine Art), nor the rate of bursary it offers. The only recognisable organisational term is 'Health', which is not the Faculty in which Fine Art is located. Pinning down the calculative implications of the computational logic requires an understanding of the grammar of Excel. A full translation of the argument is:

IF G6 = 'Health' then the value is 0; otherwise the value is 35% of the HEFCE Fee set out in D25 of Income Detail

However, the ratio of 35% for bursaries is a corporately defined standard of which managers are aware (one of their tasks is to manage the distribution of these funds). And D25 is easily looked up. This allows the manager to guess what a 'workable pidgin' translation of the argument might be; a translation that is good enough for all practical purposes.

The presumption of similar practices of pidgin translation can be seen elsewhere. Take a look at the code for the run of Indirect Space Costs at cells F32 to K32 on the Summary Sheet. This is:

=IF(H21>=1,'Cost Detail'!M52,0)

Cell M52 on the Cost Detail Sheet is the summary of space cost for Fine Art, but what is the rest of the argument about? The full explication would go something like this.

IF the relevant Total Income cell is equal to or greater than 1 then include in this cell the Total Space Cost from Cell M52 on the Cost Detail Sheet; otherwise set the cell at 0.

The pidgin version might be: 'Only calculate a space cost if there is an income to set it against.' A working familiarity with the model's pidgin is yet another required element of the locally specified lore.

## *Empirical reference*

Course costing is a consociate production process. The model's usefulness comes from the coordination of the calculative and computational models to produce a reasonable account of the course. Using and following that coordination in flight is an *intersubjective* achievement.

Costing is one process in a network of evaluative processes directed to supporting decisions. Seeing how its financial representations fit within that network requires an appreciation of its interdependency with these processes. In other words, it is necessary to have a working grasp of the operational configuration of the network. This involves scaling and, where necessary, closing the representational gap between the course as depicted in the summaries and the course as experienced – that is, the course as a complex organisational, teaching and learning consociate experience.

### Closing the representational gap

Closing the representational gap for any particular course involves determining the degree of empirical reference of the course summaries and assessing the robustness of the causal logic of the model. It also involves judging the 'realism' of the targets for *this* course and hence what the variance in performance from target actually means. This scaling allows a calibration of the course as represented with the course as experienced.

The tallies on the Summary Sheet are relatively coarse absolute and relative financial measurements. In this setting, the absolute measures of gross and net surplus and SSR are self-explanatory. Clearly, managers have expectations of where the numbers should lie relative to the size of the course. These rules of thumb reflect the well-known problem that large-scale operations have large-scale costs and demand lots of resources. So big courses can generate big surpluses, but still be poor value. Equally, small courses can have low SSRs and still be resource hungry. It is the KPIs which point to comparative performance and hence relative managerial value of the course. The summary provides a pair of tables allowing absolute performance to be 'read off' and a further table of comparative positioning. But this positioning is relative to managerially defined planning targets. They are not *course-tuned targets* in the sense of targets derived from the detailed examination of what the course could deliver. Rather, they are derived from targets set by Fiat in the Annual Plan. They are fixed by that plan. Comparability, therefore, is not with other courses and relative expectations about their performance but with the requirements of the Annual Plan. Unlike the caucus race where everybody wins, in this evaluative competition even the winners – that is, those with 'the best' scores – could fall below the derived targets set for them and so 'fail' to be viable. The question is how that judgement of 'failure' or otherwise is arrived at from the absolute and comparative numbers. How are they used to come to that determination?

The significance of variance to target turns on the weight placed on the 'realism' of the financial summaries compared to other evaluations which managers have to hand and their experience of the course as a delivered programme of teaching and learning. A course with strong income which makes a surplus and has low SSRs might be a 'good course' financially but because of factors such as the calibre of the students, the material to be taught, the physical environment of the teaching rooms, it may well be viewed as being 'difficult' because of the support demands it makes or the configuration of the teaching rooms used. Equally, despite drawbacks such as low retention rates, low progression and achievement levels, courses popular with employers may be thought of as 'good' or 'worth putting on'. For courses that have been in existence for a while, the relative balance between 'quantitative and qualitative measures' and 'objective and subjective assessments' is generally known. What is being looked for in the model is the degree of reinforcement provided for that expected balance. For new courses, or courses that have undergone major revision, such expectations are projections of the likely variance between performance and target and are based on managers' experience of similar cases rather than 'like for like' comparisons.

To make the necessary assessment, the manager uses a variety of practices to balance a number of things. First, from what is known about this course, is *this* level of variance expectable and acceptable in *this* case? Second, is the known degree of possible 'play' in the numbers spilling over into the scaling of the 'realism' of the summaries? 'Play' here refers to the tightness or 'goodness of fit' of the measure for the construct it is measuring.[17] FTEs are notorious for their potential play. As we have said already, the numbers of students registered on SITS, the number listed on the class register, and the number who actually turn up to be taught, may be very different. Similarly, classrooms are not uniform, let alone identical.[18] The 'space norms' for different courses might be satisfied by very different actual teaching arrangements, even though the standard space charge is applied. Thus the cost of a practice lab for nurses, say, or a sports science lab may be charged at the same rate as for a drama group or fine art studio, even though the quality of the space in each case is very different, the standards of maintenance very different and the expectations of those who teach and those who are taught in the space very different. Laboratory courses are known to be 'expensive' as are Drama and Fine Art, but what this 'expensiveness' means is not fixed. Drama and Fine Art might be taught in very cluttered, unkempt and overcrowded conditions compared to laboratory sciences and as a consequence are not viewed as being as hungry for facilities support.

Play is also known to apply to 'overhead charges'. One reason is the known differences in expectation about course materials, especially photocopying. Some courses such as Business Studies generate 'good numbers' in terms of income, surplus and SSRs. However, to ensure the professional accreditation of these courses, students on every module have to be provided with highly structured and standardised courses of learning based on reproduced teaching and learning materials. At this point in CU's development, big numbers here imply big reprographics costs. But reprographics as a service was funded at the corporate level and so the reprographics costs of any course are hidden in the total volume of reprographic work undertaken. At this point, no tracking process was in place to itemise the specific contribution of each course to the annual cost of the reprographics unit. The known play in this aspect of overhead meant that for a course like Business Studies to be taken to have 'washed its face' financially, it was required to over-perform against target by a considerable margin.

CU managers know their courses and most of the time the summary values fall within their expected margins. But occasionally this is not so. The response to such 'surprises' is a process of 'exceptionalising' through rolling back the computational logic. Rolling back the computational logic does not mean re-running the calculations but checking the data being input. The working assumption is that the case is 'an exception' not the symptom of global modelling error. The model is trusted but the data is not. We have seen some possibilities for this exceptionalism already (FTEs, overheads, space charges). Others are found in the character of particular course cohorts and learning experiences. A course may incur a negative outcome only when there are no obvious grounds for making an exception. This throws light on an important managerial tension in processes such as course reviews (and other reviews in other settings), namely, between the local management team's predisposition to follow a line of least resistance and where possible continue with what they have simply because change means more work, more disruption and uncertainty and, on the other hand, senior managers' predisposition to continuously tighten the margins for discretion on refreshing, renewal and change. The predisposition towards inertia is not itself entropy. It is, in fact, the preservation of current organisational structures in the face of possible entropy-engendering change. What the tension expresses is differential estimation of the risk of entropy *and a difference over who will have to carry those risks*. It is the local team and their managers who will have to manage the potential 'disruption' of re-design, re-validation and re-launch, not the senior managers of the organisation.

### *The synecdoche problem*

We said that use of the course-costing computational model involves determining calculative correctness and empirical reference. These are not steps in a decision-making process but interrelated contingent aspects of unfolding assessments. As we have just shown, in determining 'correctness for all practical purposes' or 'for all practical purposes realism' of the summaries, reference is often made to 'how the data sits' in regard to a range of complementary measures and assessments. In producing the evaluation as a standardised assessment, these themes are interwoven threads of the patterning of that displayed standardisation.

The 'assessed course' which emerges from the assessment exercise is the gestalt contexture of assessment and experience. It is not the result of a serial process, even if each individual process has a stepwise, structured feel. What the course comes to as an 'assessed course' emerges from seeing measures like course costing 'in the round', whilst at the same time gleaning what else is known about it. It is more like the *annealed crystallisation* by which frost forms than a beginning-to-end, component-by-component build-up of the final assessment from the measures, computations, resulting calculations, commonly known and locally known organisational knowledge, and so on. Whatever structure the assessment has (one way to think of it is as the topology of a phenomenal field of interpreted numbers, perceptions and understandings), that assessment emerges out of the process rather than being constructed Lego-like from component parts. The assessment is a conjoint shaping of expectations, interpreted numbers and projected outcomes cast in future-perfect terms: 'From what we have so far, this is what it looks like it will have turned out to be . . .' There is no mystery or magic in this, simply locally known and deployed artful practices producing an emergent gestalt of assessment.

## Conclusion

Our intention here has not been to deny the calculative rationality of economic decision making. Rather, we want to bring out how that rationality is undergirded by a melange of interpretive practices which tie it into and lift it out from the environment of organisational processes within which it is situated. Each and every use of the model to assess the financial viability of a course requires this embedding and extraction. This is how an operating organisation is fitted together in the understanding and planning of senior managers as the continuous outcome of everyday management. In the flow of management, this fitting is a blending of financial and other judgements to produce an annealed assessment of the 'value' of a course and the consequential folding of that judgement into the planning processes of which it is part. This socially organised ecology of standardised processes and their recognised and expectable outcomes radiates through the particular judgements being made about individual courses. In this very strong sense, then, market making – the fixing of what products should be offered on the market and at what price (and, no doubt, what products should be acquired and at what price) – rests upon a panoply of consociate practices produced and reproduced as organisational management.

## Notes

1 Often enough such objections have carried very little weight, as they tend to be variations of the Irishman's advice when he was asked for directions: 'If I was going there, I wouldn't start from here.'
2 We have had our say before in a number of places. See, for example, Anderson et al. (1988)
3 In that sense, this is a preliminary exercise in what Espeland and Stevens (2008) call the 'sociology of quantification', which, paraphrasing John Austin, they define as 'Doing Things with Numbers'. Our interpretation of their paraphrase, though, is somewhat different to their own.
4 There was an obvious rationale for this. Quality Assurance demanded that decisions about course provision be justified on academic grounds *as well as* financial grounds and be taken by academic managers. Grouping allowed managers to make those judgements rather than to apply a mechanical rule (though many, for their own local management reasons, would much have preferred the latter).
5 The model is set out in the Appendix to this chapter.
6 Standardised for CU, of course, though the forms of the calculations are not that dissimilar to those used by other HEIs.
7 See the materials provided at www.ageofsignificance.org
8 The working model's Excel spreadsheets are a calculation account of the cost modelling computations.
9 With tongues firmly in cheeks and caps reverently doffed, we might want to call this whole analysis 'Good Organisational Reasons for Flawed Computational Logic'.
10 'Pareto's Rule rules!' refers to the widespread management assumption of organisational assymetries. For example, only a small portion of the customer base usually provides the overwhelming proportion of profit, or only a small number of technological innovations yield major returns on investment. In management mythology, the discovery that the ratios are typically 80/20 is attributed to Vilfredo Pareto (2014).
11 This closing off of the open texture of questioning is a familiar characteristic of practicability. We first looked at it in Sharrock and Anderson (2011).
12 The process is never closed but is constantly being re-run and revised though with incremental reductions in the scale of change at each run.

13 The effect of 'churn' at the start of term and the importance of 'Post A-level results recruitment' were very important for CU. The variances between what was 'on SITS' and who was 'in the class' could be quite large.
14 See Anderson and Sharrock (2013; 2016).
15 See Baccus (1986) on a similar order of issue regarding the lore of work objects and tools.
16 There is another relevant aspect to trust here which we have not brought out, namely trust in the intentions of the user. The model provides no cross-checks on the deliberate use of inflated or deflated values. Although the model assumes the integrity of the data, when managers come to review outliers, odd cases, exceptions and surprises, the possibility that the numbers may have been 'massaged' or 'manipulated' is among the first, if not the very first, thing they will think of.
17 Without any embarrassment, we are borrowing this term, but not its precise use, from Derrida (1985).
18 One problem encountered in building the model was the poverty of the data which CU had on some of its buildings. As a consequence, the new data base modelled the space norms on 'standards' derived from prior experience in other HEIs.

## References

Anderson, R.J. and Sharrock, W.W. 2013. *Analytical Sociology*. www.sharrockandanderson.co.uk/the-archive/1990-present/post-2010.
—— and Sharrock, W.W. 2016. *Portmanteau Representations*. www.sharrockandanderson.co.uk/the-archive/1990-present/post-2010.
——, Hughes, J. and Sharrock, W. 1988. *Working for Profit*. Aldershot: Gower.
Baccus, M. 1986. "Multipiece truck Wheel Accidents and their Regulations." In *Ethnomethodological Studies of Work*, by H. Garfinkel (ed.), 20–59. London: Routledge and Kegan Paul.
Bittner, E. 1965. "The Concept of Organisation." *Social Research, vol. 32* 239–255.
Churchill, L. No date. *Notes on Everyday Quantitative Practices*. New York: Russell Sage Foundation.
Derrida, J. 1985. "Structure, Sign and Play in the Discourse of Human Sciences." In *Literary Criticism: A Reading*, by B. Das and J.M. Mohanty (eds), 394–395. Calcutta: Oxford University Press.
Espeland, W. and Stevens, M. 2008. "A Sociology of Quantification." *European Journal of Sociology, vol. 49, issue 3* 401–436.
Gintis, H. 2000. "Beyond Homo Economicus." *Ecological Economics, vol. 35, no. 3* 311–322.
Pareto, V. 2014 (originally 1906). *Manual of Political Economy*. Oxford: Oxford University Press.
Sen, A. 1977. "Rational Fools." *Philosophy and Public Affairs, vol. 6, no. 4* 317–344.
Sharrock, W.W. and Anderson, R.J. 2011. "Discovering a Practical Impossibility: The Internal Configuration of a Problem in Mathematical Reasoning." *Ethnographic Studies, no. 12* 47–58.
Smith, B. 1996. *The Origin of Objects*. Boston, MA: MIT Press.

# Appendix

## Screenshots of Course Costing Model

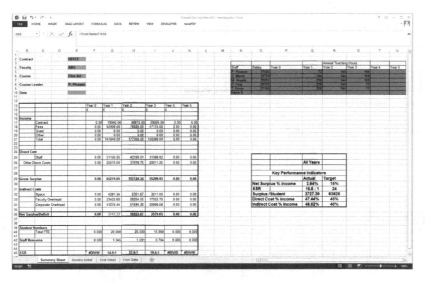

*Appendix 9.1* Cost model sheet 1

*Appendix 9.2* Cost model sheet 2

*Appendix 9.3* Cost model sheet 3

*Appendix 9.4* Cost model sheet 4

# 10 Plans and their situated actions

## Introduction

The allusion in the title of this chapter is deliberate. Apart from Garfinkel's *Studies in Ethnomethodology*, Lucy Suchman's *Plans and Situated Actions* (2007) is probably the most widely cited ethnomethodological work.[1] What matters for us here (and this is why we have chosen the paraphrase we have) is not that Suchman's book had an extraordinary impact on the technical discipline of Human Computer Interaction (HCI), but the pointers its central ideas might offer us with regard to our own materials. Whilst it is certainly true Suchman's study opened up a whole new approach of what came to be called 'ethnomethodologically informed ethnography' for researchers in HCI, Computing Science and Cognitive Science and so stimulated what was called a 'turn to the social' in those disciplines, what is of importance for us here is the centrality she gives to the problem of mutual intelligibility in her analysis.

The core of *Plans and Situated Actions* is an attack on a psychological theory called 'The Planning Model', at the time the dominant approach used in Cognitive Science (see Miller et al. 1960). This model was rooted in a conception of human action as the instrumental achievement of goals, with courses of action taking the form of a mental projection of a planned sequence of steps which serve as a means toward achieving a desired goal, those anticipated steps then being enacted in behaviour. On this view, action is the working through or implementing of planned tasks defined as 'sequences of actions designed to accomplish some preconceived end' (Suchman 2007: 52). As such, the planning model is really only a derivative of the instrumental rationalist approach to human conduct. Using arguments, examples and methods from the classical corpus of Ethnomethodology, Suchman showed the planning model is not an adequate description of our experience of interaction in general nor of human computer interaction in particular. This is because the planning model generally takes 'the problem of mutual intelligibility' for granted. Using a machine to achieve some desired end depends on both user and machine resolving the double contingency and satisfactorily interpreting each other's actions. As her experiments demonstrated, because mutual intelligibility had not been considered to be relevant, resources for its resolution are entirely missing from system designs which deploy the planning model. In episodes remarkably similar to Garfinkel's breaching experiments, Suchman's users were left to thrash around trying to work out what the machine had done, was doing, and was likely to do and so what they themselves should do next. In its turn, the machine could only respond in accordance with its pre-programmed steps. If what the user did was at variance with what the program expected, the machine had no resources with which to work out what to do, and so froze. Suchman pinned her analysis to the contrast between the users' improvisational strategies for working out what the machine was doing and the machine's fixed repertoire of responses. For Suchman, this taught a seemingly general lesson about the nature of action, that it is improvised through and through rather than planned, meaning that the usability of computational systems can only be improved by reconceiving action as the improvised, moment-by-moment, locally organised achievement of mutual intelligibility.

Suchman's demolition of an algorithmic conception of action was undoubtedly highly successful. That conception is based upon a metaphorical extension of our common sense notion of plans and planning. It translates the deliberative character of our ordinary sense of planning into a task-centred conceptual model for the psychology of human and artificial reasoning. This is taken into the model as the idea that action is the following of recipes for accomplishing tasks and, of course, it is this which fails so dramatically because it makes no provision for the plain fact that people are often working out what to do as they go along.

Suchman's eyes are on the character of social interaction and the failure of the instrumental rationalism of the planning model to provide for mutual intelligibility. The focus is on the machine's failures not the detailed constitution of the user's experience through the use of improvised methods of reasoning to resolve the meaning of the machine's actions. Her topic was not the intelligibility of formal plans and planning per se, but of machines as rule-bound interpreters.

This is not the case with Dalvir Samra-Fredericks' 'ethnomethodologically informed' investigation of strategic planning (Samra-Fredericks 2010). Here, strategic organisational planning is the locus of the interactional work of jointly reading, amending and otherwise editing a common resource, namely the written plan. Using discourse analytic methods loosely based on Conversation Analysis, Samra-Fredericks traces the sequential organisation of a stretch of meeting talk in which interpretations and formulations are agreed, sequences of topics determined and likely issues summarised. We see how considerations such as the ordering and emphasising of particular points and the management of 'the politics' of extrinsic interests are expressed as topics in the talk. The one thing we don't see is how the plan being discussed is constituted as a plan, nor what those discussing the plan bring to its interpretation as an organisational object.

Tim Dant and Dave Francis (1998) take us part way to that objective with their description of planning in a Health Authority and a school. The two organisations are chosen by Dant and Francis because they operate in contrasting ways in their planning activity. They see the two organisations as involving two different models of planning, which they term 'rationalistic' and 'contingent' models respectively. Their conception of the rationalistic model is derived from the standard rational actor model, the psychology of which strongly informed the planning model in Cognitive Science. Their identification of the 'contingent model' affiliates their conception with Suchman's arguments from Ethnomethodology. Dant and Francis are interested in how plans are used in the planning work people do. From the cases they examine, they suggest plans are used as contingent rationalisations of possible actions. Such rationalisations emerge in an ad hoc way within the flow of planning discussions and serve a number of important functions such as: offering a context for the synthesis of different activities, a means of aligning the actions of different organisations, a repository of value statements, a script for addressing political and other external considerations, and an all-purpose justification of unforeseen and approved actions. Unlike Samra-Fredericks, Dant and Francis do show plans as organisationally relevant resources in the determination of managerial and other courses of action. However, the organisational particularities of their material and managerial construction are not addressed.

The same cannot be said of Kjeldt Schmidt and Inna Wagner's (2004) discussion of the plans they observed used in an architectural office. They are very much taken with the material realisation of plans themselves in the form of blueprints, maps and diagrams and their purposeful use as locally organised coordinating and ordering devices for complex courses of action. They emphasise the heterogeneity of the plans found in their research site. These plans were designed using very different specifications, levels of precision and media, and used for very different purposes. The types ranged from 'back of an envelope' sketches to white-board displays to fully developed computer-aided design (CAD) drawings. In each case, they 'afforded' different interactional uses.

The character of CAD drawings was of particular importance. Below is a summary of a number of key features of these objects which Schmidt and Wagner identify:

A standardised format defines sets of conventions and codes for identifying and validating the plan's contents and their specification as well as for defining the scope of the document's distribution;

A layered organisation of representations allows a palimpsest of views to be built up whereby the modularised 'whole' can be seen through the serial consideration and mutual explicativeness of each individual component;

Provision of inventories of named objects and devices to be deployed as part of the construction. This catalogue offers generic description of objects which are 'localised' in the particularities of any specific drawing.

Detailed drawings offer the same localisation for abstract signifiers (boxes, names, sketches) used in the layers.

The management of the use of the objects used in planning is the function of a highly structured repository where the corpus of drawings used on the project is stored and tracked. The code system for storing, retrieving, distributing and tracking is one of the formatted conventions constituting the contents of the drawing.

Viewed as socially constructed organisational objects, the composite CAD drawings are not *post hoc* representations of the structure of the building-being-built. Rather, they are an *ex ante* mechanism for producing or imposing order on the building's construction-in-flight. They constitute a 'constructable order' which, if followed, will allow the building to be built. What makes the set of drawings a plan is the recognisability of that constructable order in the organisation of the plethora of detail they contain. Construing, adapting, detailing and amending the constructable order of the drawings is the achievement of plans as lebenswelt pairs.

The Schmidt and Wagner discussion identifies features in common with our own case, the revised strategic plan put together in 2008 by the senior team at CU. We will demonstrate how, as a written-read lebenswelt pair consisting of the plan account and the planning undertaken, the revised planning document provided the 'constructability' of a sustainable future for the newly launched venture. The plan provides instructions for producing planning as a constructable order for the future of CU. The set of integrated and related documents and activities making up the revised plan is a complex construction. We concentrate only on one component, the part labelled 'Review of Core Assumptions', which designates the first steps in the planning process.

## The Review of Core Assumptions

The Review of Core Assumptions was produced as input to the kick-off meeting for a typical management activity, a mid-cycle review of strategy. A reminder of a little historical context may be helpful for the understanding the issues in play:

> CU became operational in 2005 in preparation for its launch in 2006. A small management team had guided the development of the organisation and its related capital planning. The original strategic plan adopted a three-phased planning horizon:
> Phase 1: 2005–07. This was the start-up phase and included the first year of full operation. The initial purpose built facilities would be constructed.
> Phase 2: 2007–12. This was the expansion phase when student number growth was to accelerate and the second round of capital development would take place.
> Phase 3: 2012/13. This was the stabilisation phase. Student numbers were projected to reach 5,000 FTEs at the end of the period, the campus build would be complete and the institution would be seeking independence from its university sponsors.
> The mid-cycle review was undertaken during late 2008 and completed early 2009. The resulting plan was to be implemented in the academic year 2009/10. Its outcomes were to be any necessary strategic course corrections required as a result of the experience of operating CU in 'shadow mode' during 2006/07 and full mode in 2007/08. The review team were the most senior managers of the organisation. In the end, the mid-cycle review gave rise to a major re-organisation.

The kick-off meeting for developing the revised strategy was held in October 2008. During the day, the management team reviewed the assumptions underlying the original plan and undertook SWOTs[2] on the academic, organisational and market strategies. The CEO had circulated a briefing setting out objectives for the day along with the agenda. Each section of the agenda had its own bundle of background documents. We will look at the review of the assumptions underlying the original plan and will cite relevant sections from this document in the text.

Like the workbook of financial forecasts discussed in Chapter 5, the Review of Core Assumptions[3] (RCA) was produced *for* a meeting, not *in* a meeting. Its character as a management object is shaped by the fact it was to be read prior to a meeting. In the meeting, it was subject to much face-to-face discussion (and not a little wrangling) during which its central thrust was formulated and re-formulated several times. The ultimate review of core assumptions was the lebenswelt pairing of the written-read document (the RCA 'review account') and the revised assumptions feeding into the revised strategic plan.

## Methods for co-producing the review of core assumptions

As a written-read document, the RCA trades on taken-for-granted understandings about the state of the organisation formulated in the rest of the circulated package of documents. It also trades on shared assumptions about the roles and attitudes of its presumed readers. In that sense, every element of the package is replete with things it does not have to say in so many words. The managers for whom it was written know what the review is about and what are the issues. They also understand the process they are engaged in. This shared knowledge is visible in the methods used to co-produce the review. To bring out their character, we will cast these methods as instructions for finding the written-read review in the RCA and its assemblage of documents.

### *Decipher the agenda in the Agenda*

The RCA is designed to be read alongside the general agenda, the briefing and the other documents provided for this agenda item (the original assumptions and a schedule for the review). Its character (along with the other documents) projects an 'agenda' in the Agenda. This agenda configures what this meeting is about in the sense of what the topics might actually imply in detail and what outcomes they might lead to. This projected agenda is often described – for instance, by John Law (1994) – as marking a difference between the formal specification of the meeting and its actual performativity. The circulated papers are to be construed as providing the rationale for the Agenda (that is, the rationale behind the decontexualised list of things specified to be done) and a bundle of projected courses of action. This rationale is the CEO's agenda in (or behind) the circulated agenda. Setting the agenda in the Agenda is what the assemblage of this written-read document does.

Strategic planning is a well-known, standard, specific, recognisable and 'routinely structured' management activity. It has well-known phases, well-known types of inputs and well-known types of outputs and consequent actions. The relevances attributable to the RCA are derived from where in the course of planning it is introduced. As the review proceeds, some things will be found to be routine. Others will turn out to be less so. Part of the work of the review projected in the RCA is to re-frame how the course of the whole strategic planning exercise will unfold.

One of the documents circulated was a schedule. Although the steps this sets out are the conventional ones, a quick skim of the detail shows rather than

*Table 10.1* CU planning schedule

| Action | Responsibility | Timeline for completion | Process connection |
|---|---|---|---|
| Review and amendment of current assumptions and driver statements for strategies | Executive | Kick-off mtg | |
| Approval of amended assumption and driver statements | Executive | 25 Oct. 2008 | |
| Review of implications of revisions for 2007–12 targets | Executive | 4 Nov. 2008 | |
| Consideration of flow through of target changes to Business Unit plans and targets | Faculties, LN & Portfolios | 19 Dec. 2008 | Outbound to Planning |
| Modelling of implications for 2007–12 business plan | CD/EF | 19 Dec. 2008 | |
| Approval of revised Business Units 2007–12 targets and plans. Approval of revised 2007–12 business plan | Executive SMG | 14 Jan. 2009 | Outbound to Planning |
| Approval of Academic Strategy Statement for consultation | Executive | 31 Jan. 2009 | Inbound from Academic Strategy |
| Re-drafting 2007–12 Strategy Statement | CD | 27 Mar. 2009 | |
| Approval of revised 2007–12 Strategy Statement including Academic Strategy Statement | Executive | 30 April 2009 | Inbound from Academic Strategy |
| Review of revised 2007–12 Strategy Statement | LN Strategic Management Meeting | 18 June 2009 | |
| Approval of revised 2007–12 Strategy Statement | P&R Committee | 2 July 2009 | |
| Approval of revised 2007–12 Strategy Statement | CU Board | 24 July 2009 | |

simply running over a standard, lightweight process, the aim is to deliver a completely revised plan.

From the number of approval steps and the range of bodies to be consulted, it is clear that this is not a 'light touch', 'steady as she goes' process. Significant change is being proposed with the rationale for the scale of change being presented to numerous bodies in order to secure their involvement and support. The Briefing Note circulated by the CEO in the package similarly carried messages about the need to manage a complex decision process:

> The process for developing the academic strategy must be an inclusive one, embracing staff at CU and across the Learning Network. Inevitably, this will mean that the process will be lengthy and complex. To prevent progress on the academic strategy delaying immediate planning for 2009/10 and the review of more operational aspects of the overall strategy, I propose to run these processes in parallel. They will be brought together in early spring 2009 to ensure alignment for the 2009/10 plan. AB will continue to lead the planning process. I will lead the processes for developing the academic strategy and the overall strategy. My expectation is that all these processes will be driven and coordinated by the Executive.

The circulated documents are 'first formulations'. They are working documents rather than 'throw aways' or 'formal records'. They are first descriptions or enumerations of the forces shaping the organisation's strategy. These first formulations are important because no matter where in the plan-in-production process the discussion reaches, the only record of the planning process is the produced plan itself. The plan-as-record stands for the decisions taken but not the work of taking them. The RCA will not appear within the revised strategic plan but will, of course, be immanent in it. The review it articulates sets 'the boundary conditions' on the objectives adopted in the plan.

First formulations are important organisational objects. They circumscribe the space of discussion they nominate. In the RCA, this circumscription is contained in the answers to 'Where are we now?'. This question has a dual character: where are we now with regard to progress on the strategy? And where are we with regard to completing the planning of the strategy? These are different but very closely related questions. Fixing their answers is a crucial first move in setting the bounds of any revision to current objectives and targets, as well as the selection of a strategy for achieving such revisions.

Objectives, targets and proposed actions are the standard constituents of a review. What the RCA says about those 'givens' defines the progress made thus far on the strategy. The field of possibilities for the review is, thereby, a narrowed, not an open, one. The purpose of the organisation is fixed, as are the global objectives. All managers in the organisation know these, at least at the level of summarising slogans: year on year 10% per annum growth in student numbers; financial sustainability in five years; in-year balanced books. Whatever senior managers decide to do next, whatever strategies are revised or unveiled, continuity of purpose regarding these objectives will be assumed and is what the proposed actions will be measured against. Because they were agreed by all the stakeholders and laid out in the foundation documents submitted to the various approval and funding agencies, a mid-term review cannot, on its own initiative, decide to scrap them. The set will remain the 'ostensible objectives' unless or until they are manifestly not going to be achieved. Second, defining the organisational implications of 'managing for financial sustainability' as opposed to 'managing so the books balance' is known to be a central 'unresolvable' (a 'wicked problem') in the rolling planning process. The difference between the two management strategies centres on the generation of the level of investment required to allow CU to become financially self-sufficient, and the length of time over which it might be achieved. In the planning undertaken so far, what sustainability might entail has never been clarified and was recognised to be unclarifiable because both the relevant data was not available and the organisation had not yet garnered enough experience of running in operational mode. For those undertaking the review, what the idea of sustainable development at CU might actually mean in terms of the necessary real-world management actions was entirely opaque.

The timing of the meeting and its package of documents are important in other ways. The strategic plan is still being worked through. Everyone shares a common organisational history and the plan-in-production (like many other documents which will be used during its construction) will be treated as a summary historiography of that production. The constructable order of changes to strategic direction will be discoverable as the formal account of the plan. The historiography is carried by the use of 'perfect' and 'future perfect' tensing. One of the central tasks in constructing the plan as historiography will be arriving at formulations which enable a range of projected future organisational gestalts to be construed so everyone 'can at least live with' what the review proposes.[4] The RCA is the first formulation of the historiography of the organisation's current position. For the manager encountering this historiography, it raises the key questions: 'Can everyone live with it?' and 'What does the answer to that question imply?'

*Solve the synecdoche problem*

The 'first formulations' are designed to be read against one another. Reading the RCA in the light of these other documents also means reading the others in the light of the RCA. What they import, their implicature, is grasped from this iterative reading.[5] All these first formulations are read as intentional documents. They have a coordinated character. Relative play in that coordination will be used as a resource for the pursuit of particular interests and concerns. In that sense, a planning process is a design process. First formulations are used to fix things in place so they can subsequently act as constraints on later fixings.

There is a second aspect to the synechdoche problem. Everyone knows planning (and especially strategic planning) is path dependent. It is impossible to deliver an implementable plan if prior decisions are constantly revised. Recursive decision re-visiting through re-interpretation in the light of later decisions of what original decisions mean and what implications they have, will cause the process to implode. Everyone knows and accepts this.[6] The RCA specifies the first steps on the path. Once agreed, these will be hard to revise.

One of the background agreements preceding the start of the strategy review was the need to integrate academic and organisational plans. The organisational strategy was to be designed to lock into the academic strategy. The approach to this was largely unfamiliar to most of the participants. The idea of interlocking was not intellectually challenging. At the general level, it was clear it meant the academic and organisational strategy should be complementary both in terms of the objectives set and general implementation plans formulated. What was new and challenging was how to ensure and manage it *all the way down* to specific lines of action that might be taken by particular management teams whilst, at the same time, undertaking the first major strategic review. Thus each bundle of documents was to be taken as draft instructions for achieving interlocking. This strategy exercise was not a development process or a dummy run. The degree of integration visible in the two strategies at the end of the strategy process would be the degree of integration in the strategic plan, and hence the degree of integration the team and the organisation would have to construct, manage and live with.

The RCA is the first item on the agenda. Strategising is path dependent so part of the meaning of this document is to be found in the implications of its positioning for the trajectory of whole planning process. It is the projection of what the list of steps in Table 10.1 will actually turn out to be. This is not just a 'political with a small p' observation. Quite what the document finally means, implies, or determines will be discovered retrospectively in the historiography of the unfolding planning process. Proposals developed later will be compared to the revised core assumptions. However, the core assumptions also imply some of those actions. The RCA offers a preview of 'what this planning process will turn into' and 'what we will find ourselves having to do'. Pairing the review account and the review is the work of shaping outcomes and their actions in the context of the projections to be found in the RCA.

*Follow the standardised format*

The RCA is a table of summary statements of assumptions, dependencies, proposals and their rationalisation. Here are the first two rows.

Reading left to right, the table follows a familiar 'then' and 'now' linearity. The commentary rationalisation lays out a proposed historiography for each row. Each assumption is allocated to a strategic 'component': governance, student numbers, strategic partnerships, and sustainability. For the team, this structure is novel but transparent. In the 2005 plan, the assumptions were gathered differently. This new structure provides for a different way of locating the components in the strategic architecture. This is, then, a reframing of the discussion and planning undertaken prior to 2006. It allows triangulation on 'Where are we now?' by thematising how planning will proceed. In other words, the heads of terms for the draft plan are

Table 10.2 RCA governance

| Domain | Assumption 2006 | Dependency | PROPOSED confirm/revise/open | Commentary 2008 |
|---|---|---|---|---|
| Governance | Increased collaboration but no mergers between regional HEIs. Pattern of HE provision fixed | HEFE national strategy and HEI strategic and financial positions | Confirm | Nationally RAE outcomes will lead to some re-alignments. Regionally, we are likely to see strategic relationships develop. Not clear what New University Challenge will mean. Also future of Oldborough not clear. Seeside and CU big enough challenges on their own for RUN and RUS. Lack of certainty regarding policy post-2010 and potential change in Govt. However, any impacts will be towards the end of the strategy period. |
| | CU model remains in place over the planning period | Assumption 1 | Confirm | Scale of deficits for start-up period together with uncertainty over future development will act as a barrier to any change in relationships. Positively, the CU initiative is a flagship collaboration around which others can be built. Reservations within both universities will be overcome if 'competitive independence' is not seen to be on the agenda. HEFCE will be unlikely to support changes until future is certain. Need 4,000 FTEs for degree-awarding powers. Independence pointless without this. |

148  *The practicalities of executive management*

laid out in the structure of the RCA. The RCA is a formulation of what the revised plan will come to be.

The structure of the table carries considerable freight.

1   The row listings might appear to be of equal importance, but they embed an organisational model and hence have a causal texture. The logic is an unfolding, containing, or waterfall one. The first three (Governance, Student numbers and Strategic partnerships) are mutually interdependent. The fourth, Sustainability, depends on the previous three. The top-down order of the row lists portrays causal relationships.
2   The left-to-right reading of the table provides for both the formulation of possible revisions in the strategy and how they might be implemented. Hence it configures the constructability of the organisation which is the core of the plan. It points forward to the plan with each cell formulation transforming shared knowledge, understandings and actions into unfolding lines of consequences which will have (more or less) obvious implications over the planning period. Once those implications are agreed (or reformulated so everyone 'can live with them'), the pathway to achieving the objectives can be set (or, if absolutely necessary, the row can be looped and the objectives revised).

The RCA is nothing less than a working architecture for the developing strategy. With this architecture in hand, planning can begin. The degree of agreement on the work the document sets out foreshadows and scales the first tasks to be achieved.

### *Find a plan for the planning in the RCA*

The structure provides an architecture for strategic planning. It also is a plan for that planning. The contrastive pairs of assessments indicate the extent of the exercise. The unfolding implication of the table is the need for complete revision. That is the agenda in the Agenda.

The written-read RCA structures the planning process by formatting how the review is to be carried out. In that sense, it is 'instructional' and the planning it proposes would be a course of 'instructed action'. The instructions are carried in the implications of the 'then' and 'now' statements and make up the format of the plan. The original format of the existing strategic plan was developed for Phase I and an understandable preference for representational continuity will encourage close approximation to that format.[7]

### *Resolve the modal transformations of the cell entries*

The review applies the usual tabular grammar. The left-right, top-down organisation is its syntax. The ordering of rows (1 to 13) is not just a device for referencing the assumptions. It is also a process ordering. This is not a funnel

*Table 10.3* RCA sustainability

| Sustainability | | | |
|---|---|---|---|
| Curriculum development and associated recruitment will provide the basis for growth in academic culture | Assumption 4<br>Assumption 5 | Revise | Growth trajectories look more difficult to achieve and so levels of recruitment will not be of a scale and pace originally envisaged. This will hamper growth in academic culture and may lead to internal competition across the LN and hub.<br>Investment in new academic staff especially in new discipline areas is already severely constrained and likely to become more so over the next 3–4 years. This will hamper opportunities for growth in new areas. |
| Economies of scale and increased efficiencies will release investment to support academic development | Assumption 10 | Open | Projected salary, pension and other inflation costs could consume any efficiency gains. In any event, to achieve such gains there will need to be investment and major re-organisation and rationalisation. The perceived limitations of the SHA contract mean efficiency gains in HWS may be limited. The rigidity of the contract may limit capacity to re-organise. |

(from the macro to the micro, or from the political to the financial). It is a causal sorting of 'drivers' on the final two rows, 12 and 13. The logic runs across the rows (domain → assumption → dependency → proposal → commentary) and matches the expected institutional due process of assessment. It provides a normative model for how each decision should be made. The meaning of the option choices (confirm/revise/open) cannot be 'understood' (that is, what they might imply cannot be grasped) without reading the rationale. At this point, though, it is not clear what the terms 'revise' and 'open' do actually mean. During the discussion of each line, what the decision implies will be projected back onto the table. The 'proposed' column becomes, then, a crucial fulcrum on which understanding the table turns. It is the 'revise' and 'open' rows to which attention is being directed. The 'proposed' column provides a path through them. The design of the column uses a known range of possible decisions to throw focus on the implications of 'revise' and 'open'.

What the transformations in the cells, rows and columns are about is, of course, common knowledge. Known events, decisions, processes and their histories are being reformulated as historiography. To see how this is done, let's look at two examples.

The organisational model is a star network.[8] The balance between the hub and the network and between the network members themselves has become an emerging issue. This had two components. Some partners wanted to start courses which appeared to be duplicates of offerings the hub had or was planning. In addition, one centre was growing much faster than the others (as well as faster than the hub). The notion of 'balance of growth' implied exercising control over the distribution of student numbers. The original assumption was that balance meant uniform growth rates everywhere. This was no longer the case. One partner was surging whilst the delay in new build was holding the hub back. Two other centres were historic competitors. Finally, in one centre, HE was a major

*Table 10.4* RCA network growth

| 3 | Balance of growth between the Hub and LN remains broadly constant | Continued broad parity in growth rates | Open | In initial period, growth in the LN (especially B) may be easier to achieve than in the Hub (proportionally if not in volume terms). This may over time lead to a reduction in skewing. There may also be issues arising over internal competition. |
|---|---|---|---|---|
|   |   |   |   | Two important factors are the future of O (small numbers but in potential growth areas) and the G and L arrangements |
|   |   |   |   | Outcomes of Local Govt review may also impact G and L. |

cost rather than a revenue stream. On the other hand, it was felt that the site's specialism might support development of potentially attractive courses. What this row stands for is a debate over the distribution of student numbers. The numbers have to be put where they would be used. But that would inevitably shift resources around. These decisions would be important, and not just politically. With further significant increase in the burgeoning partner would come demands for greater infrastructure support. That would stretch the support organisations. Row 3, then, intimates a briar patch of issues which will have to have been resolved as part of producing a workable plan.

A second set of modal transformations relate to assumptions underlying the original growth model. It had been assumed initiatives undertaken by the County and the regional Learning and Skills Council (LSC) would contribute to the raising of aspiration among the local 18–21 population, which aggressive CU marketing could take advantage of. However, this is a long-term strategy at best. At the point at which the review was initiated, it looked as if this strategy wasn't working. The LSC was in turmoil after the announcement of its closure. The County's proposal to re-organise its schools had failed. Moreover, the new CEO of the County was seeking to reduce not enhance the County's role in managing service provision. 'Revise' here is an instruction to assume this potential driver is inoperative or weak. The local level of HE aspiration among 18–21-year-olds was

*Table 10.5* RCA external drivers of growth

| | | | |
|---|---|---|---|
| 8 | LSC and SCC initiatives will raise aspiration and achievement sufficiently to offset demographic down turn | Success and speed of policy implementation | Revise | 18–21 population will decline post-2012 but 25–49 population will increase. This will mean likely increase in pt and WBL. In 18–21 population, proportion of females will continue to grow. Also differential birth rates mean high proportion of middle class in 18–21. Non-EU recruitment will fall. Not clear what the impact of Eastern European immigration will be. Raising aspiration and achievement is a long-term process. Current momentum will only be impacted marginally by LSC and County re-organisation. However, continued uncertainty about local arrangements will start to have an effect. A number of key initiatives have been initiated and CU has taken a watching brief on them. |

Table 10.6 RCA internal drivers of growth

| | Sustainability | | |
|---|---|---|---|
| 12 | It will be a challenge to enable curriculum development and associated recruitment to provide the basis for growth in academic culture | Assumption 4 Assumption 5 | Growth trajectories look more difficult to achieve and so levels of recruitment will not be of a scale and pace originally envisaged. This will hamper growth in academic culture and may lead to internal competition across the LN, College and hub. Investment in new academic staff especially in new discipline areas is already severely constrained and likely to become more so over the next 3–4 years. This will hamper opportunities for growth in new areas. |
| 13 | Economies of scale and increased efficiencies must be achieved to release investment to support academic development | Assumption 10 | Projected salary, pension and other inflation costs could consume any efficiency gains. In any event, to achieve such gains there will need to be investment and major re-organisation and rationalisation. The perceived limitations of the SHA contract mean efficiency gains in Health may be limited. The rigidity of the contract may limit capacity to re-organise. |
| 14 | Diversification of income and revenue streams will take place only slowly | Assumptions 9, 12, 13, | CU lacks the skill base, facilities and processes to rapidly expand and diversify its non-HEFCE and non-SHA income base. |

and is chronically low. To 'Accept' this assumption would mean to accept that the policy drivers were (at least to some extent) ineffective. The implication of adopting 'Revise' is that even if the organisation was awarded more student numbers, it would be unlikely to use them. Such an outcome would threaten confidence at the Funding Council in the organisation's potential. When row 8 is seen in the context of row 3, clear tensions emerge about the shaping of the plan. The burgeoning centre is a middle-class town with lots of residents working in a nearby boom city. It can fill its numbers and more. Funding all the growth possible there would provide a counterweight to the lack of aspiration elsewhere but would severely strain the agreed delivery model. The question raised by these two rows is simply 'How much strain will the model stand?'

The rows in the table set out budgets of issues to be resolved. As with all such budgets, the key questions will be 'How much of an issue is it?' and 'What can be done about it?' The tabular formulations transform what everyone knows about the issues (the common history) into proposed answers to these two questions. Some (the 'revised' options) attract potentially straightforward answers and hence decisions – for example, revise = scale back growth aspirations. Others (the open ones) are labels for scoping exercises which will have to be carried out. Working through the table is a shaping or profiling of the meeting's agenda and an initial specification of the agenda in the Agenda.

The critical rows are the last three.

These rows construe the central problems of the organisation. The terms 'academic development', 'academic culture', 'economies of scale' and 'efficiencies' are management codes for what has been endlessly discussed as three of the major barriers to growth. For lots of historical reasons, staff tended to see themselves as solely teachers of the institutionalised body of knowledge defined for their disciplines, rather than active contributors to that body of knowledge. As a consequence, the urge to develop 'new courses' outside the scope of the standard or traditional curriculum was often resisted. Increased resources would be needed to change this by bringing in 'new blood' and by funding 'research time', 'career re-direction' and the like. The only way to generate such resources was to find efficiencies, but the nature of the organisation and its adopted delivery model severely restricted options here. Neither the academic nor the support organisations were running with spare resource. To finance the development of the academic culture, cost would have to be reduced across the whole organisation. But that can only be done by massive re-structuring. This conclusion is what rows 12, 13 and 14 imply. If the organisation doesn't re-structure, then it will not survive the changes to its environment listed in rows 1–11. What are presented as simple revisions to the basic assumptions of the strategy turn out to be proposals for major re-organisation. And that *is* the agenda in the Agenda.

## Summary

The RCA and the schedule of steps are not a plan; they are a critical pre-figuring of what a plan to provide constructable future for CU should be. This pre-figuring is the agenda in the Agenda, an interpretation of current state and tasks to be undertaken which constitutes the scale of the planning task and its outcomes. Arriving at this interpretation is the closing of praxeological gap between the planning account given in the RCA and the schedule and the planning to be undertaken. The recipient-designed nature of the RCA and the schedule facilitates that gap closing work by means of the methods we have identified. As written-read documents, the RCA and the schedule enable the consociate achievement of mutual understanding. Those who are 'proper readers' of the document (that is, the senior management team embarking on the Mid Term Review) can find the 'proper reading' (the agenda in the Agenda) put there for them to find. Once again, mutual intelligibility and the coordination of action is achieved. In saying this, we are *not* saying that having understood what was being proposed, all the team (or indeed, any of them) accepted it. That is not what we are claiming. Significant debate did, indeed, ensue. What we are saying, and this is all we are claiming, is that for the debate to be had, *first* mutual understanding of what was in hand had to be achieved and the greater part of that understanding was accomplished outside the meeting through the co-production of these written-read documents as an exercise in consociate management – that is action at a distance.

## Notes

1 It was originally published as Suchman (1987). The second edition was retitled *Human Machine Reconfigurations* (Suchman 2007) and included reflections on the subsequent debates as well as the original text. It is the latter version we have used.
2 Summary assessments of strengths, weakness, opportunities and threats.
3 We will use capitalisation when referring to the circulated document titled 'Review of Core Assumptions' and lower case when referring to the in-production and completed activity.
4 To the working manager, this is the only sensible way of interpreting what 'stakeholder analysis' is about. You need to figure out who the relevant stakeholders are and what they 'can at least live with' in order to write an approvable historiography.
5 It is taken for granted that a key part of the meeting will be taken up with figuring out what exactly (for here and for now) these implicatures are and how they impact on the constructability of sustainable future set out in the plan. We have borrowed the term 'implicature' from Paul Grice (1981).
6 This is accepted as a general policy. Decisions cannot be treated as endlessly revisable. This does not mean, in the midst of the process, managers will not argue strongly that some particular decision ought to be revised or has been inadvertently and wrongly revised.
7 Finding continuity in the midst of radical change is an unsung managerial skill and one of the techniques used to keep the threat of entropy at bay.
8 That is, a network with a central hub and peripheral points.

## References

Dant, T. and Francis, D. 1998. "Planning in Organisations: Rational Control or Contingent Activity?" *Sociological Research Online*, vol. 2.
Grice, P. 1981. "Presuppositions and Conversational Implicature." In *Radical Pragmatics*, by P. Cole (ed.), 113–128. New York: Academic Press.

Law, J. 1994. *Organising Modernity*. Oxford: Blackwell.
Miller, G., Galanter, E. and Pribram, K. 1960. *Plans and the Structure of Behavior*. New York: Holt, Rinehardt and Winston.
Samra-Fredericks, D. 2010. "The Interactional Accomplishment of a Strategic Plan." In *Organisation, Interaction & Practice*, by N. Llewellyn and J. Hindmarch (eds), 198–217. Cambridge: Cambridge University Press.
Schmidt, K. and Wagner, I. 2004. "Ordering Systems: Coordinative Practices and Artifacts in Architectural Design and Planning." *Computer Supported Co-operative Work*, vol. *13* 349–408.
Suchman, L. 1987. *Plans and Situated Actions*. Cambridge: Cambridge University Press.
——. 2007 (originally 1987). *Human Machine Reconfigurations*. Cambridge: Cambridge University Press.

# Part III
# Conclusion

# 11 Ethnomethodology: a First Sociology?

## Introduction

Ethnomethodology has been a lively research endeavour for well over half a century, so it is hardly surprising that over time new initiatives, emphases and outlooks have emerged. Equally, since Harold Garfinkel remained at its heart for most of that period, it is also unsurprising his view of how Ethnomethodology should be defined shifted and developed and, given the erratic sequencing of his publications, that his readers should have difficulty pinning down precisely what those changes might have been. Lately, then, Ethnomethodology's direction of travel has come under increasing scrutiny, with a number of experienced members of the field questioning whether the path currently being followed is not only more conservative than originally envisaged, but actually involves a reneging on the foundational principles. We think these suggestions are misplaced and, using the notion of Ethnomethodology as a First Sociology, in this final chapter we summarise why. We will then use the same conception to position the studies presented in previous chapters. Finally, albeit very briefly, we will address some residual issues entangled in but not central to the debate over Ethnomethodology's current state. These issues mostly turn on what some identify as the unambitious character of the studies currently being carried out.

## A First Sociology

For some little while, we have been arguing the most reasonable way of approaching Ethnomethodology is to conceive it as one Sociology among others. There is no given way of investigating the social world. Diverse assumptions can be integrated into coherent pre-investigative postulates and operationalised in studies, which is exactly what Ethnomethodology has done by developing its own distinctive set of principles. What it has chosen to study are features of the social world other forms of sociological research have hitherto largely passed by. This is not a defect on their part though. Given their standpoints and their investigative methods, not only are these topics unavailable to them, they are irrelevant too. Ethnomethodology and conventional Sociology can sit alongside one another without the need for sibling rivalry. Each has its own programmes and its own preferred procedures.

Such tolerance does not catch everything about the relationship though. Whilst they should not be conceived as competitive, nonetheless there is an ordering. It is not temporal (Ethnomethodology was certainly not first on the sociological scene), explanatory (sociological phenomena do not 'reduce' to Ethnomethodology's) nor conceptual (Sociology's concepts do not presuppose Ethnomethodology's). It is *ontogenic*. Ethnomethodology concerns itself with the primordial social facts on which Sociology's research depends. In that sense, as a *First Sociology*, Ethnomethodology occupies a position analogous to that Husserl intended Phenomenology should stand in vis-à-vis the natural sciences and Philosophy. It discloses what Sociology presupposes.

The question which preoccupied Husserl was what made the natural sciences possible? What does the scientific understanding of the world rest on? He perceived that to answer this question we have to step back beyond the practices and findings of science to the point in analytic reflection at which scientific conceptual schemas are introduced. Rather than starting by giving the scientific representation of the world logical priority over our pre-theoretical understandings, Husserl sought to begin from the historical priority of those pre-theoretical understanding in relation to scientific ones – the latter arose in a world already experienced through the terms of the former. Understanding how those scientific understandings could arise in an environment experienced in pre-theoretical terms was a way of understanding more clearly the relations between pre-theoretical and scientific understandings. Marvin Farber summarises this proposal:

> For Husserl, the 'final measure' of all theory is that which is 'originally' given in simple seeing. The term 'original' applies to that which can be experienced in direct observation; the 'originally given' is something that is 'naively' meant and possibly given as existent. That which can be 'grasped' by simple looking is prior to all theory, including 'the theory of knowledge'.
> (Farber 1943: 203)

Aron Gurwitsch particularised the analysis to the case of Formal Logic.

> While the technical logician is engaged in constructive work... the philosopher of logic raises questions as to the very sense of the constructive... procedure. *The perceptual world as it presents itself in pre-predicative experience appears* in our analysis *as one of the fundamental presuppositions of logic.*
> (Gurwitsch 1966: 353; emphasis in original)

In much the same way, Ethnomethodology's questions concern how the social world is understood independent of and prior to its construal within sociological schemas. These understandings comprise the common ground on which those sociological schemas stand; a common ground which existed before Sociology and continues to exist independent of it. In that sense, Ethnomethodology's concern is with the understandings which make sociality possible and hence available for sociological investigation and analysis. Husserl's conclusion was that although the sciences saw themselves as breaking with the 'naivety' of pre-scientific thinking, their conceptual apparatuses actually incorporated much of it. In a similar way, vernacular modes of discriminating social institutions, for example, have been taken directly into Sociology's own conceptual structure in categories such as its conventional divisions between sociologies of the family, work, religion, education, science, and so on. This dependence on vernacular concepts allows non-sociologists to understand in the most superficial but nonetheless reasonably correct ways, just what those domains encompass. It is also vital when, as much of the profession professes to want to do, the discipline sets itself an ambition to have relevance for the formation of policy. Without a reliance on vernacular understandings, those who have no training in Sociology's technical apparatus could struggle to understand both what is being said to them and its significance.

The articulation of a First Sociology is what motivates Ethnomethodology's interest in the investigation of social affairs exclusively in the terms these are understood by those engaged in them. The purpose is not to measure members' understandings against the ones a sociologist might offer, thereby calibrating 'robustness', 'objectivity', 'factuality', or 'generality' against the standards Sociology adheres to, and certainly not to seek ways of replacing such understandings with those drawn from Sociology. This does not mean issues of assessment cannot be a matter for investigation, but only when framed in the terms the participants in a setting use when seeking to determine how robust their understanding is and whether it will yield what is expected. How do they see a case as an 'instance' of some category and how do they tell if their expectations about that category are fulfilled in any actual case? Finally, how do they determine the dependability of the information on which they make such judgements? Undoubtedly, these are questions sociologists ask about their own social data, but what motivates their framing and what would count as satisfactory answers are entirely different to those of other members of society.

The determination to step back beyond sociological frames means the settings of social action have to be conceived in ways which allow participants to interpret activities and events and share their understandings without recourse to Sociology's technical apparatus. In particular, 'what things are' and 'what they mean' must be recoverable from the activities themselves, such recovery being part and parcel of engagement in the flow of action. This has an initial and very important implication. Since those engaged in the activities under view determine what is going on and what it means within the flow of their activity, the distinction between being an investigator sitting apart from the action, and being a member immersed in it, collapses. Gaining a working understanding of social life does not require abstracted Cartesian reflection nor an 'objective method'. Neither does it depend upon the design of special interventions to gather material. Looking at what is available to those in the setting is sufficient to determine how they came to the understandings they patently did.

## First Sociology and the current state of Ethnomethodology

As we set out in Chapter 1, Garfinkel's early thinking derived from an attempt to align, if not integrate, Alfred Schutz's (1967) social philosophy with Talcott Parsons' general theory of action (Parson and Shils 1951). His conclusion was that Parsons' schema could not accommodate a line of development based on Schutz's principles. The reason, as Schutz himself had observed to Parsons (Grathoff 1978), was because trying to do so would require 'one more radical step', namely the bracketing of the presumptions of the schema itself. This would be necessary if a way of theoretically grounding the interactions between sociological investigators and their informants was to be found. Since such interactions were necessary to the gathering of materials and the interpretation of data on which analysis depended, for rigour to be maintained, such grounding within the investigation's theoretical premises was required.

Ethnomethodology was forged by taking that 'one more radical step' and with the step, a First Sociology became possible. The body of work which has built up since then has been in service of identifying, working out and working through the range of topics and analytic avenues made available by that radical move.

In recent discussions, though, the epithet often used to mark the current state of the discipline is a supposed 'loss of radicalism' consequent upon a redirection in, or even retreat from, the original impetus. This loss is said to be taking place across three different fronts:

1   From roughly 1967 to the millennium, Garfinkel fundamentally changed his view of Ethnomethodology. This change involved a retreat from the direct challenge to fundamental views on the nature of social life not just in the profession of Sociology and associated disciplines, but in society in general. Instead, what emerged was a point of view which simply acceded to conventional outlooks in social science and society.
2   Ethnomethodology has tended to adopt a less combative stance towards the rest of the Sociology profession. Instead, many working in the field actively seek collaboration and partnership. This has led to the suggestion Ethnomethodology increasingly accepts professional Sociology's image of what it is to be an academic discipline even though part of Garfinkel's original concern with regard to sociological schemes was not their substance but the way they were framed in terms of general academic presuppositions. Garfinkel's radicalism has, then, been interpreted by some as a resistance to academisation. Although the issue is couched in terms of a concern over the image projected, for us it seems more motivated by the belief that increasing accommodation will necessarily moderate the challenge being made and so undercut one of Ethnomethodology's foundational principles. Certainly it is true Ethnomethodology's traditionally obdurate stance is felt to be unhelpful at best for those seeking cooperation and close working.

3   Although not central to the first two concerns, associated with them is a worry that the studies being carried out these days have little of the 'edge', the novelty and energy seen in the very early work. As a result, the vast body of contemporary work is felt to be unexciting and conveying the sense of a discipline becalmed.

What gives these observations especial force is that they are not just the disparaging allegations of those lacking sympathy for the field, but come from highly respected members of Ethnomethodology's own community. If these people are worried, shouldn't we all be?

## Taking the long view

In this section, we will run over the above list. Unfortunately, we do not have the space to do much more than offer a limited recital and rehearsal of the issues involved. We will start with the last.

### A sense of lassitude

This issue is the least intellectually consequential though, as we will see, because it implies a reservation about how lively and hence attractive the discipline might seem, it is the one which ought to prompt the community to immediate remedial action. As sociologists, none of us should be surprised to see an enterprise born of a determination to make a radical break with the status quo begin to show signs of 'routinisation'. With continual explication and demonstration, what once was surprising and exciting becomes less so. Familiarity breeds not so much contempt as contentment. There is another aspect though. While conventional Sociology hardly regards it as *kosher*, Ethnomethodology has become generally accepted. It is taught and taught about (though whether it is well understood is another matter entirely). This gradual institutionalisation has meant in orders of magnitude more students have been exposed to it, considerable numbers of whom, having taken up research and other professional careers, have sought to align their work with it. Routinisation is associated with a loss of challenge and innovativeness. The explosion in the researcher base has meant what innovation there might be gets drowned out in the volume of work being produced. Contemporary academic culture with its emphasis on the publication treadmill only makes the situation worse. The studies are bland, to be sure, but their blandness is not testimony to the loss of the gene for radical investigation, simply a correlate of increased mass.

### A methodological disjunct

It was a prominent ethnomethodologist, the late Melvin Pollner, who first publicly questioned Ethnomethodology's apparent shift from confrontation to absorption within Sociology. Caustically, he referred to it as 'settling down in the suburbs'

(Pollner 1991: 370). Although he saw it had many dimensions, for him what was critical was the tendency to conflate the roles of ethnomethodologist-as-analyst with ethnomethodologist-as-member.[1] Pollner thought this tendency had been given momentum in the period between the publication of *Studies in Ethnomethodology* (Garfinkel 1967) and *Ethnomethodology's Program* (Garfinkel 2002). For Pollner, it constituted no less than a re-conceiving what it was 'to do' Ethnomethodology. Originally, the adoption of the Schutzian distinction between the scientific and natural 'attitudes' and the pre-suppositions on which they are based meant ethnomethodological investigation was predicated on setting aside the assumptions underpinning ordinary life. To use phenomenological terminology, the ethnomethodological attitude 'bracketed' the pre-suppositions of normal social life.

For Pollner, this bracketing is the core of Ethnomethodology's radical stance. It carries a conception of social life and social reality orthogonal to that of ordinary members of society. In Chapter 3, we briefly mentioned one of the implications he felt could follow. Someone who grasped the import of this bracketing is likely to be confronted what he called an 'ontologically fatal insight' (Pollner 1987: 88). Lynch suggests this often takes the form of

> an insight sometimes arrived at in a moment of heady delight, but often as a horrifying realization – that the world we take for granted as an independent environment of action is not what it seems; instead, it is a product of our own constitutive practices and 'it could be otherwise'.
>
> (Lynch 2013: 449)

Because the heart of Sociology's analytic practice retains the natural attitude, such 'insight' poses a profound challenge. Under the natural attitude, the social world is taken to be an external, constraining reality which shapes our experience. Under the ethnomethodological attitude, social reality is re-framed as the construction, the conjoint output, of our interpretive actions. Ethnomethodology's phenomena are the 'methods' by which that reality is constructed.

For Pollner, Garfinkel's promotion of the research agenda known as 'the studies of work', and especially the studies of science, marks where the erosion of the distinction between analytic and natural attitudes becomes really obvious. In outline, his argument goes like this. The strategy of refusing to adopt the pre-suppositions of ordinary life was in service of making them visible and analysable. In the studies of work (and this is especially true in the studies of the sciences), investigators are charged with turning themselves into competent members of the local, often highly specialised, communities being studied. *Prima facie*, this is a significant demand. It means researchers have to acquire and then be able to enact the distinctive competences possessed by those communities. The measure of success is the degree of approximation between the understandings the researcher possesses and can convey and those of the community members. Calibration between researcher and member is the only means of determining the quality of the findings. Rather than demanding a distancing of investigator and the investigated, the studies of work require the investigator to be submerged as a fully practising member into the local community. The distinction between analyst and member central to Ethnomethodology disappears entirely.

We can see how Pollner can come to this conclusion from the way the studies of work are talked about in *Ethnomethodology's Program*. It is also very easy to find in that book whole stretches of text which appear to be given over to making a decisive break with Sociology as a discipline and brutally re-fashioning Ethnomethodology as studies of the 'classical accounting' other disciplines give of their own work. However, we suggest that if the later work is viewed in terms of exploring new and different possibilities for a First Sociology, the perception of a shift fades and the claims about a severing of relations with Sociology become much less substantial.

To begin with, radical re-direction or not, the moves being discussed were in train well before *Studies in Ethnomethodology* was published. They involved not so much a revision of theoretical principles as an adjustment of practice. This can be traced in the published sources, though the following personal anecdote offers equally strong evidence for our view:

> Late in his life, Garfinkel made regular telephone calls to Jeff Coulter. When Jeff told Wes [Sharrock] about these, Wes said, 'I've spent years trying to work out the logic in Garfinkel's move from the highly theoretical – commonly deductive – reasoning in his earlier work to the insistence on studies, but I've never been able to pin it down. Can you ask him about that?'
> 
> A few days later, Jeff rang Wes. His opening line was: 'Saul Mendlovitz. That's your answer.'
> 
> 'What are you saying?'
> 
> 'One day Mendlovitz said to him "Harold, you've got to stop this theory shit."'
> 
> 'And that was it?'
> 
> 'That was it.'

Mendlovitz worked with Garfinkel on 'the juror study' and we take it his advice was offered around that time. In essence, he was suggesting what was needed was more than simple identification of the theoretical possibilities in Ethnomethodology's transformative position. Those possibilities had to be demonstrated through empirical investigations – that is, in actualising a First Sociology. This was the reason Mendlovitz advised Garfinkel to stop theorising and undertake studies, advice Garfinkel accepted and followed. Doing so involved moving from a preoccupation with Sociology's modes of creating theoretical schemas to a focus on its methodology and data collection. Both in the *Studies* and after, Garfinkel seems to have had much less interest in the content of findings and what they might imply for Sociology than in how the studies were actually being carried out. The widely used soubriquet 'the coding study' carries the point well. Ostensibly, this was a study aimed at using the records of a psychiatric clinic to demonstrate how it operates. What was actually presented was a study of the ways members of the research team combed through, interpreted and shaped up the material in the records to provide the necessary condensed rendition of the clinic's activities which the research objective required.

The form the rendition took did not seem to be of much concern to Garfinkel either. What did arouse Garfinkel's interest was the device of using the lens of strict conformity with the standard principles of methodological practice to bring out the work required to mount a sociological investigation. As is well known, the study showed much of the research activity undertaken was not specified by the standard procedures even though such activity was indispensable to collecting the data needed for the study. The insights offered by 'the coding study', then, are about what happens in sociological investigations *prior to* the sociologising getting underway. Attention is directed to what in Husserl's terms we would call the 'original' activities which facilitated the undertaking of sociological investigation.

If the transition to an interest in studies is a turn, it is one which, to use the oft-cited phrase, transforms Sociology from a resource for ethnomethodological studies into a topic for them. In Sociology, theoretical and methodological issues are largely conceptualised in terms of the relationship between theory and data. By framing his stance as a First Sociology, Garfinkel's studies (as well as those of others) threw the problematic relationship of data and phenomena into relief. That this relationship is often problematic, with a slippage between the 'intended' and the 'actual' object of investigation was not, however, to be taken as a *discovery*. It was something every practising sociologist was aware of and the topic of endless advice sharing and conversations at professional gatherings. Every researcher has come up against the same impasse Garfinkel observed in the coding study. Although the object of investigation was the clinic, what was being examined were the residua of the clinic's organisational activities captured in the records, together with the common sense understandings held by the research team of how psychiatric clinics might work. Equally, every practising researcher is well aware of the inscrutability of the transformation process by which materials collected in someone else's investigation are turned into the data presented in published reports. Both materials and means of their transformation are necessarily filtered from the sociological findings. Although every researcher was familiar with both these features of sociological research, until Garfinkel's intervention they were not topics for sociological investigation in their own right.

What Garfinkel did not do, though, was frame his investigations as a search for remedies to salve Sociology's theoretical and methodological ambitions. Rather, he sought to avoid the one and ignore the other. Instead of treating social life as a plenum of intrinsically unorganised activity only rendered orderly by the shaping given it by sociological schemes of empirically real categories, he uses Schutz's description of the natural attitude to postulate 'There is order in the plenum!' (Garfinkel 2002: 94).[2] This allowed him to treat the materials on which sociological investigation and analysis depend as the embodiment of understandings used by ordinary members of society in living their everyday lives. To conceive of activities as social action is to conceive of them as organised responses which members of society exhibit to their experience of the social environment.

In so far as Sociology posits social action as its fundamental phenomenon, that assumption is only possible because there is a prior organisation to the ways social affairs are carried on. The order produced by the understandings members use must be *conceptually prior* to the order produced by Sociology. But not only that. The work of finding an order in the social world cannot be exclusive to Sociology's methods of systematic data collection. If there is an order to the social world, such order must be available to and findable by ordinary members of society going about their ordinary everyday affairs. Social order is not simply or only the result of systematic sociological enquiry. It is to be found everywhere from the most fragmentary to the most extended routines in everyone's daily lives. In Harvey Sacks' memorable phrase: there is 'order at all points' (1984: 22). Describing how that order is produced is the remit of a First Sociology.

This line of thinking forced two notable changes in Garfinkel's investigative procedure. First, rather than continuing to seek alignment between collected materials and a preconceived phenomenon, it was possible to take fragments of material and, from their close inspection, ask what phenomena they could instantiate. A key part of investigation, therefore, became identifying what was to be analysed. Second, the examination of materials could be directed to determining the internal coherence of specific runs or stretches of activity, a procedure which suits the treatment of the in-course-organisation of lines of social action. Taken together, these two imply there is no need for the investigator to be equipped with any specialised repertoire of practices to identify the features of social order and so there is no need to differentiate between the professional sociologist and ordinary members of the society with regard to the organisation of the setting of action. The twin suppositions (a) analysts are extensively members, and (b) members are practical analysts, do not entirely eradicate the difference between members and analysts, but they do reduce it to differences in the types of interest characteristic of the two. Analysts have an interest in seeing how the order of ongoing social life relates to scholarly or theoretical themes – an interest which is irrelevant for those intent on getting on with their lives. The idea of erasing the distinction between 'the sociologist' and 'the member' of society was effected as part of a turn to undertaking studies to demonstrate Ethnomethodology's phenomena and not as a result of those studies. As a consequence, what Pollner and others have highlighted are not really markers of any profound change in direction.

What is being cast as fundamental change is better seen as adaptive modification and adjustment in the light of changing circumstances in the development of Ethnomethodology as a First Sociology. Much the same can be said in regard to another of the supposed markers of fundamental change: the introduction of the requirement for 'unique adequacy'. The earliest studies were predicated on the assumption that investigations of such ordinary things as answering the telephone, playing tick-tack-toe and engaging in talk, required the investigator to have enough knowledge and skill to recognise what was happening. There was no need to emphasise this simply because these competences were part of most people's cultural resources. Most investigators were also members of the particular society from which the materials for study are taken.

That straightforward presumption no longer holds when attention is focused on Mathematics and the rest of the natural sciences. Here, investigation requires the acquisition of competences very different to those usually held by sociological investigators. In addition, acquiring them is no easy matter. Investigators are expected to do precisely the same when mounting these studies as they do when describing 'the missing interactional what' characterising talk, children's games and telephone conversations which members of society rely when doing those things. However, grasping the 'missing interactional what' of quantum tunnelling experiments or jazz improvisation, and seeing 'directly' and 'originally' as the scientist or jazz musician does, are not everyday competences. What is demanded is greater not because the investigative rationale has changed but simply because the domain has. Being an ethnomethodologist, a sociologist, or an ordinary member of society is no preparation for playing jazz piano sufficiently well to pass muster among other musicians nor for being adept enough to aid in carrying out a chemistry experiment.

As Lynch (forthcoming) points out, the key to unique adequacy is the difference between speaking *of* the work being carried out in the setting and speaking *about* it. This is the distinction carried by Husserl's 'directly' and 'originally'. The aim is to move the investigator over the line demarcating a well-informed commentator from a member of the community under investigation. The concern about unique adequacy amounts to a fear that the investigator will be reduced to simply repeating what the subjects of the investigation would say. We see it as more a measure to ensure that whatever the investigator does say, at least they have acquired enough of the necessary competence to be able to speak authoritatively on behalf of those whose activity it actually is.

Looking at the history of Ethnomethodology as an unfolding development of a First Sociology leads to the conclusion that the idea of a complete rupture between earlier and later versions of Ethnomethodology is overdrawn. First, what happened was more a re-shaping which occurred prior to the publication of the *Studies*. Second, it took the form of sustaining continuity through the adaptation and adjustment to extant approaches in order to apply them to a new set of investigative domains.

### *An intellectual caesura*

But what of the other suggestion? Does *Ethnomethodology's Program* mark a complete break with Sociology as a discipline? Well, it is true Garfinkel repeatedly insists that Ethnomethodology is independent and incommensurable. At the same time, though, ethnomethodological work (including Garfinkel's own) is routinely positioned by using standard sociological themes as foils. The situation, it seems, must be more nuanced than the melodramatic claims might allow.

To begin with, taking Schutz's radical step did not supply answers to the questions which Parsons had posed. Rather, it raised many questions Parsons' schema did not and could not ask. To do so, Parsons' scheme would have had to have been so thoroughly revised it would have lost its integrity and identity. The coining of the term 'ethnomethodological indifference' refers to this disjunction and is, in effect, a policy of self-denial. Ethnomethodology sets aside the questions asked by Sociology because, given its own pre-suppositions, it cannot answer them. The relationship between Sociology and Ethnomethodology is often presented as a face-off rooted in the latter's 'critique' of the former. This formulation is only acceptable if 'critique' is taken to mean the examination of the conceptual foundations of an intellectual enterprise in order to see whether, when suitably developed, new and different possibilities can be derived from it. Ethnomethodology is not a *correction of* or *replacement for* Sociology's theories and findings, but a systematic *critique* of them – a critique which led to a First Sociology. It is not a better way of doing what Sociology wants to do, but a way of doing sociological research which professional Sociology (both at the time and later) most definitely does not want to do.

What this begs, of course, is the question: 'Can Sociology do what it says it wants to do?' Once again, things often get muddled here. Proponents and critics alike usually present Ethnomethodology as mounting an attack on Sociology by denying it can. It is also true Garfinkel often appears to be traducing what he claimed were Sociology's shortcomings. Given its placement in the midst of a discussion of sociological reasoning, a classic example of this attitude appears to be the paragraph heading 'The unsatisfied programmatic distinction between and substitutability of objective for indexical expressions' (Garfinkel 1967: 4). Surely this and the discussion it headed are tantamount to an attack by claiming Sociology cannot do what it says it wants to do? Sociology wants to construct formal theory but such formalisation requires precisely the substitution of forms of expressions identified in the heading. Since the distinction between the two cannot be made, the substitution is impossible.

This is another misconstrual. Rather than identifying a hitherto unrecognised problem, Garfinkel is, once again, pointing to a challenge which was, and is, well known among those trying to develop formal theory in Sociology and elsewhere. Innumerable remedies have been offered, not by ethnomethodologists, but by sociologists and the practitioners of other disciplines deeply committed to the ideal of formalisation. As with the slippage between data and phenomenon, the irredeemably indexical character of expressions is a familiar practical, original fact of research life. It is not that sociologists have no way of managing these problems and working around them, but that the work-arounds investigators use are work-arounds, and not in-principle, theoretically justified solutions.

The idea that Ethnomethodology was constructed to be an existential threat to Sociology is a myth. The myth rests on the premise that what Ethnomethodology says about Sociology came as a complete surprise. This is nonsense. Sociology has long been troubled by the deficiencies in the premises of its modes of theorising, its procedures for operationalisation of investigations and the methods it uses to collect data, especially when these are compared to the rubrics and standards used in other disciplines, particularly the natural and physical sciences. And yet addressing these deficiencies has remained a far lower priority than undertaking studies themselves and developing theoretical categories on the basis of the findings. This is what Ethnomethodology and Sociology are at odds over: the significance to be attributed to the familiar features just outlined. For Ethnomethodology, they are central and pressing matters, crying out to be addressed and resolved. For Sociology, they are expectable, not to say routine, limiting facts of research life. Ethnomethodology's own methodological prescriptions do not provide remedies Sociology might use. Rather, they are designed to displace the very assumptions which give rise to the deficiencies in the first place.

If Ethnomethodology is not an attack on Sociology, what is their relationship? A weak sense of the term 'foil' used earlier makes Sociology out to be an easily invoked straw man against which some ethnomethodological study or argument can be positioned – a rhetoric of 'They say this... but we say that.' And, to be fair, a number of studies (many of which we had in mind earlier) do suffer from this. A much stronger conception, though, would link the ideas of 'foil' and 'hybrid studies'. Given what we have said about Garfinkel's re-thinking of the foundations of Sociology, the consequences of the move of methodology to centre stage alongside (and perhaps in place of) theory, and the way both fed through to the interest in the operationalising of investigations, a strong case could be made for proposing rather than a rupturing of the relationship between (professional) Sociology and Ethnomethodology, the initial realisation of Ethnomethodology as a First Sociology was actually as a hybrid 'ethno-sociology'. The introduction of the studies of work simply extended the range of opportunities and possible disciplines with which hybrid relationships might be sought. Where once the source of investigative topics was derived from Sociology but not cast according to Sociology's conventions, now topics can be drawn from Mathematics, Chemistry, Physics, Philosophy and practically anywhere else. With the adoption of the idea of hybrid disciplines, the notion of using a discipline as a 'foil' comes to mean a detailed explication and triangulation of Ethnomethodology's 'radicalising' interest in the common sense constitution of some set of relevant topics against the interest generally shown towards them within the discipline being studied. Whereas once this was done solely with regard to Sociology, now it is to be carried out with a range of disciplines. As with Sociology, what this means is a drawing out of why the very matters which usually are taken to be of little scientific interest to the discipline concerned are of central investigative concern to Ethnomethodology as a First Sociology.

We are left, though, with the question of the strategic advantage to Ethnomethodology of a stress on hybrid studies. To be sure, more topics are made available thereby, but will the successful undertaking of these studies make a significant, long-lasting difference to Ethnomethodology itself? Where, to coin the phrase, is the ethnomethodological beef? At this point, it is difficult to say, in part because there are so few, if any, fully authenticated examples. Take what many regard as the leading case. Is the pay-off supposed to be that ethnomethodological studies of Mathematics can provide mathematicians with novel ways to pose and solve problems they grapple with? Or, is it expected that after sufficient joint work, ethnomethodological studies of theorem proving and the like will offer modes of mathematical reasoning which can be integrated into the portfolio of practices mathematicians invoke? From what is on offer so far, both seem unlikely. Far more likely is that the relationship will turn out to be civil toleration between two cooperating disciplines which, without any intention of fusing their disciplinary standpoints, are seeking ways of working together for mutual benefit.

If this is (all) the turn to hybrid studies amounts to, it is important but not radical reformulation.[3] Moreover, it also implies the myth of a necessary and endemic antagonistic relationship between Ethnomethodology and Sociology will have to be re-thought. Just as with Mathematics, we can imagine, for example, the findings of ethno-sociological studies of surveys might help improve question formulation and response rates. This would hardly require either party to review the integrity of their investigative frameworks and theoretical presuppositions. Studying surveys is not done by using the survey method, nor does administering surveys need to involve Conversation Analysis or third person phenomenology.

One recent initiative, however, does not seem to fit so easily with this ecumenism, nor within the general rubric of a First Sociology. Although the work carried out in 'epistemics' seems to fit very closely with what was and is done in Ethnomethodology and Conversation Analysis under the heading of 'the social distribution of knowledge', it has been received with some considerable suspicion.[4] The source of this suspicion is a conviction that the wish to forge epistemics is actually a desire to bring Conversation Analysis into line with the requirements of proof and analysis found in Linguistics. This would require both the relaxing of conversation analysis's foundational requirement for the traceability of the phenomenon being analysed in the specifics of the materials being reviewed and the acceptance of Linguistics formalisations as the premises for its descriptions. If so, both would seem to involve stepping away from the stipulation to focus on the primordial set out by Husserl, Schutz and Garfinkel, which is why so many of its critics accuse it of 'constructivism'. At the moment, the best one can say about epistemics is that its results do not appear to be offering any order of improvement on traditional conversation analytic descriptions of talk. Indeed, on occasion, given the moves mentioned above, the policies invoked occasionally seem to exhibit the familiar sociological substitution effect we described in Chapter 3.

To summarise: the conclusion we draw from the debates over the supposed retrenchment in Ethnomethodology is a sanguine one. On close inspection, points of rupture and discontinuity of principles appear to be more adaptation and evolution of an emerging First Sociology than anything else and, as a consequence, the idea of necessary antagonism with Sociology is more myth than reality.[5] Seeking cross-disciplinary connections, be they be in search of hybrid disciplines or with somewhat more modest ambitions, does not seem to us to be either a new radical innovation nor a slighting of the autonomy of Ethnomethodology's own foundational position. In these cooperative ventures, neither partner needs to feel under threat and so any mutual learning which does eventuate should not be sniffed at.

## Action at a distance, and studies of consociation

We have argued taking Ethnomethodology to be a First Sociology opens up an investigative space within which the understandings ordinary members of society have of the social world they are immersed in can be made visible, accessible and analysable. The coherence displayed by these understandings is to be determined by reference to the context in which they are deployed. This context is constituted not simply by the material world they inhabit and the nexus of streams of activity in which they are engaged, but also by their perceptions and motivations, the outcomes they seek and their judgements concerning all these things. Such perceptions, outcomes, motivations and judgements shape the ways courses of action unfold and the circumstances to which they give rise. All this sense making takes place without recourse to the formal schemes of interpretation afforded to analytic investigators by the disciplines of the social and related sciences.

The studies presented in this book are essays in applying the ethnomethodological approach of third person phenomenology to instances of sense making undertaken by senior managers. We have identified a number of modalities under which this sense making proceeds. By means of the device of holding a range of 'management objects' up for scrutiny, we have illustrated the practical reasoning underpinning financial planning and decision making, organisational structuring, price setting, forward planning, and so on as matters of co-produced, recipient-designed courses of action exhibiting schemes of value, continuity of purpose and discoverable due process. What the studies reveal is the complex detailed organisation by which senior managers provide for and literally 'manage' the real-world problems they face on a moment-by-moment, day-by-day basis. It is this 'management' and their success in accomplishing it which gives their routine practices the significance they have for those engaged in organisational life and allows them to be the resources they are for the social and management sciences which study them.

From time to time, we have tried to draw appropriate connections between the orders of social organisation which we have been concerned with and those of interest to the social sciences more broadly. Drawing such conclusions marks one way in which, separate, autonomous and incommensurable though they might be, Ethnomethodology and formal or classical social science can be coupled. Our findings do not provide solutions to the investigative problems set by sociologists and management scientists. What they indicate is how, as a practical matter of their daily lives, senior managers perceive, grapple with and resolve much the same problems sociologists and management scientists (and philosophers, accountants, and lawyers, to name but a few) set themselves in theirs. All are investigators. It is the only the domains in which these investigations take place and the auspices under which they are carried out which differ.

Even though the expertise we drew upon in developing our studies was that of senior executives at CU, we will not justify our ethnomethodological contribution by defending its 'unique adequacy', nor by promoting our work as the initiation of a 'hybrid discipline'. As we have made clear, neither adds materially to the identification of what makes Ethnomethodology distinctive. Instead, our claim is this. As a First Sociology, the investigative space which Ethnomethodology occupies is distinctive enough, interesting enough and, as yet, unexamined enough to warrant its systematic exploration. That others find the issues we attend to trivial is no reason for us to be reticent about making our materials and analyses available. If the phenomena we present are not gripping enough, nothing we can say about them will make any difference.

## Looking forward

The burden of this chapter might be summarised as 'Beware the fallacy of the immediate!' Ethnomethodology has been around for a long time and while there have been shifts in emphasis, vocabulary and interest, there are also strong skeins of consistent reasoning which preserve its radicalism. By treating it as a First Sociology, we emphasise Ethnomethodology's primordial, self-contained structure; one which facilitates a line of investigation which does not compete with more conventional sociologies. Given this separation and insulation, it is hard to see what detailed topical continuities there might be between them nor how they might be integrated. In our work, we have sought little more than loose coupling and indicative identification.

Even if we don't see Ethnomethodology as entering a death spiral, that does not mean we think there are few problems and issues to be addressed. The most important (and this is certainly associated with the sense of ennui many feel) is the problem of capitalising on the achievements made thus far. The body of studies faithful to working out the original impulse have clearly demonstrated the fertility of the approach and its character as a distinct form of sociological investigation. Unsurprisingly, as the momentum of the work began to pick up, differing clusters of emphases and interests have emerged. The most important of these was Conversation Analysis, although video analysis and ethnography should not be overlooked. The evident success of Conversation Analysis, though, may have owed much to the nature of the phenomenon being studied. The early identification of the centrality of turn taking within the analytic object, 'a single conversation', certainly allowed the development of a programme of focused studies wherein each could see itself codifying distinct aspects of a unified and generalised organisational structure. How cumulative this programme actually is remains less clear. Whatever the case, it is plain the studies undertaken are exemplifications of the close analysis of ordinary phenomena.

Determining progress and cumulativity in the enormous range of studies framed as following Garfinkel's own work is a far greater problem. Taken en masse, it is hard to say exactly what their overall cumulative force is – apart, that is, from repeated identification of the viability and fertility of the standpoint. Whilst Garfinkel himself may have insisted on the primacy of studies and the absolute necessity of undertaking them for oneself, it may be time to review what has been achieved in the accumulation we have and to ask what order of success this achievement really displays. Once we know how far we have come, we ought to be able to decide where we need to go next and how we might get there. With this stocktaking in hand, our hope is the studies we present here and the approach we have used in this book will prove useful pointers to one of the paths which deserves to be followed.

## Notes

1 In the final pages of *Mundane Reason* (1987), Pollner points to the dilemma he sees Ethnomethodology facing. Either it can extend its own 'radical' agenda to itself, thereby threatening any claims to empirical realism, or it can exempt itself from its own tenets and adopt the objectivist stance of the rest of Sociology. By 1991, he became convinced it had chosen the latter.
2 In classical and medieval philosophy, the plenum was the chaotic universe of fundamental matter which filled the cosmos. Time and space were not real but simply 'figments of the mind' used to order our experience. Enlightenment thinking, especially following Newton, asserted fundamental properties such as time and space were real and ontologically coeval with matter. Kant's metaphysics of 'empirical realism' tried to give a philosophical grounding to this view and became the consensus. Kant's philosophy was the backdrop against which the sociologies of the nineteenth century were developed.
3 Indeed, 'interdisciplinary studies' would do just as well as 'hybrid studies' and would have the added advantage of drawing attention to the extent that such studies are commonplace across Sociology and other disciplines.
4 The debate is ongoing. See Heritage (2012a, 2012b) and the papers in *Discourse Studies, vol. 18, no. 5 (2016)*, especially Macbeth et al. 2016, and Macbeth and Wong 2016.
5 We want to place emphasis on the word 'necessary' here. We think the undoubted antagonism is unnecessary. It could be that Pollner himself may have put his finger on its cause when he suggested the bracketing of a mode of enquiry such as Sociology's frame of reference could provoke a questioning where the sociological investigator comes to doubt, what as an ordinary member of society, it means to be a social actor and to live in the social world. This is just the kind of reality disjuncture examined by Pollner (1987) though not one of his examples. To take just one instance, a dispassionate review of some of the responses to Garfinkel and Sacks in *The Purdue Symposium* (Hill and Crittenden 1968) might well conclude this is precisely what is happening.

## References

Farber, M. 1943. *The Foundation of Phenomenology*. Albany, NY: State University of New York Press.
Garfinkel, H. 1967. *Studies in Ethnomethodology*. Englewood Cliffs, NJ: Prentice Hall.
———. 2002. *Ethnomethodology's Program*. New York: Roman and Littlefield.
Grathoff, R. 1978. *The Theory of Social Action*. Bloomington, IN: University of Indiana Press.
Gurwitsch, A. 1966. *Studies in Phenomenology and Psychology*. Evanston, IL: Northwestern University Press.
Heritage, J. 2012a. "Beyond and Behind the Words: Some Reactions to my Commentators." *Research on Language and Social Interaction*, vol. 45, no. 1 76–81.
———. 2012b. "Epistemics in Action: Action Formation and Territories of Knowledge." *Research on Language and Social Interaction*, vol. 45, no. 1 1–29.
Hill, R. and Crittendon, K. (eds). 1968. *Proceedings of the Purdue Symposium on Ethnomethodology*. West Lafayette, IN: Purdue Research Foundation.

Lynch, M.E. 2013. "Ontography: Inventing the Production of Things, Deflating Ontology." *Social Studies of Science, vol. 43, no. 3* 444–462.

——. Forthcoming. "Garfinkel's Studies of Work." In *Harold Garfinkel: Praxis, Social Order and the Ethnomethodology Movement*, by J. Heritage and D. Maynard (eds). Oxford: Oxford University Press.

Macbeth, D. and Wong, J. 2016. "The Story of 'Oh', Part 2: Animating Transcript." *Discourse Studies, vol. 18, no. 5* 574–596.

—— and Lynch, M. 2016. "The Story of 'Oh', Part 1: Indexing Structure, Animating Transcript." *Discourse Studies, vol. 18, no. 5* 550–573.

Parsons, T. 1951. *The Social System*. London: Routledge and Kegan Paul.

—— and Shils, E. (eds). 1951. *Toward a General Theory of Action*. Cambridge, MA: Harvard University Press.

Pollner, M. 1987. *Mundane Reason*. Cambridge: Cambridge University Press.

——. 1991. "Left of Ethnomethodology: The Rise and Decline of Radical Reflexivity." *American Sociological Review, vol. 56, no. 3* 370–380.

Sacks, H. 1984. "Notes on Methodology." In *Structures of Social Action*, by J. Atkinson and J. Heritage (eds), 21–27. Cambridge: Cambridge University Press.

Schutz, A. 1967. *The Phenomenology of the Social World*. Evanston, IL: Northwestern University Press.

# Index

5 year projections and cash flow workbook 58–71

absolutes 78–79
academic strategy 146
accountability 12–14, 75
achieved representativeness 107
actor network theory (ANT) 30
ad hoc generalisation 109
additional student numbers (ASNs) 56, 93
agenda: meeting documents and 58, 142–145; setting 6
annual company accounts 46–47
arbitrage opportunities 62
attitudinal world 87–88
audit culture 75
authorisation, level of 77–78
authoritativeness, social construction of 103–109

background knowledge 45, 47
Ball, M. 46–47
baseline 91–93
benchmarking 100–117
Bishop Grosseteste University 112–116
Bittner, E. 19–21
breaching experiments 11–12
Bucciarelli, L. 29, 30–38, 44, 47
Buckinghamshire New University 112–116

calculative order 123; correctness of 124–129
calculative rationality 118
Canterbury Christ Church University 112–116
carry around documents 54
cash flow 62–63, 65, 66, 68–71
cell linkage 67–68
Chester, University of 112–116

Chichester, University of 112–116
closed configurations 80
closed flow governance 82–83
coding study 165–166
collaboration 162
common culture 10–11, 11–12
common sense constructs 16, 19–26
completeness 78
composite depiction, authority of 103, 109
computation 122–124
computational order 123
computer-aided design (CAD) drawings 140–141
conceptual play 9, 11, 13
condensate of local knowledge 59–64
consociation 4, 16, 21, 172–173
constraints, change in 63
contingencies: double contingency 10–11, 16; governance chart 82–85
contingent model of planning 139–140
continuity of purpose 22–23, 24–25
conversation analysis 171, 173
coordination 10–11; degree of 77–78; market coordination 118–137
core data sheet 122, 127, 137
co-selection 80
cost detail sheet 122, 126–127, 136
costs: course-costing model 120–133, 135–137; sensitivity analysis 92, 95–96
Coulter, J. 165
County University (CU): benchmarking document 101–109, 111–117; course-costing model 120–133, 135–137; financial forecasts 56–71; governance chart 74–86; HESES reconciliation 56; review of core assumptions 141–154; sensitivity analysis 87–99
course-costing model 120–133, 135–137

course renewal 120
Cumbria, University of 112–116

Dant, T. 139–140
data: ecology of 124–126; evidence in benchmarking 106–108; relationship with phenomena 166; trust in 125–126
data authority problem 106–107
decision linkages 81–82, 86
decision processes 74–86
definition of the situation 9, 10, 12
design and implementation 31–34
designed readership 104–105
determinism 34
displays of professional practice 46
diversity 74
documents 44–52; as displays of professional practice 46; ethnography of 45; formats and parts 55; managers' knowledge about 49–51; ownership of 67; re-positioning 30, 44, 45–46; re-specifying 46–51; substitution effect 29–43; types of 54–55; as worksites 46; *see also under individual documents studied*
double contingency 10–11, 16
downside risk 93–94
due process: contingencies of 74–86; discoverable 22–23, 25–26

ecology of data 124–126
efficiency 120; benchmarking 114–116, 117
egologicality 14
embedding 123
empirical reference 124, 129–132
end/means rationality 10, 11
engineering mentality 36–38, 44
engineering pedagogy 29, 30–38, 47
entropy, organisational 6, 56–57, 87
epistemics 171
ethnography of documents 45
ethnomethodological attitude 164
ethnomethodological gaze 13–15, 48
ethnomethodological indifference 169
ethnomethodology 8–13; current state of 162–171; 'discovery' of ethno-methods 10–13; as a First Sociology 4, 159–175; and third person phenomenology 8–10
*Eurobarometer* 38–41, 44
everyday quantitative practices 128
evidence 103, 106–108
exceptionalism 131–132
expectations 104
external drivers of growth 151–153

extraction 123
'eyeballing' 67–68

Farber, M. 160
files 54
filters 91
financial forecasts 56–71
financial model 90
first formulations 144–145
First Sociology 4, 159–175; and the current state of ethnomethodology 162–171
flow closure 82–83
'folklore' 5
formal logic 160
formalisation 169
format, standardised 146–148
format-constructed documents 54, 55–71
formatted courses of action 54, 55–71
formatted structure 67–68, 126–127
fragmentation 4–8; external logic of 4–6; internal logic of 6–8
Francis, D. 139–140
FTEs (student full time equivalents) 56, 93, 131

Galileo's inclined plane experiment 47–48
Garfinkel, H. 8–10, 159, 162, 164, 166, 168, 169, 173; breaching experiments 11–12; changed view of ethnomethodology 162; changes in investigative procedure 167; conceptual play 9; ethno-methods 11–12; lay sociology 15; lebenswelt pairs 47–48, 48–49; natural language 15; praxeological rule 9; studies of work 164–166
Gödel's Theorem 48
Goodman, N. 102
governance 25–26
governance chart 74–86
Grice, H.P. 102
Grint, K. 19
growth drivers 151–153
Gurwitsch, A. 160

Hacking, I. 97
Hales, C. 5, 8
Harper, R. 45
HEFCE 61, 68, 93, 101, 102
hermeneutics 71; of spatial distributions 77–78
HESES reconciliation 56

# Index

hidden assumptions 38–41
homunculi 9, 14
Husserl, E. 160, 161
hybrid studies 170–171

IMF 45
income detail sheet 122, 136
incompleteness of data sets 107
incongruity procedures 109
indexical expressions 169
input measures 114–116
insight, ontologically fatal 40–41, 164
institutionalisation 163
integration of academic and organisational plans 146
interior configuration 13; of management 15–16
internal drivers of growth 151–153
iteration 32, 34

Kotter, J. 5, 6, 8
Kroes, P. 35–37

lassitude, sense of 163
Law, J. 29, 38–41, 44, 142
lay sociology 15
learning and teaching assessment (LTA) 75–76
lebenswelt pairs: benchmarking 102–103; course costing 123; observability of 46–49; sensitivity analysis 89–90; written-read documents 54, 55–56, 56–71
Lewis, D. 88
linkages 81–82, 86
Livingston, E. 48
loan covenants 61–62
local knowledge 59–64
local relativities and absolutes 78–79
locatability 78
logical grammar of narratives 103, 105–106
loss of radicalism 162–163
Lynch, M.E. 40–41, 48, 164, 168

managed re-direction 96
managed start up 95–96
management: challenges faced by 6; as a common sense construct 16, 19–26; external views of management work 4–6; interior configuration of 15–16; internal views of management work 6–8; as a management construct 21–26; managers' knowledge about documents 49–51; nature of senior management 3–18; re-thinking management work 8–15
management model 90
market coordination 118–137
market positioning 120
materiality 124–126
maxims 14
means/end rationality 10, 11
meeting documents 53–73; review of core assumptions 141–154; workbook of financial forecasts 56–71
meetings 55
membership linkages 81–82, 86
Mendlovitz, S. 165
methodological disjunct 162, 163–168
Mintzberg, H. 4–5
mission reports 45
modal transformations: benchmarking 108; revised strategic plan 148–153
modalities: of accountable senior management 22–23; of material form 77
mode of orientation 10
modified flow closure 82–83
motivated compliance 10–11
motivated document 102–109, 111–117
motivation 67
mutual intelligibility 11, 12, 138–139, 154

names and naming 127–128
narratives, logical grammar of 103, 105–106
natural attitude 164, 166
natural language 15
necessary and sufficient conditions 65–66
network building 6
network growth 150–151
normativity 21
numbers 127–128

object world 31–33, 36, 44
objectives: benchmarking 103–105; revised strategic plan 144–145
one pagers 77
one world metaphysics 38–41, 44
ontologically fatal insight 40–41, 164
operational management 76
organisation, as a common sense construct 19–21
organisation charts 74–86
organisational acumen 20, 84, 125
organisational cartography 77–79
organisational distance 79
organisational entropy 6, 56–57, 87

## Index

organisational fictions 83
organisational knowledge, displays of 46
organisational strategy 146
output measures 116
overhead charges 131
ownership of documents 67

Parsons, T. 10–11, 162, 168–169
path dependence 145–146
performativity 30
Perrow, C. 6
phenomenology 160; third person phenomenology 4, 8–10, 13–15
piety 20
planning model 138
planning schedule 143–144
planning support documents 89; *see also* sensitivity analysis
plans and planning 138–155; *see also* strategic planning/plans
play: conceptual 9, 11, 13; empirical reference 131
Pollner, M. 40–41, 163–164, 164–165
possible worlds 87–98; construction of 90–94; managing at 94–97; pairings and their constitution 89–90
practices 38, 41; documents as displays of professional practice 46; documents as residue of typical practices 64–65
praxeological gap 48–49, 89
praxeological rule 9, 13, 22
predisposition towards inertia 132
Prior, L. 30, 44
problem-solution document pairing 56–71
proceduralising 9, 10
professional practice, displays of 46
professional sociology 15
propriety, sense of 25

Quality Assurance Agency (QAA) audits 75–76, 82, 84, 85
quality enhancement 120
quality positioning 120

radicalism, loss of 162–163
rational actor 118
rationalisation drift 23
rationalistic model of planning 139–140
readership: designed 104–105; types of 67
reasonableness of comparisons problem 106–108
reciprocity of perspectives 14
re-design 94–95
relativities 78–79

relevance 67; governance chart 78, 79–81
representations: closing the representational gap 129, 130–132; managed representation 84–85; and realities 29–43; without metaphysics 44–52
re-purposing 107
research agenda (studies of work) 164–166, 170
re-specifying documents 46–51
revenues 92, 93, 95
review of core assumptions (RCA) 141–154
rigour 8, 9
rolling back the computational logic 131–132
routinisation 163
Rumsfeld problems 24

Sacks, H. 13, 15
Samra-Fredericks, D. 139
scenarios 91–97, 99
schedule, planning 143–144
schemes of values 22–23, 23–24
Schmidt, K. 140–141
Schutz, A. 4, 9, 14, 162
sciences, natural 47–48, 160, 161
scientific attitude 164
scientism 38–41, 44
self-explication 14; meeting documents 67–71
semantic rule 14
senior managers *see* management
sensitivity analysis 87–99
sequencing 80–81
shared culture 10–11, 11–12
'skimmability' 67–68
Smith, B. 123
Smith, D. 45
Smith, J.H. 19
social order 8, 9, 166–167
socialisation 10–11
sociological gaze 9
sociology: First *see* First Sociology; lay and professional 15; relationship with ethnomethodology 162, 163–171
space charges 131
staff timetabling data 125
standardisation: of depiction in benchmarking 107–108; standardised format 146–148
star network 150–151
strategic planning/plans 89–90, 91, 139–140; revised planning document 141–154

structure 33–34
structured formatting 67–68, 126–127
student numbers 56, 93, 125, 131
studies of work 164–166, 170
study policies (maxims) 14
substitution effect 29–43
Suchman, L. 138–139
summary sheet 121, 126, 130, 135
surveys 29, 38–41
sustainability 114, 145
symbols 81–82, 86; alternative readings of 84
synecdoche problem 21; course-costing model 123, 124, 132; revised strategic plan 145–146
syntactic rule 14

tacit knowledge 45, 47
textbooks 31–36
thematisation 104–105
third person phenomenology 4, 8–10, 13–15
throw away documents 54
time 33

tolerance limits 85
traceability 75; course-costing model 128–129
transformations of form 103, 108–109
transparency 75
trust in data 125–126
turn to the social 37, 138

underspecified calibration of topologies 83–84
unique adequacy 167–168
unit act 10–11
universal locatability 78

values, schemes of 22–23, 23–24
vernacular understandings 161

Wagner, I. 140–141
'we-relationship' 4
Winchester University 112–116
workbook of financial forecasts 56–71
worksites, documents as 46
written-read format-constructed documents 54, 55–56, 56–71

PGMO 05/07/2018